M000317819

THEATER
IN THE
AMERICAS

A Series from
Southern
Illinois
University
Press
ROBERT A.
SCHANKE
Series Editor

STAGING
SOCIAL
JUSTICE

Collaborating to Create Activist Theatre

Edited by Norma Bowles and Daniel-Raymond Nadon

With a Foreword by Bill Rauch

Southern Illinois University Press
Carbondale and Edwardsville

Copyright © 2013 by the Board of Trustees,
Southern Illinois University
"Teaching without Lecturing: A Lesson in (Re)Writing History" copyright © 2012
by Flint; "Do Not Try This at Home!" copyright © 2013 by Michael Ellison; "Creating
Space for Intergenerational LGBT Community and Movement Building" copyright
© 2013 by Diane Finnerty; "Pushing without Shoving: Ethics of and Emphasis on
Target Participation in TSJ Institutes" copyright © 2011 by Bryan C. Moore; "We
Are Who We Are: Theatre to Confront Homophobia and Transform Education
into Social Praxis" copyright © 2013 by Tracey Calhoun; "It's Safe to Say" copyright
© 2013 by Bernardo Solano and Paula Weston Solano; "Creativity or Carnage: An
International Theatre for Social Justice Project" copyright © 2013 by Selina Busby
and Catherine McNamara; "Adapt the Space! Working with People of Diverse
Abilities" copyright © 2013 by Kathleen Juhl and Lindsey Smith; "Ripples over the
Great Barrier" copyright © 2012 by Rod Ainsworth and Jude Pippen; "Voicing Your
Gender, Gendering Your Voice" copyright © 2012 by Rebecca M. Root (Rebecca
M. Root has asserted her moral right to be identified as author of the work "Voic-
ing Your Gender, Gendering Your Voice"; permission is granted to reproduce for
personal and educational use only; commercial copying, hiring, and lending are
prohibited); "The Wizdom of Us: Reconsidering Identities and Affinities through
Theatre for Social Justice" copyright © 2012 by Brooke Kiener
All rights reserved
Printed in the United States of America

16 15 14 13   4 3 2 1

Library of Congress Cataloging-in-Publication Data

Staging social justice : collaborating to create activist theatre / edited by
Norma Bowles and Daniel-Raymond Nadon ; with a foreword by Bill Rauch.
pages cm. — (Theater in the Americas)
Includes bibliographical references and index.
ISBN-13: 978-0-8093-3238-0 (pbk. : alk. paper)
ISBN-10: 0-8093-3238-8 (pbk. : alk. paper)
ISBN-13: 978-0-8093-3239-7 (ebook)
ISBN-10: 0-8093-3239-6 (ebook)
1. Theater and society. 2. Theater—Political aspects. 3. Community
theater—Social aspects. 4. Social justice. I. Bowles, Norma, [date] editor of
compilation. II. Nadon, Daniel-Raymond, [date] editor of compilation.
PN2049.S48 2013
306.4'848—dc23   2012039092

Printed on recycled paper. ♻
The paper used in this publication meets the minimum requirements of
American National Standard for Information Sciences—Permanence
of Paper for Printed Library Materials, ANSI Z39.48-1992. ∞

The *Staging Social Justice* collaborators dedicate this book . . .

to the artists and activists whose lives and work reflect their belief in equality and justice;

to the professors and teachers who challenge their students to think critically, to open their minds and hearts, and to engage thoughtfully with the world around them;

to the students and youth who dare to envision other possibilities and to pursue their dreams;

to the outsiders, the marginalized, and the oppressed who face injustices, both "petty" and daunting, and who still manage to stay inspired and inspiring;

to all who share the belief that through theatre we can work together to create a peaceful and loving world, and who generously contribute their time, energy, expertise, or funding toward making Theatre for Social Justice a reality.

We dedicate this book to you!

Contents

Foreword

BILL RAUCH

When I first encountered Fringe Benefits over twenty years ago, I was delighted to find both camaraderie and inspiration. I had just moved to Southern California with Cornerstone Theater Company, and so it was especially heartening to discover a fellow theatre that shares many of Cornerstone's and my core beliefs. A belief in the power of collaborative, community-based theatre. A belief that through theatre, we can air our differences and collectively shape a new set of images of how the world does and doesn't function. A belief that theatre can be a rehearsal for changing the world.

In its early years, Cornerstone, the theatre company that I cofounded with Alison Carey in 1986, traveled around the country, collaborating with people in isolated rural communities to adapt classic plays to reflect the realities of their lives. Up to fifty of the cast members in each project we produced were local men, women, and children, the vast majority of whom had never acted before. In 1992, we settled in Los Angeles in order to expand our work to include original and oral history–based plays in a series of collaborations with urban communities, each sequence of which would culminate in what we called a bridge show, designed to bring people together across as well as within community boundaries.

During my years at Cornerstone, in both rural and urban settings, I learned that every community contains painful divisions. Sometimes these divisions are self-evident, in terms of socioeconomics or race. Other times, the divisions are less visible, and all the more insidious for their invisibility. A seemingly homogeneous, all-white community in the Pacific Northwest was the most sharply divided town in which Cornerstone worked during our early years. Half the community gathered for song and drink in a bar on Saturday nights, while the other half worshiped in a fundamentalist Christian church on Sunday mornings. There was simply no way to step into the bar and then into the church the next day. As outsiders, though, we were able to cast both parts of the community, making it possible for them to participate together in the cooperative venture of our play, a play that took on the question of how to live a moral life. As always happens in Cornerstone's work, lives were changed, including those of us who were temporary interlopers. In every project, every community, we always found surprisingly courageous individuals willing to cross borders, especially the hardest of all to cross: the internal ones that exist in our own hearts.

One of the most profound lessons I learned from my time with Cornerstone involved how to measure the effectiveness of our work. In our early years, we measured our success in terms of whether or not the community continued to do plays after we moved on (we always left behind some of the pay-what-you-can box office proceeds for the community to continue to produce theatre). In Port Gibson, Mississippi, we had produced a biracial adaptation of *Romeo and Juliet*, filling seats in the town's movie theatre beyond capacity and landing our company on the cover of *American Theatre* magazine and in the Sunday Arts and Leisure section of the *New York Times*. After we left town, however, the community produced only one biracial play, and I carried this fact as a knot of shame in my stomach. We had failed this community while increasing our own reputation.

A few years later, when Cornerstone returned to Mississippi, both African American and European American community members pulled us aside excitedly to tell the same story again and again. Port Gibson had become a Main Street, USA, town, designated so by a federally funded program for small towns to revitalize their main streets. Moreover, they had recently been honored, out of a field of over four hundred Main Street towns, for having the most racially integrated board in the United States. "It was because of the play," was the constant refrain. "We all met and learned to trust each other through the play." We realized that social change created through artistic projects is not always immediately apparent and that we had to redefine our own tools of evaluation. This is a subject that *Staging Social Justice* tackles with terrific clarity. The book is bursting with inspiring examples of the transformative impact of similar community-based endeavors along with numerous examples of the myriad ways such impact can be evaluated. More importantly, perhaps, the writers discuss how artists and community members can work together to ensure that they are in alignment about their social change goals from the moment a project is conceived through the entire collaborative play-making process. These stories will be one of the anthology's most important legacies.

I'd like to add my own impact story to this rich compendium. Right after moving to Los Angeles in the early 1990s, I attended a performance by Fringe Benefits. As a young gay man who had grown up in relatively safe suburban environments, I was engaged, challenged, and emotionally shattered by the accounts of the lives of the homeless LGBT (lesbian, gay, bisexual, and transgender) urban youth who stood before me. My mind was further blown by the fact that the performers were telling each other's and not their own stories, an aesthetic choice that carried great political and poetic meaning. As these young people bravely bared their souls in a small black box theatre, my world expanded in a way from which I knew, even then, that there would be no turning back.

After seeing the performance, I wanted to connect with the artist who had organized this remarkable work. As a founding artistic director of a community-based arts organization myself, I immediately bonded with Norma Bowles. We compared notes and shared raucous laughs over meals and coffees. We co-taught a performance workshop with a multilingual group in the nation's largest housing project for low-income senior citizens in downtown Los Angeles. When I was on faculty at the University of California, Irvine, Norma guest-lectured in my community-based theatre class, completely captivating my students with her war stories and irresistible charisma. She rigorously dealt with the complex ethical issues around theatre and social change practices and rallied the students to action. I have continued to learn from Norma and from all the good women and men of Fringe Benefits for over two decades now.

One of the Fringe Benefits programs that most deeply affected me was *Cootie Shots*, short plays for elementary school students that are "theatrical inoculations against bigotry." Like other strong arts efforts, Fringe Benefits is an organization that is always learning and growing, continually building in its current work on what has come before. Years of experience—adventures considered failures as well as successes—have helped the company develop, rework, and refine its unique approach to devising, which has been gradually distilled into the five-day Institute process. I am full of admiration for this evolution, and frankly, I have been taking notes. One of the joys of becoming a middle-aged practitioner is that you get to compare methodologies with more and more people whom you respect. In that spirit, I consider Fringe Benefits a national treasure.

In 2006, after twenty years of serving its vital mission, I left Cornerstone Theater Company and have moved to the Oregon Shakespeare Festival. I consider this new chapter of my professional life as a grand experiment, applying the values that were developed through my community-based work to a larger-scale arts organization. How can racism, homophobia, classism, and gender and ability bias be addressed both internally and externally within the context of a company that draws over 400,000 audience members a year, with an operating budget of over $30 million? The lessons that I have learned from observing Fringe Benefits over the years glimmer in my thoughts and help shape my actions with surprising frequency in my current work.

Ironically, collaboratively developed activist theatre—theatre that at its very essence is inclusive—can easily become overwhelming and even lonely. As you confront the seemingly impossible task of being equally responsible to so many parties and priorities, you have to be careful to not lose yourself. In encountering the voices captured in this book, I found that wonderfully specific joy of an electric connection to kindred spirits, as well as the equally wonderful sense of being shaken out of my complacency by bracing challenges from people whose paths and perspectives are different from my own. I hope that you will find, as I did, that this anthology makes you feel less alone and more ready to open your heart to the next day's challenges.

The authors of the twenty-eight essays that follow include individuals whom I am proud to call my colleagues and friends; and based on reading their insightful reflections, the other contributors are all people whom I want to get to know and to work with, too! I trust that you will feel the same desire to meet each writer as you delve into their provocative and entertaining reports from the front lines of the arts-based social justice movement.

The essays are refreshingly diverse in their points of view, but they all share some wonderful qualities: they are lively, accessible, and *readable*. I am especially moved by the recurrent exploration of the dynamics of privilege that arise in activist and community-based theatre work. Privilege is often masked, even protected, by good intentions. It is almost always invisible to those who enjoy it. These writings will prove especially invaluable in helping to make practitioners more aware of the power dynamics within each room we enter at each point in our process.

My husband and I are the loving parents of two adopted sons. As I watch my mixed-race children, the children of liberal gay parents, grapple with social pressures in terms of gender and dominant culture norms, I am stunned and dismayed by how deeply embedded bias is in our twenty-first-century society. In such moments, I am especially mindful of the power of the work of Fringe Benefits and all artist-activists who work tirelessly to end discrimination.

This anthology is a vital contribution to the effort to make the world a safer and better place than we found it. *Staging Social Justice* is *useful.* Can higher praise be given? As an arts leader and artist, as a citizen, and as a parent, I am so grateful that it exists.

Preface

NORMA BOWLES AND DANIEL-RAYMOND NADON

What follows is a lively assortment of essays about a unique approach to the collaborative development of activist theatre. The contributing writers describe and critique the theories behind and the play development process involved in Fringe Benefits' Theatre for Social Justice Institutes, as well as their impact on participants, audiences, and communities in the United States, Australia, Canada, and the United Kingdom. Many of the writers also use their experiences with the Institute as a springboard for considering larger issues such as community-building, activism and empowerment, aesthetics and ethics, and the ever elusive Safe Space. All of the articles were written by individuals who have firsthand knowledge of Fringe Benefits' innovative devising process from participating in and/or facilitating one or more of the Institutes. Scholars and community members, youth and adults, theatre artists and activists, a psychologist and a lawyer—the diversity of contributing writers reflects the diversity of collaborators in each Institute. Imagine something analogous to a book about *The Laramie Project* comprising reflections from the Tectonic Theater Project artists/interviewers who devised and performed the play *and* from their Laramie, Wyoming, interviewees, as well as critical analyses from scholars in a variety of disciplines. In a field that valorizes working in a nonhierarchical, inclusive manner and giving voice to marginalized and disenfranchised people, the presence of a wide range of voices in this anthology not only is harmonious with these values but also aspires to embody them.

Our inclusive approach is inspired in large measure by the pioneering scholarship of three extraordinary editorial teams: Jan Cohen-Cruz and Mady Schutzman, Linda Frye Burnham and Steven

Durland, and Robert H. Leonard and Ann Kilkelly. The first two editorial teams bring together dazzling arrays of scholars and practitioners in their work, mirroring the rich diversity of voices in the multidisciplinary field of "Art in the Public Interest." Leonard and Kilkelly's *Performing Communities*, a book that, in the words of Cohen-Cruz, is "based on 1,000 pages of interviews with artists, staff, audiences and extended community members of eight theatre ensembles" (3), is grounded in the premise that "the many participants in an artistic enterprise—the artist, the audience, the community sources and partners—are essential voices in the development and understanding of the theories and practices of community art making" (Leonard and Kilkelly 26). Leonard and Kilkelly thoughtfully weave these voices— primarily the voices of the ensembles' artistic directors and artists— through their essays in the form of quotations, dialogues, and script excerpts. They also interpret and synthesize the project participants' experiences, reflections, and feelings for the reader. We hope we have been able to do honor to and build on the groundbreaking work of these editorial teams by providing community collaborators, as well as collaborating scholars and practitioners, with the opportunity to frame their own arguments, to speak directly to the reader, to be the authors of their own stories.

Our Editorial Process

Making this pure, theoretical ideal a reality posed a number of challenges. It is undeniable that, as editors, we have played a significant role in determining which participants' voices are heard in this anthology and how they articulate their arguments. We believe, therefore, that it will be helpful to the reader for us to provide a glimpse into how this text was constructed.

When we began working on this collection in December 2008, we reached out to all of the more than 1,000 individuals who had participated in the twenty-five Institutes that had taken place by that time and invited them to submit essays or abstracts about the theatre/activism work we have all done together and the impact it has had on us and on our communities. The response was exhilarating: dozens of Institute collaborators submitted essays and abstracts! Many of the writers addressed issues we had hoped to tackle; many others zeroed in on areas we had not yet identified. All of the submissions were thought-provoking and compelling.

Norma Bowles and Daniel-Raymond Nadon

We then faced the daunting challenge of determining which essays could be included in the anthology and how best to organize the collection. We also discussed the possibility of collaborating with the contributing writers to determine the structure and content of the anthology, an approach that would have mirrored our inclusive, democratic play-devising process. We soon realized, however, that it would be extremely challenging to facilitate such a complex editing process fairly and effectively—and within a reasonable time frame. After some consideration, we decided to employ a more traditional, hierarchical approach to structuring and editing the anthology—no international "Dramaturgical Quilting Bee"! In the end, although many noteworthy pieces needed to be left out in order for the text to be a manageable size, we are thrilled with the exciting range of voices, writing styles, perspectives, and expertise we have been able to include in the twenty-eight essays that make up the collection.

It is also important to note that, because of our own historical involvement with the work being discussed, we, as editors, found ourselves in uniquely strong, complex, and awkward positions vis-à-vis working with the contributing writers as they developed and polished their articles. As the founding artistic director of Fringe Benefits, the person primarily responsible for developing the Institute methodology, and a co-facilitator of most of the Institutes (Norma), and as a professor of theatre, youth theatre, and LGBT studies, a scholar who has both directed and written about Fringe Benefits' work and, on one occasion, served as an Institute project coordinator (Daniel), we discovered, in a number of instances, that we had different memories, points of view, and/or questions about the projects being discussed. Through "comment balloons," emails, phone calls, and in-person discussions, we had lively conversations with the writers about these issues and together discovered exciting solutions. These dialogues deepened our understanding and regenerated our conviction to continue to do this work and to improve upon it.

A Few Thoughts about Using this Anthology

We are deeply honored and thrilled to be able to share with you the contributions of the writers in this anthology. They discuss various aspects of the Institutes, from initial conception, through the play-development workshops, to the performances, post-show discussions, surveys, and beyond. They tackle many of the political, ethical, psychological, legal, and aesthetic issues we have encountered while working collaboratively to address social justice issues through theatre.

Some of the writers have contributed *descriptions* of the Institute planning and script-development process, as well as roadmaps for outreach and coalition building and for designing and facilitating post-show discussions. Some have shared *reflections* about frustrating, exciting, problematic, and thought-provoking moments in the collaborations. And a number of the writers have offered *critiques* of the Institutes in relation to other theatre activism work, specifically in terms of central concerns in the field: devising and community-building methodologies, aesthetics, activist and educative impact, Safe Space, inclusivity, and empowerment. We have organized our chapters so that each comprises essays presenting diverse perspectives on these central concerns.

There are myriad ways this anthology can be read and utilized, beyond exploring the issues discussed in each chapter. If you are looking for smart and extremely helpful brass-tacks/"how-to" guides, we highly recommend the essays by Acevedo and Thornton, Ardern, Armstrong, Juhl and Smith, the Solanos, and Tacconelli, as well as coeditor Daniel-Raymond Nadon's "By Hook or by Crook!" essay. The first four appendixes also provide practical information and ideas.

Thoughtful scholarly analyses of the Institute play-devising and community-building methodologies can be found in the essays by Busby and McNamara, Calhoun, Finnerty, Halse, and Nadon (in "Sympathy vs. Stigma"). Persuasive evidence of the activist and educative impact of the work is woven throughout the anthology—especially in Ainsworth and Pippen, Calhoun, Goodson, Hanley, Kaye, and Nadon, to name a few—and with detailed quantitative analysis in Iverson's "Inspiring Change and Action: Measuring the Impact of Theatre for Social Justice."

Theatre artists curious about questions of aesthetics and dramaturgy will find exciting food for thought in the pieces by Ellison, Kaye, and Pippa and in Nadon's "Sympathy vs. Stigma." Those grappling with ethical questions that can arise when collaboratively developing activist theatre will appreciate the insightful interrogations of the practice and the candid self-reflections shared by Brusilovsky, Busby and McNamara, Ellison, Flint, Hanley, Juhl and Smith, Kiener, Moore, the Solanos, and Walker. And finally, if you are hungry for an inspiring story affirming the positive, transformative, empowering impact of the work on participants and facilitators, you will definitely enjoy reading Brusilovsky, Calhoun, Finnerty, Goodson, Grills, Kiener, Root, Tacconelli, and Walker. Brief overviews of each essay are included in the chapter introductions.

We would like to see artists, activists, scholars, and revolutionary spirits of all stripes use this book as a springboard for their own work in support of existing social justice movements, or perhaps to help start a movement or two. However this anthology may serve you and your school, organization, or community, and whichever issues you feel inspired to address, we wish you well. There is much to do.

Bibliography

Burnham, Linda Frye, and Steven Durland, eds. *The Citizen Artist: 20 Years of Art in the Public Arena: An Anthology from "High Performance" Magazine, 1978–1998*. Gardiner, NY: Critical Press, 1998.

Cohen-Cruz, Jan. "The Ecology of Theater-in-Community: A Field Theory." In *Performing Communities*, by Robert H. Leonard and Ann Kilkelly. Edited by Linda Frye Burnham. Oakland, CA: New Village Press, 2006. 3–24.

Cohen-Cruz, Jan, and Mady Schutzman. *A Boal Companion: Dialogues on Theatre and Cultural Politics*. New York: Routledge, 2006.

Leonard, Robert H., and Ann Kilkelly. "Findings: Knowing the Secrets behind the Laughter." In *Performing Communities*, by Robert H. Leonard and Ann Kilkelly. Edited by Linda Frye Burnham. Oakland, CA: New Village Press, 2006. 25–43.

Schutzman, Mady, and Jan Cohen-Cruz. *Playing Boal: Theatre, Therapy, Activism*. London: Routledge, 1994.

Acknowledgments

The collaborative process requires us to rely on the kindness of strangers, friends, family, colleagues, and mentors. We began work on this volume in 2008. Along the way, many lovely people have given us their generous support. First, we would like to thank our spouses, Juhl (Norma) and Jim (Daniel), whose sacrifices often left them in a situation akin to widowhood. We are also grateful to the Kent State University administration and to the Fringe Benefits board of directors, staff, and community of contributors for their unstinting support.

This book is an extension of Fringe Benefits' many and varied Theatre for Social Justice Institutes. For their inspirational leadership and thoughtful collaboration as Institute co-facilitators, we would like to thank the following talented and delightful artists/activists/educators: Amanda Dunne Acevedo, Donald Amerson, Blaire Baron Larsen, Natalya Brusilovsky, Flint, Sara Monica Guerrero, Suzy Martinez, Bryan C. Moore, Cristina Nava Perez, Paula Weston Solano, Alex Suha, Jan Tattam, Lindsey Barlag Thornton, Lorely Trinidad, and especially Cynthia Ruffin (Lady Justice) for helping launch the Institute program. We are also greatly indebted to the 1,000-plus project partners and Institute participants, whose wise and creative contributions to the plays we collaboratively devised and to the Institute process are incalculable. And of course the international Institute program would not have been possible without the generous financial support of Fringe Benefits' donors and princely multiyear grants from The Gill Foundation, Liberty Hill Foundation/Queer Youth Fund, the Mukti Fund, and the New Generations Program, funded by The Doris Duke Charitable Foundation and The Andrew W. Mellon Foundation and administered by Theatre Communications Group, the national organization for the American Theatre.

From the moment we first envisioned this anthology through our proofing of the galleys, numerous colleagues and friends came to the rescue with writing and editing assistance. We would like to acknowledge the work of a few of these angels. First and foremost, we want to express our deep appreciation to the contributing writers for their brilliant essays and for their unbelievably gracious patience with our lengthy editorial process! It is also important to recognize Andrei Malikov, whose early, astute, and thorough editorial feedback helped enormously with getting the anthology on its feet. It also gives us great pleasure to thank the following individuals whose sage advice we enjoyed at many key points in the process: Ann Elizabeth Armstrong, Adina Avery-Grossman, Rosemarie K. Bank, Dalia Basiouny, John H. Bowles, Norma Bowles, Sr., Linda Frye Burnham, Flint, Suzi Hoffman-Kipp, Susan Jonas, Kathleen Juhl, Joshua Karton, David Miller, Cathy Plourde, Domnica Radulescu, Carol L. Robinson, Mark E. Rosenthal, Amy Sarno, Bernardo Solano, Paula Weston Solano, Christopher Swan, Jan Tattam, and Leigh Zona.

Hearty thanks are also due to Kathleen McHugh and Chon Noriega for their winning book cover image concept; to Craig Collins and Cynthia Ruffin for a brilliant and fabulously fun photo shoot; to Sara Adelman, Chris Anthony, BJ Dodge, Michele Manzella, and Mark Seldis for their logistical support of the shoot; to Kathleen Juhl for finding the "ChalkDust" font; and to Mary Rohrer for putting it all together so beautifully. For further support zeroing in on the "perfect cover," we are also tremendously grateful to the "sages" mentioned above, to all of the contributing writers, and to Jane Abernethy, Betty Bernhard, Sharon Green, Martin Harries, Virginia Jackson, Alma Martinez, Bill Rauch, Sonja Berggren Seaver, and Nancy Williams.

Norma would like to express her appreciation to her Loyola Marymount University students—Bianca, Caitlin, Cameron, Charles, Corinne, Emily, Joy, Kate, Kimi, Leslie, Natalie, Rebecca, and Thomas—for exploring *Staging Social Justice* as a required text in our Theatre and Social Change class. Their feedback, suggestions, and questions—along with their imaginative applications of the readings to a variety of community-based activist theatre projects—provided us with priceless guidance for fine-tuning the anthology.

We would also like to thank Kristine Priddy, Southern Illinois University Press acquisitions editor, for her gentle and masterful management of the publication process. We are also happily beholden to the entire SIU Press team, including Bridget Brown, Wayne Larsen, Barb Martin, Hannah New, Lola Starck, and Paula Durbin-Westby, and especially Mary Rohrer, for her beautiful book design, and our delightful, judicious, and painstaking copy editor, Julie Bush. Most important, however, we would like to recognize the invaluable (and undying) support and encouragement of our mentor, Bob Schanke, without whom this book might not have been realized.

STAGING
SOCIAL
JUSTICE

Introduction

NORMA BOWLES

We're all back on dry land now—more or less—and we're enjoying a wee rest from our crazy-wild and definitely eventful odysseys. We've navigated bumpy roads, treacherous waters, and political, ethical, psychological, legal, and aesthetic minefields. We've crisscrossed the United States, from union halls in California to Rotary Clubs in New Hampshire, from high school cafetoriums in Texas and homeless shelters in North Carolina to university theatres in Iowa and Ohio. We've tested our mettle in all-too-brief forays across our northern borders into Canadian black box theatres, across the ocean into British classrooms, and across two hemispheres into Aussie schools, theatres . . . and pubs. We've joined together in small, tireless bands—artists and activists, teachers and students, outsiders and insiders, youths and adults—striving arm-in-arm, cheek-by-jowl, enduring endless hours of talking and listening, writing and editing and reediting, and re-editing, and finally rehearsing and touring in hopes that we might Change the World! We've taken on diverse pernicious and ignoble adversaries—racism, classism, sexism, homophobia, and discrimination based on size. And we've championed various weighty and noble causes—immigration rights, marriage equality, and the employment of formerly incarcerated women. And we're a little tired—but undaunted!

"We" are Fringe Benefits,[1] Dan, Norma, and the twenty-nine other individuals who have contributed their reflections and analyses to this anthology, all participants in one or more capacities in one or more Theatre for Social Justice Institutes. "We" are also the other 1,000-plus artists, activists, teachers, students, youth, and adults who collaborated to create activist plays in these twenty-five Institutes and/or to produce and present one of those activist plays to audiences we hoped to inspire to join our fight for social justice.

Perhaps by reflecting on our experiences and sharing them in this anthology, we can provide a navigational chart of the challenging terrain we traversed while working together to address social justice issues through theatre. Perhaps our methodology, developed and refined in the course of twenty-five collaborations over a period of five years, can be of use to other theatre activists. It's a complex and demanding but replicable and effective process.

Perhaps, too, some of the positive outcomes we have achieved— creating friendships and coalitions within our Institutes; changing hearts, minds, even votes; and launching new theatre and/or activist groups on our campuses—may inspire others to do this crazy, hard work as well!

Where We're Coming From

"Theatre for Social Justice" is an umbrella term for a wide range of work, including activist community art, agitprop, community cultural development, community-based theatre, devised theatre, grassroots theatre, participatory arts projects, political theatre, Theatre for Civic Engagement, Theatre and Social Change, and Theatre of the Oppressed, to name only a few.[2]

Theatre for Social Justice and community-based theatre are, arguably, as old as the art of theatre itself and as widespread and diverse as the communities from which they spring. Broadly speaking, these art forms can be described as "creative expression that emerges from communities of people working together to improve their individual and collective circumstances, . . . 'communities' that include not only geographical places, but also groups of people identified with historical or ethnic traditions, or dedicated to a particular belief or spirit" and/or who share certain social or political concerns (deNobriga and Schwarzman 3).

Theatre for Social Justice practitioners and companies run the gamut from Augusto Boal's Center for Theatre of the Oppressed in Rio de Janeiro to the San Francisco Mime Troupe; from Zambia's Chikwakwa Theatre to Reverend Billy and the Church of Stop Shopping, based in New York City; from Appalshop of West Virginia to Los Angeles–based Cornerstone Theater Company; and from Pakistan's Interactive Resource Center to the Peryante street players in the Philippines to the international "Women in Black" antiwar movement.[3] Over the years, Fringe Benefits has drawn guidance, ideas, and inspiration from these and myriad other activist theatre individuals and groups.

Collaboratively Developed Activist Theatre

We are living in scary times. It is becoming more and more challenging every day for most of the world's population to have our voices included in the decision-making processes that affect every aspect of our lives. Now, more than ever, it is imperative for marginalized individuals and communities to come together, listen to each other's concerns, stories, and ideas, and work together to frame our own narratives, not have them silenced, co-opted, distorted, or "Hollywood-ized." If we can work together, we stand a better chance of being heard and heeded.[4] Many of Fringe Benefits' diverse programs, along with countless other groups and individuals around the globe, bring people together to create theatre that frames our own narratives and uses our own words to promote social justice. I would define this work as "collaboratively developed activist theatre." *Staging Social Justice* is a collection of essays about a specific version of collaboratively developed activist theatre, Fringe Benefits' Theatre for Social Justice Institute program.

Activism

I'll start with "activism" because that's where we—Fringe Benefits—start. When we work with our community partners to plan an Institute, we devote a great deal of time and attention to determining the problem we wish to address, the target audience we need to reach in order to effect positive change, and very specific and measurable outcome expectations. For example, our 2006 Institute with the Darwin Turner Action Theatre of the University of Iowa, Iowa City, and the Iowa City Community School District (ICCSD) was designed to stop discrimination based on race/ethnicity in Iowa City public schools. Our target audience comprised 1,200 ICCSD educators, whom we could reach during their professional development day. More specifically, we decided to focus on reaching high school teachers, especially those who might be resistant to addressing these issues. Our goal was to give these teachers some tools and additional motivation to address racism both responsively and proactively and to create safer, more inclusive, and more respectful schools. We then measured the impact of our work through a post-show survey through which the teachers could indicate to what extent they were already dealing effectively with diversity and discrimination issues in their schools, what new tools they'd gained, and how motivated they felt to use these tools to improve their school environments.

Our primary goal for all of our Institutes is activist: we want to raise our audiences' awareness about social justice issues affecting their communities, equip them with tools for addressing these injustices, and inspire them to take action.

Collaborate

> My son and I were watching *Apollo 13* not too long ago. There was a crisis in space and you heard one of the astronauts say to NASA, "Houston, we have a problem." The person in charge, seeing a complex problem, assembled a diverse group of people, each of whom had different skills and different strengths to offer. He said, "You've got to figure this out." They were able to convert what could have been a tragedy into a triumph. That is the challenge that I am trying to leave with you. How can we collaborate, brainstorm creatively, put the big issues on the table and come together as a community so that we can convert what could have been a tragedy into a triumph? (Guinier)

Fringe Benefits works collaboratively because we have found that is the most effective way to ensure that our plays are accurate, effective, and dramatically strong. Over the years, we have come to see that collaborating with a diverse coalition of individuals and organizations is crucial as doing so helps us grapple with the complex issues involved in the projects we take on and navigate the institutional and attitudinal minefields we need to traverse in order to reach our target audiences.

For example, in Fringe Benefits' earliest years, we decided to collaborate with homeless lesbian, gay, bisexual, and transgender (LGBT) youth to address the impact of homophobia on youth; we wanted to ensure that the work accurately reflected current concerns of LGBT youth, not just concerns we might imagine based on research or on our own past experiences. The diversity of the participating youth— diverse not only in terms of their sexual orientation and gender but also in terms of their race/ethnicity, socioeconomic status, beliefs, abilities, and interests—as well as their fierce commitment to authenticity helped us keep the characters, situations, and dialogue realistic. Later, as we began to take our shows into schools, we reached out to a wider range of youth, straight as well as LGBT, and in-school and at-home as well as homeless. We wanted to include as broad a representation as possible of our target audience in the play development process to ensure that the show would really "speak to" that audience.

At that juncture, we also started to recruit high school teachers who showed us some of their strategies for proactively addressing LGBT issues. They also shared personal stories as well as lesson plans and readings from a variety of disciplines, such as English literature, social studies, and science. Some teachers also gave us access to swabs of culture (often toxic!) from faculty lounge gossip. Many of their experiences and ideas were incorporated into our scripts and our study guides. Parents also joined in discussions and improvisations, helping us anticipate concerns that might come from more conservative parents. Both parents and teachers helped ensure that adult characters in the plays sounded like adults. Many also served as our "ambassadors," paving the way for us to come into their schools and helping resolve problems as they arose.

LGBT studies experts advised us concerning how to define key terms and how to portray characters and situations in ways that would broaden and deepen our audiences' understanding of the issues. Administrators advised us regarding what kinds of supporting materials and references would be useful and what compromises would need to be made when portraying discriminatory slurs, jokes, and behavior. Legal consultants helped ensure that we were on target regarding our understanding of relevant discrimination and equal protection laws—laws to which we might wish to draw attention in our scripts or handouts or which might influence when and where we could present our plays. They also vigilantly oversaw our work, helping us avoid violating copyright, libel, and slander laws in our plays. The participation of legal consultants in our projects has provided invaluable support and protection for us, for our project partners, and for the individuals and institutions who host our shows.[5]

Since our earliest years, we've also included theatre artists as well as social workers or counselors in our collaborations. It probably goes without saying that the participation of theatre artists in the script development process—playwrights, actors, directors, improvisers, designers, stage managers, and so on—tends to lead to the creation of work that is more dramatically effective, theatrical, and, yes, easier to produce than might be possible without their involvement! Their expertise is particularly valuable vis-à-vis dramatic structure, character development, mise-en-scène, and helping theatre newcomers feel more at ease with improvising/playwriting on their feet. Their participation also helps ensure that the resulting script is "producible" given the producing organization's available resources, expertise, and time.

Including at least one social worker or counselor in our workshops is one of the steps we take to create as safe a space as possible for the work. Sometimes recounting, listening to, and/or reenacting discrimination stories can trigger powerful emotions. Sometimes, too, working at such a fast pace to dramatize personal stories for the consumption of a potentially hostile audience can be a harrowing experience. Imagine mustering the courage to talk about a time when you were race-baited or gay-bashed and then trying to stay objective as you work with forty people to determine how your experience will be presented—perhaps as the central plot of the play, perhaps as a "throw away" comment; potentially for maximum dramatic impact but also potentially for comic relief. The counselor is present and available to any participant who might want to leave the workshop space for a spell to talk through feelings or concerns. As the Institute facilitators aren't licensed counselors, they don't try to facilitate discussion about emotional issues but instead keep the group focused on the work of creating the play.

Additionally, although the primary purpose of the Institutes is to create plays that promote social justice, community building is an integral part of the process and the outcome. Our Institutes are designed to help build and strengthen communities and relationships between communities by bringing together diverse individuals, helping them discover common ground, and giving them tools and guidance to work together to develop creative solutions to social justice issues. The coalition of people who come together in an Institute sometimes becomes a mutually supportive community with friendships that endure long into the future. Often, too, the coalition of individuals and organizations continues to function as a network of allies, assisting each other with additional activist, educational, and/or artistic endeavors.

Develop

Our Theatre for Social Justice Institute play-development process includes months of planning and outreach followed by a brief on-site, concentrated collaborative script-development process.[6] The Institute is co-led by two or three Fringe Benefits teaching artists who travel to a partnering organization's school or community center, where they conduct a series of five intensive, fast-paced workshops with a group of about thirty-five participants. The participants share stories of incidents wherein they've witnessed or been involved in some form of discrimination. Everyone works together in what we call a "Drama-turgical Quilting Bee," using storytelling, discussion, brainstorming, improvisation, and collective dramaturgy to create a dialogue-pro-moting play about the discrimination issue selected by the group. For most of the four-hour-long Institute workshops, even when we're doing improvisations, we work in one big circle so that we can all see and hear each other. Between workshop sessions, the facilitators invite any and all of the participants who have time, energy, and inclination to join us in our hotel room, where we transcribe the audiotapes of our workshops and continue the work of writing, editing, and shaping the script. Following the Institute, we offer email and telephone consul-tation as the partnering organizations move forward with designing, rehearsing, marketing, and presenting the play and post-show dis-cussion for their target audiences. Many of the Institute participants continue to be involved in the project following the play-development process; often they invite (and/or audition) others to join them in these later stages of the work. Some or all of the participants perform the play they have created (followed by a post-show dialogue and/or workshop) for an audience of their choosing.

Theatre

We use theatre to achieve our activist goals because it is an art form through which people can communicate stories to each other in an in-finite variety of powerfully affecting ways. As Jill Dolan has expressed so beautifully, "Live performance provides a place where people come together, embodied and passionate, to share experiences of meaning and imagination that can describe or capture fleeting intimations of a better world" (2). Theatre, unlike film, television, or radio, brings performers and audience members together in time and space. We can experience each other's presence with all of our senses. We can affect each other. We can relate to each other. Being present with our audiences helps us quite literally put a human face on the issues we're addressing. This is especially important in relation to the Institute plays discussed in this volume as they tackle discrimination issues.

The presence of "the other"—the people who have been the targets of discrimination—portrayed by live, three-dimensional, multifaceted, likable human beings, helps break down any stereotypical conceptions the audience may have held and potentially helps replace fear and prejudice with understanding.

Telling personal stories is one of the most effective ways to change hearts, minds, and behavior (see Iverson's essay in this volume). In our plays, we dramatize the stories that Institute participants share about their experiences facing discrimination, often tying the stories together in ways that reveal connections—especially how relatively minor manifestations of hate, left unchecked, can create a toxic environment in which increasingly harmful discriminatory events are more likely to occur.[7] Through our dramatizations, we can "unpack" the stories, illuminating how various personal, sociopolitical, and cultural factors might influence discriminatory behavior.

The structure and tone, as well as the situations and characters, of each Institute play are unique. Participants are asked to approach creating the play for their target audience in much the same way as they might approach selecting a birthday present. It's relatively easy to select a present for someone whose taste is similar to our own. Often, however, it can be difficult to select an appropriate gift for someone, either because we don't really know the person very well or because our tastes are so different that we almost have to hold our noses all the way to the cash register. Similarly, while many Institute participants (and facilitators) might prefer more avant-garde approaches, we try to create plays that more closely resemble the kinds of entertainment we think our specific target audiences would enjoy. Over the years, we have created plays borrowing structure, style, tone, and/or characters from television shows as varied as *The Colbert Report*, *Sex in the City*, *CSI*, *Total Request Live*, and *The Best Damn Sports Show Period*, as well as from dramatic literature such as *The Laramie Project*, *The Colored Museum*, and *Stop Kiss*.

Still, there are some characteristics all of our Institute plays share. Each is a short play, generally thirty to forty-five minutes long, designed to precede a longer discussion with the audience. All are much more text-based than image-based. Focusing on language allows us to be as precise as possible when addressing complex issues and helps us make sure that we're all "on the same page" when vetting scripts vis-à-vis tone, accuracy, and legality. Although all of our plays are message-driven, we work to make that less obvious and to make them feel more character-driven (or at least plot-driven!). Most important, we tend to inject as much humor as possible into all of our scripts.[8] Each play tends to open with a relatively light, comedic scene. We want audience members to feel welcome, at ease, included. We don't want them to brace themselves against a lecture or sermon. Still, while humorous moments are woven throughout the scripts, the plays tend to grow darker toward the end, as with *As Seen on TV,* our play tackling racism in Texas high schools. In the course of that play, we follow a group of youth who are at first transfixed by and aping what they're watching on TV. Gradually their racist joking gets uglier and uglier until a Holocaust "joke" hits them all like a ton of bricks. At that point, they begin to reflect on their language and behavior. The play ends with a news report about the anniversary of the hate crime committed against James Byrd Jr. in 1998. Following each of the performances of *As Seen On TV,* the writer-performers facilitated intense, lively discussions with their high school audiences about the role of media and humor in creating a sociopolitical climate in which hate crimes might be more likely to occur.

Impact of the Theatre for Social Justice Institutes

In addition to creating tolerance-promoting plays, Fringe Benefits' objectives for the Institutes have been to introduce participants to theatre activism, to provide them with creative tools to address discrimination in their communities, and to help our partnering organizations broaden and diversify their networks of allies. Although many Institute participants have had previous experience with either theatre or activism, at least two-thirds have told us that our project was their first engagement with activism *through theatre.* Almost all said they had developed a greater appreciation for theatre, the collaborative process, and the importance of working to promote social justice. Most of the partnering organizations expanded and diversified their network of allies as they reached out to various organizations and schools to cosponsor the Institute; as participants invited friends, colleagues, and family members to join them for workshop sessions; and as they marketed and toured their shows.[9]

We reached over 12,000 school and community audience members through the dedicated work of over 1,000 youth and adult theatre activist partners who gathered to collaboratively write plays in twenty-five Theatre for Social Justice Institutes throughout the United States and in Canada, the United Kingdom, and Australia, from 2004 through 2009. Following are a few examples of the impact of the Institutes and the plays created through them:

- The play we created with homeless youth in North Carolina helped raise funding for and offers of emergency housing (Goodson, this volume).
- The youth activists we worked with in Ohio got their pro–marriage equality play into more than twenty-one college classes and used it to help draw press and progressive allies to a demonstration against a right-wing senator who had come to campus to speak against the university's health benefits for domestic partners. Four years later, Miami University students were still receiving requests to tour that play (Acevedo and Thornton, this volume; see also Armstrong in this volume).
- An Institute play promoting a progressive approach to immigration rights helped convince California educators and legislators to support the "Dream Act" (Sara Monica Guerrero, personal communication).
- When asked, "What can you do regarding LGBT issues in your community?" after seeing our freshman Week of Welcome show at another Ohio university, all but two of the 282 students who responded to this post-show survey question expressed increased motivation to educate themselves and others or to serve as an ally for LGBT persons (Iverson, this volume; see also Nadon in this volume).
- California Rotarians hosted our production promoting the employment of formerly incarcerated women, and New Hampshire Rotarians hosted a statewide tour of our play promoting marriage equality (Hanley and Kaye, this volume).
- Inspired by an Institute addressing racism, university students in Texas founded their own student-run, campus-based Theatre for Social Justice organization. Their first production prompted an audit of the university's accessibility issues, which resulted in the installation of automatic doors, ramps, and curb cuts throughout the campus (Juhl and Smith, this volume).
- A team of youth and adults in Queensland, Australia, toured their play about LGBT diversity issues to local high schools and garnered an unprecedented level of positive press and support for LGBT youth

in the region (Ainsworth and Pippen, personal communication; see also their essay and Grill's essay in this volume).

- In London, university theatre students and faculty collaborated with transgender youth to create a play addressing anti-LGBT discrimination and then to tour it to secondary schools throughout the United Kingdom. The play and accompanying workshop were so successful that they were remounted and toured for three years (Busby and McNamara, this volume; see also Halse, Root, and Tacconelli in this volume).

Fringe Benefits' Institutes have functioned at times like boot camps, helping arm participants with verbal and physical, individual and collective strategies for contending with seemingly inevitable battles with bigotry. More often, however, they have functioned like consciousness-raising, radicalizing USO troupes, preparing a show either for the "good guys" (the targets of discrimination), for the "bad guys" (discriminators), or for bystanders, who actively or passively collude with discriminatory behavior. The specific target audience and battle plan for each project is always determined by the diverse group of people who gather together to address discrimination in their community. But regardless of the intended outcome of any specific collaboration, our itinerant theatre company seems to operate somewhat like a MASH (mobile army surgical hospital) unit, creating, at least for a moment, a relatively safe space where healing can begin.[10]

After five years traveling the world, honing our Institute process, and helping collaboratively develop activist theatre, and after several more years of reflecting on this work, we are ready to share what we have learned. And we have some fascinating tales to tell and war stories to recount! We—Dan and I and our fellow "ship-builders, captains and sailors"—all hope that our stories and ideas work together to create useful construction plans and navigational charts for anyone interested in working collaboratively through theatre to promote social change. We also hope our anthologized tales will aid in the exploration and discovery of new trade routes of collaboration, shipping lanes of shared experience, refueling points of understanding, and as-yet-uncharted archipelagos of connection. To borrow loosely from Homer, whatever odysseys you may be inspired to embark upon: Launch out on your own stories! Start from where you will! Sing for your time, too!

Notes

1. Founded in 1991, Fringe Benefits is a groundbreaking theatre company with a strong track record of collaborating with school and community groups to create plays that promote constructive dialogue about diversity and discrimination issues. Fringe Benefits' theatre activism workshops and residencies, the two published anthologies of our plays, *Friendly Fire* and *Cootie Shots*, and the award-winning documentary film about our work, *Surviving Friendly Fire*, narrated by Sir Ian McKellen, have earned the commendations of artists, educators, activists, and community leaders. Find out more at www.cootieshots.org.

2. For excellent definitions and illuminating examples of these and many other forms of theatre for social change, please refer to Cohen-Cruz (*Radical Street Performance*, *Local Acts*, and *Engaging Performance*); Cohen-Cruz and Schutzman; Goldbard; and Schutzman and Cohen-Cruz.

3. While the activist work of Women in Black groups generally is conducted in the form of vigils, marches, demonstrations, and sit-downs, some Women in Black groups use more performative approaches, including masks, giant puppets, and drums. See http://www.womeninblack.org/en/about.

4. For more about diverse approaches to and advantages of devised theatre, see the March 2005 "Devising" issue of *Theatre Topics*, including Bowles's article "Why Devise? Why Now? 'Houston, we have a problem.'"

5. For more information about the diverse issues that legal consultants can help theatre activists address, see appendix D.

6. Appendix A gives a brief overview of the Institute process, including planning, devising sessions, and follow-up.

7. For further information and clarification, see the "Pyramid of Hate" diagram in appendix E and visit the Anti-Defamation League website.

8. To read more about Fringe Benefits' use of comedy to tackle discrimination, refer to Bowles's "A Few More Thoughts About Aesthetics" (in this volume) and "Running the Gauntlet" as well as to Radulescu's *Women's Comedic Art as Social Revolution* (216–22).

9. The assertions in this paragraph regarding impact on participants are estimates supported by the responses to "Institute Participant Feedback Forms," which Fringe Benefits collected after all but two of the Institutes discussed in this volume (unpublished).

10. For a more detailed discussion of Fringe Benefits' theatrical strategies, please see Bowles, "Running the Gauntlet."

Bibliography

Baird, Robert M., and Stuart E. Rosenbaum, eds. *Hatred, Bigotry, and Prejudice: Definitions, Causes, and Solutions*. Amherst: Prometheus Books, 1999.

Boal, Augusto. *Legislative Theatre: Using Performance to Make Politics*. Translated by Adrian Jackson. New York: Routledge, 1998.

Bowles, Norma. "Running the Gauntlet: Battling Sexism in Academia with Greasepaint, Bed Sheets and Mardi Gras Beads." In *Feminist Activism in the Academy: Essays on Personal, Political and Professional Change*,

edited by Ellen C. Mayock and Domnica Radulescu. Jefferson, NC: Mc-
Farland, 2010. 61–77.

———. "Why Devise? Why Now? 'Houston, we have a problem.'" *Theatre Topics* 15, no. 1 (2005): 15–22.

Brandt, Eric. *Dangerous Liaisons: Blacks, Gays, and the Struggle for Equality.* New York: New Press, 1999.

Cohen-Cruz, Jan. *Engaging Performance: Theatre as Call and Response.* New York: Routledge, 2010.

———. *Local Acts: Community-Based Performance in the United States.* New Brunswick, NJ: Rutgers University Press, 2005.

———, ed. *Radical Street Performance: An International Anthology.* New York: Routledge, 1998.

Cohen-Cruz, Jan, and Mady Schutzman. *A Boal Companion: Dialogues on Theatre and Cultural Politics.* New York: Routledge, 2006.

deNobriga, Kathie, and Mat Schwarzman. "Community-Based Art for Social Change." Community Arts Network, October 1999. wayback.archive-it. org/2077/20100906201249/http://www.communityarts.net/readingroom /archivefiles/1999/10/communitybased.php.

Dolan, Jill. *Utopia in Performance: Finding Hope at the Theatre.* Ann Arbor: University of Michigan Press, 2005.

Freire, Paolo. *Pedagogy of the Oppressed.* New York: Continuum, 1970.

Goldbard, Arlene. *New Creative Community: The Art of Cultural Development.* Oakland, CA: New Village Press, 2006.

Guinier, Lani. "Educational Opportunity and Democracy." Lecture at the University of Wisconsin, Madison, February 11, 1998.

Homer. *The Odyssey.* Translated by Robert Fagles. New York: Viking Penguin, 1996.

Leonard, Robert H., and Ann Kilkelly. *Performing Communities: Grassroots Ensemble Theaters Deeply Rooted in Eight U.S. Communities.* Edited by Linda Frye Burnham. Oakland, CA: New Village Press, 2006.

Radulescu, Domnica. *Women's Comedic Art as Social Revolution: Five Performers and the Lessons of Their Subversive Humor.* Jefferson, NC: McFarland, 2012.

Schutzman, Mady, and Jan Cohen-Cruz. *Playing Boal: Theatre, Therapy, Activism.* London: Routledge, 1994.

Devising Text: Collaborative Decision Making

Central to Fringe Benefits' Institute play-devising methodology is our "Dramaturgical Quilting Bee," the painstaking, democratic process through which the participants collaboratively conceive, devise, and edit the script. The essays in this chapter describe and respond to aspects of this process and examine how individual and institutional stakeholders negotiate diverse aesthetic, sociopolitical, educational, ethical, logistical, and personal considerations to develop their plays. Before delving into these articles, it would probably be helpful to read our soup-to-nuts "Theatre for Social Justice Institute Overview" (appendix A), which includes the agendas for the five workshop sessions.

We open the chapter with creative nonfiction writer and teacher Flint's "Teaching without Lecturing: A Lesson in (Re)Writing History," which explores some of the complex power dynamics that arose when a group of Aboriginal and white students and adult theatre practitioners collaborated to develop a Forum Theatre piece addressing racism in Winnipeg, Canada, high schools. Next, British performance artist and educator Carly Halse gives us "Brief Encounters between Disciplines and Cultures: An Analysis of the Dramaturgical Quilting Bee," in which she discusses various practical, aesthetic, and ethical implications of the interdisciplinary Institute process. Halse vividly describes a number of cross-cultural negotiations that were integral to crafting an effective piece of activist theatre with a diverse group of LGBTQ (lesbian, gay, bisexual, transgender, and queer) and straight students, educators, artists, and activists from the United Kingdom and North America.

Sometimes the devising process can hinge on a single word. In "Are You an Inmate? Collective Decision Making in the Development of *If Yes, Please Explain . . . ,*" New York–based theatre activist Megan Hanley explores diverse points of view about the use of one key word in a scene from a play created to encourage business owners to hire formerly incarcerated women. Using verbal "snapshots" from interviews with the Institute's lead facilitator, legal advisor, one of the community representatives, and a fellow student participant, Hanley creates an almost cubist, multiperspective montage of a pivotal moment in the devising process.

While Flint examines Fringe Benefits' dramaturgical approach through the eyes of a forensic cultural anthropologist, Halse through the prismatic glasses of a scholar of interdisciplinarity, and Hanley from diverse vantage points and through multiple lenses, Cristina Pippa offers a rare glimpse of the corpus of her Institute's script through a playwright's X-ray vision. In her "Writing Conflict Out of Schools," Pippa vividly describes how Boal's Forum Theatre technique, an Anti-Defamation League's pedagogical tool, and a television sports show were "Frankensteined" together to create the flesh and bones of a play designed for high school educators.

Though sometimes fraught with painstaking negotiation, angst-laden conflict, and an often frustrating attention to detail, our Dramaturgical Quilting Bee methodology creates space for all collaborators to have their voices included—to hear each other and to be heard—throughout the devising process. The interplay of a rich diversity of perspectives and ideas helps ensure that the resulting plays are as accurate, effective, and dramatically strong as possible.

Teaching without Lecturing:
A Lesson in (Re)Writing History

FLINT

I know how I got here—curiosity, eagerness, an interview of sorts, a three-legged flight from Los Angeles to Winnipeg—but now that I am here, I am not quite sure what to expect from my first time working with the Theatre for Social Justice Institute. I reach for the illuminating comfort of my lived experience and expertise and shine it in search of an open pathway through this thicket of the unknown. As an academic and a writer, my ear is trained to hear silence: the muffled echo of the marginalized, the stifled shrieks of the disenfranchised, the rumble and whisper of the story as it slips through the cracks between the lines. As a performing artist and activist, my voice is trained to shatter that silence with articulate pleas, howls of rage, impassioned protests, and boisterous joy.

This is the light that must guide me—listening to everything that is said, and all that remains unspoken, and helping the Institute participants give voice to exactly what they believe needs to be heard.

Day One

The air crackles with anticipation and uncertainty. Curiosity has pulled us out of our everyday lives and drawn us together in this bright rehearsal room, where we will pool our energies and talents in the service of changing the world, or at least shaking up the status quo in this little corner of it. One by one, we take our seats in the circle, and burbling pockets of small talk are swallowed by the spreading hush. The door closes, and we begin.

The Institute participants form an ethnically diverse group of middle and high school students, actors, activists, and community partners, ages ranging from thirteen to mid-fifty, albeit overbalanced with women and whites. I cannot help but wonder how this wonderfully motley crew will weave their different voices together and speak as a unified and singular entity. We have a mere handful of days in which to collectively conceive, structure, write, revise, and edit a play that tackles the thorny issue of racism against Canada's Aboriginal and First Nations students in the high schools of Winnipeg, Ontario, introduces its target audience of students to fresh strategies for positive intervention, and engenders a sense of empowerment and agency.

Introductions and icebreakers and little games help us loosen up our breath and our bodies, but we don't know each other yet, so our trust is still wobbly and our hope is still a personal thing, a gangly fledgling we hold close to the heart. We learn the guidelines for speaking and listening to each other in order to create a space safe enough to withstand the risks of self-disclosure and working with strangers in the constructed intimacy of the Institute. We articulate our particular reasons for participating as well as our common goals. And then we plunge headlong into the muck with an explosive set of exercises that blasts apart the social niceties that keep us at a polite distance from one another. Fast and furious, the group throws racist slurs and stereotypes and jokes into the middle of the room, and as the stinking pile grows higher, so does the laughter, the groans of disgust, and the sharp gasps of horror at the sheer volume of hateful words we are capable of recalling and repeating. Getting the ugly out and putting it on collective display instantly humanizes every participant, and the group bonds in that moment of raw and honest vulnerability.

When the time comes to share stories—of discrimination, of violence and rage, of sorrow and neglect, of racial and ethnic myths built and broken, of strength and resiliency—the participants speak in turn or shake their heads and take a pass as they shape their courage into a bundle of words and wait for the turn to come around to them again. We will build the final play out of the bones and the breath of some of these stories. They stutter and spill and tumble out, enriching our collective understanding and expanding our sense of the possible, until the room fills up with so many stories we cannot squeeze in even one more.

Until this moment, we have held the stories in equal regard and treated them and their tellers with deference and respect, but as we wrap up the story-sharing session and move on to a series of improvisation exercises, it is clear that what was value-neutral is about to become value-loaded. We can get all the Institute participants up on their feet, but not all of the stories. Suddenly, we have a surplus of stories, more stories than we can possibly use, so we start to whittle them down. This is my first hint at what a sticky wicket this situation could become, for it seems wrong to silence someone by setting their story aside right on the heels of encouraging them to use their voice, especially if that participant belongs to a marginalized or minority population. We facilitators casually pick a few stories with a certain charged quality and choose another that seems meaty enough for the group to sink its teeth into, and for the time being, we set aside the rest.

We record everything that goes on during the Institute's working sessions, and our little facilitation team of three goes half-mad transcribing it all before the next day's session. We type up every single word, every *hmm* and *um* and *I dunno*, and go through the transcripts with a careful eye, underlining noteworthy passages and stories and snippets of language that had clearly churned up the participants' interest.

Day Two

We start today's session with a reminder about the purpose for this Institute: all of us in the room want to effect positive social change by theatrically depicting the harsh reality of racism against Aboriginals in Winnipeg's high school system and by opening a solutions-oriented dialogue that will guide high school students, teachers, and administrators to an array of strategies for prevention, intervention, and empowerment.

We pass copies of the transcripts around the room, and while everyone reads and underlines, I am completely confident (perhaps even a wee bit smug) that what the group finds most important in the text will be in clear alignment with my own findings. No matter that I have never been to Winnipeg before, no matter that it has been more than a handful of years since I was a high school student myself, no matter that the oppressed and denigrated population at the heart of our efforts is a people I know next to nothing about—I know about racism, I know who needs to be given a voice and from whom we have heard more than enough already, and I know how to find the gold hidden in a rubble of words. It is my job, and I am quite good at it.

Except, of course, for those times when the gaps in my knowledge are spotlighted in the glare of my false assumptions. Almost immediately, it becomes clear that the stories and moments I found most meaningful and rich with possibility were not the stories and moments that resonated with the group. Not that all of the participants' choices were identical—there were some narrative nuggets that garnered more than a fair share of interest, as well as a great deal of variance in individual preference—but my choices barely found a match or two in the group at large. A humbling moment, to be sure, but also an incredibly liberating moment: suddenly, I am curious to discover everything else I don't know; suddenly, I have a deeper understanding of the value of collaborating with individuals who each bring a different set of skills and perspectives and experiences into the mix; suddenly, I see that the whole of the Institute is far greater than the sum of its individual parts. It is not that I shrug myself out of the familiar skin of my expertise and experience so much as that I recognize my great good fortune in having an unprecedented opportunity to listen, and to learn, from the expertise and experience of my co-collaborators.

The Institute runs as a democratic creative collaboration, and before we launch into the task of narrowing down the foundational stories for the play, we define and clarify the rules of our decision-making process. Every participant's voice carries equal weight and is treated with equal respect. Every participant is entitled to wield veto power by way of raising a moral objection to any element the group has collectively approved, be it narrative, historical, sociopolitical, or any other troubling aspect. If you abstain from voting or are absent from the proceedings, you forfeit the opportunity to cast a ballot after the fact or to otherwise attempt to influence or alter the results of the group's democratic decision. The rules are simple and transparent and designed to keep the robust pace of a process—one that tends to veer toward the chaotic, contentious, and rambunctious—from completely derailing.

We do not talk about the invisible rules—rules based on the power and authority, whether actual or perceived, that is conferred or denied by virtue of an individual's age, gender, race, ethnicity, socioeconomic status, or education. We do not talk about how that imperceptible conferral or denial of power and authority silvers certain tongues and silences others, gives certain voices and votes more ballast, and thins other voices, other votes, to wispy inconsequentiality.

We do not talk about them because they have not yet come into play. But they will.

As a group, we plunge ahead with great optimism and gusto. We vote and argue and discuss and defend, and vote and vote and vote, until we sort the story wheat from the chaff and narrow our focus to four agreeable storylines with two more held as emergency backup options. We zero in on the particular characteristics of our target audience and construct its demographic profile. We come clean about the stereotypes we hold and confess our fears and beliefs about the target audience. We identify areas of similarity, overlap, common ground, and cultural points of reference our target audience is keyed into—films, television shows, music, video games, sports, and the like. We use this information to brainstorm different possibilities for the content and the structure of the play. Then we break into small groups to further develop the most popular concepts, flesh out the skeleton of a structure, and then pitch it to the group as a whole—highlighting its strengths and target-audience appeal and welcoming suggestions for ways to fortify any areas of narrative, structural, or conceptual weakness.

The breakout group I am assigned to has six participants: four students of low to mid-low socioeconomic standing, ages thirteen to sixteen, including an Aboriginal female, a gender-transitioning white, and two white females; and two college-educated white males of mid-range socioeconomic standing, ages twenty-nine and fifty-one. The younger of the two white males is trained in Theatre of the Oppressed / Forum Theatre principles and techniques and is an ardent advocate for youth and Aboriginal rights. He is well regarded in the local Canadian social justice theatre scene, and his participation has been a great boon in helping to ensure our United States–based Institute is so well, and so enthusiastically, attended.

With the group's approval, the Aboriginal teen readily assumes the leadership role, and she invites open discussion and presents her ideas with zest and passion and an unfortunate tendency to digress into off-topic territory. At first, she and the other teens are vocal and able to back up their proposals with evidence and an emotional rationale; in fact, they are quite a formidable force—at least until the two well-educated white male adults bring their thoroughly un-self-aware (and seemingly unintentional) sense of privilege into the conversation and their ability to advocate for their positions by advancing more nuanced and persuasive arguments. Unwittingly, and so pleasantly it hardly seems to be happening, the men's arguments gather force and heft.

It is up to me to perform the delicate operation of using firm, gentle diplomacy to ensure that the voices of the younger members of the group are not squelched, without antagonizing or shaming the well-meaning men. It boils down to a matter of balancing perspectives. In order for the play to be as effective and engaging as possible, we need to make room for more than one kind of wisdom. The younger members of our small group are exposed to the racist behaviors exhibited by some of their middle school and high school classmates day in and day out, and the authority of their daily experience will imbue the play with a contemporary currency to immediately connect the target audience to the material. The adults in the group can provide lessons learned from their lived experience and allow the audience the sense of clarity and expanded options that come with self-reflection over time and distance. For the greatest impact on our target audience, the play needs to deliver both a bird's-eye view of the forest and the chance to see the beauty and feel the rough bark of the trees right up close.

So, gently and firmly, I remind the youth that they do not need to bend their opinions, experience, and beliefs beyond recognition, and I ask the adults to stretch a little and loosen up their time-stiffened beliefs so that we can come together to create something powerful and true.

Nobody does it perfectly, but when I listen to the tapes later on, they are filled with good-faith evidence of my group, and the others, reaching toward mutuality and relinquishing the mulish desire to be right at all costs.

Day Three

After the intensity of yesterday's session, it is a delight to be up on our feet, improvising scenes to see what catches our fancy and can be further developed when we set out to write our script. Once again, the process is fast, furious, and flat-out fun, and we regularly collapse into fits of laughter before collecting our wits and returning our focus to the task at hand.

We use the two-day break between Days Three and Four of the Institute to engage in a transcribe-a-thon of epic proportions. Our hotel room is crammed with Institute facilitators and participants, all of us with laptops in lap, typing away at breakneck speed as the words from yesterday's seemingly endless tapes race down the wires of our headsets and into our ears and out through our fingers. We are eager to finish the transcriptions so that we can move on to the next creative phase of the process, where we divvy up the scenes to put some flesh on their skeletal frames and take a crack at turning our transcription into a first draft of the play.

We scribble and scratch things out, type and delete, sigh copiously, let out little yips of delight when we hit upon a clever turn of phrase, and type and type and type until we have done all we can to put our scenes together. We share and review our drafts, giving feedback and suggestions. We are a team. We are in this together. Except for the one person who is not.

With the approval of the lead facilitator, he has elected to draft the decisive classroom scene, which surprises me because yesterday he had stepped out of the room while we were in the heat of improvising and hashing out details of this exact scene and had not returned until long after we had moved on to other scenes. It surprises me, too, to learn that he has taken great liberties with the scene by changing stories and facts that the group voted to include and by adding information that was never presented to the group at all. His lone wolf stance is perplexing because he has attended the Institute every day and knows how our democratic decision-making process operates and has had ample opportunity to raise objections and present alternatives for the group's consideration, approval, or rejection.

It is especially perplexing in light of his commitment to social justice activism, and still more perplexing that the key elements he is trying to squash in the scene come directly from stories shared by one of the Aboriginal teenage girls in the group. Yet he is trying to slip past the group's one-voice, one-vote guard because he believes *he knows* what needs to be said and believes he knows how to say it better than they can themselves. *Which is exactly what I believed at the start of the Institute.*

I feel an unexpected sense of camaraderie and wish I could confer on him the rush of liberation I felt with my earlier self-discovery, but my empathy cannot withstand the hot flare of my frustration with his antidemocratic tactics and the nimble eloquence of his defense. It should be easy enough to say, "Thank you for your contribution, Kind Sir; however, we cannot allow you to undermine the defining principles of the Institute, or to mute the hard-won words forged in the heat of a diligently democratic process." Easy enough, except that if he walks away from the Institute, we don't know how many people will follow him, and we don't have the time or resources to repopulate the group so far along into our process.

As facilitators, we are confronted with two equally unpalatable risks: sacrifice our principles to keep the peace, and thereby keep the Institute participants, or speak up and possibly sacrifice a goodly number of attendees, and thereby sabotage our efforts thus far. A perk of my low totem position as a novice co-facilitator is that I do not pose much of a threat to the egos of anyone involved, so we ratchet down the tension level by tossing the hot potato scene smack-dab into my lap, and I sit down with the draft to see what I can do and what I must undo.

It is a real powder keg of a scene, with the pressure building and building as the teacher and students make their way through the day's Aboriginal history curriculum, with the lesson functioning as the fast-burning fuse that ignites the act of explosive racial violence at the heart of the play.

There are so many elements to juggle: the classroom scene must be realistic and believable; the historical facts presented must be accurate and balanced between the familiar and the thought-provokingly novel in a way that honors the Aboriginal oral history traditions as subjectively reliable rather than as automatically suspect; the scene must also include alternative perspectives on racial violence and provide opportunities for positive intervention in the post-show Forum Theatre improvisations. And I must find a way to blend a lone wolf voice into the voice of the group in a way that creates harmony rather than discord.

The play itself has its own structural and storytelling needs: I have to cram in all the histories that a history lesson can hold, knowing full well that I cannot include every story and incorporate every perspective or the play will collapse in on itself; the characters cannot stagger and flatten out, nor can the narrative pace be dragged to a crawl, under the weight of history and information; it should be serious enough to be taken seriously and funny enough to keep audience members from feeling as though we are hitting them over the head with a hammer; and I certainly cannot have a teacher standing at the front of the classroom, wagging an admonishing finger at her wayward students, and shoving an unpalatable lesson down their throats.

One of the most challenging aspects is that the educational information in the play is not fresh and enticing new material—the kids have been hearing about the history of the First Nations people in their school classrooms for years, so they just groan and roll their eyes and tune out the lessons. The scene must teach without lecturing or losing one whit of narrative integrity, and for the first time in the Institute, I find my footing and am wholly in my element.

I make lists of essential information and interesting tidbits with which to accessorize the stories. I figure out strategies for energizing the historical information by putting more words in the students' mouths than in the teacher's and for personalizing the information by connecting it to the students' extracurricular lives. I get stuck and ask for help. My co-facilitator suggests adding a countdown "warning system" in which the teacher expresses her increasing exasperation and displeasure with the students' ennui and outbursts. This neat trick accomplishes the three-pronged task of (1) making the teacher's behavior believable and consistent, (2) escalating student tensions and bad behavior, and (3) clearly alerting the audience to how fast and far each student is willing to risk getting in trouble for verbal attacks, defenses, or attempts at diversion. I think of the lone wolf's insistent bluster and listen for what he couldn't bring himself to say and discreetly slip those words into the mouths of two different student characters—the light-skinned Aboriginal male class clown and the scared and sneering white girl who throws the first punch. I look for funny bits and try to make them funnier. I return to the transcripts and our tally of votes. I enter the slipstream of the collective voice and write, and write, and write. Our lone wolf suggests a couple of minor edits and gives the draft a cautious nod of approval. I make the changes and hand the scene back to the care and handling of the group.

Day Four

We bring in the first full draft of the play and begin our "Dramaturgical Quilting Bee,"[1] which has us going through the play scene-by-scene, line-by-line, and word-by-word. We make all decisions by group consensus, and the day passes in a blur as we hunker down to pull out the loose threads of repetitive or unnecessary information, patch in tighter phrasing and more colorful language, and stitch the separate pieces together when their edges finally match.

Day Five

We have incorporated all the changes into a fresh draft, and the script undergoes the Dramaturgical Quilting Bee process one last time. The group does some high-speed tinkering and tightening. Participants drop in two "bitches" to amplify the anger and escalate the violence in the key fight scene. Snip the hind end off the word "bullshit" so that the play doesn't close with the lead character packing all her righteous indignation into an expletive. Vigorously debate the relative merits of "ho" versus "ho-bag" and reach a compromise by including both. An otherwise unanimous vote is trumped by a moral objection to giving a lead character the same name as that of a family regularly portrayed in the local media in a less than flattering light.

Finally, we read the script from start to finish, round-robin style, and we are all tickled a perfectly lovely shade of pink to witness the culmination of our collective efforts. The completed play is smart and funny, provocative and thoughtful, sparkling with the light of the tremendous care every participant brought to the challenging task of creating a story that speaks on behalf of the entire group, and in a singular, unified voice, it says exactly what its audience needs to hear.

Collectively, we have reached the heart of the transformative potential of social justice theatre. Collaboratively, we have unearthed hidden stories and unbound the tongues of silenced and silent voices. Together, we listen as our joined voice floats and soars and sings our story with a beauty and conviction no single voice can muster on its own.

Editors' Note

1. Flint refers to our Day Four and Day Five "Zen Cuisinart" collaborative editing process as the "Dramaturgical Quilting Bee," the name we currently use for the entire Institute devising process (appendix A).

Brief Encounters between Disciplines and Cultures: An Analysis of the Dramaturgical Quilting Bee

CARLY HALSE

In 2007, the UK-based gay rights organization Stonewall published a document titled "The School Report," designed to highlight and tackle homophobic bullying in schools. Alarmingly, it revealed that 65 percent of young lesbian, gay, and bisexual pupils had experienced homophobic bullying in their schools.[1] A year later, I participated in a London-based Theatre for Social Justice Institute collaboration between Fringe Benefits, the Central School of Speech & Drama,[2] and Gendered Intelligence. The Institute set out to tackle this widespread homophobic behavior and language. The participants developed the script for a "25-minute piece of theatre on LGBT-related issues" eventually titled *Brief Encounters*, which toured secondary schools throughout the United Kingdom.[3]

In the first workshop, it became evident that members of the Institute group were hugely diverse not only in terms of age, gender, physical ability, culture, and sexuality but also in terms of their various chosen disciplines.[4] Facilitators, teachers, writers, actors, directors, applied theatre students, researchers, administrators, a psychologist, a legal advisor, and a vocal coach were all in attendance, along with many young people from the London area, both queer and straight. Overall, approximately fifty people participated.

We were a multidisciplinary group, but what role, if any, did interdisciplinarity play in our work? Interdisciplinary work, which has been hailed as the key to solving complex research questions and issues, "occurs when the research question or problem has no compelling home discipline [and] requires the contribution of several disciplines" (Lattuca 117). The task of creating a play to address homophobic behavior in schools certainly presents this kind of complex challenge and would, therefore, seem to call for an interdisciplinary approach. But was that, in fact, how the project was facilitated? By analyzing some aspects of Fringe Benefits' devising methodology, with particular reference to the London Institute, I will evaluate in this essay whether we can consider this process an example of interdisciplinarity. Additionally, I will discuss whether the intercultural transposing of this American process into a British community was embraced and effective.

Interdisciplinarity in the Work of Fringe Benefits

Fringe Benefits' approach to facilitating relies on collaboration between individuals and seeks "to integrate the contributions of several disciplines" (Kaufman, Moss, and Osborn 6). Defining the group's work as interdisciplinary can be problematic, however, simply due to the variety of meanings of "interdisciplinarity." In order to assess the process, I will use the definition of "pure interdisciplinary form" as provided by S. R. Epton, R. L. Payne, and A. W. Pearson. The form is defined as a process in which "the elements of the task are carried out within a single organizational-unit consisting of the practitioners of the disciplines necessary for the completion of the task. The members of the unit share the responsibility for integration of individual contributions into a coherent whole" (Epton, Payne, and Pearson qtd. in Lattuca 13). Within the Institute process, there is a clear "shared space" where disciplines can contribute their varying methods, language, and knowledge toward a final project. Rather than work in groups defined by discipline, we worked as a unified group with the rules of the Institute guiding us.

Democracy as Methodology

Throughout the Institute, democracy was fundamental to giving voice to each individual and furthering the script. It provided a clear structure and equal opportunity for each person to put forward his or her own body of knowledge or discipline. Rather than use a hierarchical structure with a director making decisions, Fringe Benefits uses a collaborative "artistically democratic collective" (Oddey 42). Norma Bowles refers to this process as a "Dramaturgical Quilting Bee," a phrase that denotes a multilayered, multiparticipant process that leads to a quantifiable outcome, in this case our play (16).[5] Democracy is essential to developing and tailoring this "quilt." Dudley Cocke suggests that "the vitality of democracy itself . . . rests on the participation of not just a few, but many." In order to achieve the goal of the Institute, a variety of individuals need to contribute their perspectives, talents, and expertise (172). By using a democratic process, participants can, from the tangled threads and scraps of historiography and knowledge offered by each individual, vote which pieces they would like to sew into a final product. A continual voting process allows the text to be tailored gradually until, theoretically, a majority agrees that the "quilt" is complete.

Particularly interesting throughout the process that I participated in were the changes in the style of voting.[6] In the first workshops, after participants had shared their personal stories of homophobia, anonymous voting was used to determine which stories might be included in the play. This anonymity allowed all participants to be honest without worrying about appearing to be dismissive of others' personal histories. Later in the process, anonymity was dissolved as participants had the opportunity to raise their hands if they had issue with any word, line, or action in the script. After stating their concerns, they were invited to offer alternative solutions. Other participants could then raise their hands and offer their suggestions or defend the original text. All were then invited to vote, by a show of hands, which contribution to implement. By this method, majority wins. Toward the close of the process, the group speed-read through drafts, and the voting was even more rapid.

Perhaps the groundwork for this relatively fast evolution toward increasingly transparent and rapid decision making was laid on the first day as the group began to feel a collective bond or trust as members shared their personal histories. One participant wrote, "[Sharing] seemed like quite a natural thing to do and [it] felt like quite a safe environment straight away."[7] Having discovered that they could trust each other with pieces of themselves, participants felt they could also trust the group to make appropriate decisions concerning the final play. As such, "visual voting" could be used without fear of bias or accusation.

Following these public votes, the Fringe Benefits facilitators and volunteers from the group met between official Institute sessions in the facilitators' hotel room to "re-touch" the script and incorporate changes that had been voted in by the full group. Occasionally, changes voted in refused to fit overall narrative or character. At these points, it was necessary for the people in the hotel room to "mini-vote" and find alternatives that fit yet remained faithful to the changes agreed upon by the larger group. Some sections required numerous rewrites, which were tackled by individuals single-handedly. Although this might not be considered "collaborative," the product itself was still subject to a democratic vote, first by the small group in the hotel room, then by the entire Institute group, until an agreement was reached.

By the end of the Institute, we had collectively created a finished script. Through the use of democracy as a methodology, fifty individuals from hugely diverse backgrounds and disciplines were able to work quickly and collaboratively. Furthermore, allowing individuals to use their own knowledge to sculpt, edit, and create resulted in a final product that was not only truthful but also successful.[8] The inclusion of a variety of perspectives created a piece that could resonate with a variety of audiences. Although the style of voting changed throughout the process, it hinged considerably on the "harmonious relationship" developed. With this trust in place, each participant was able to feel included and integrated within our final "quilt."

When Disciplines Collide

At times, the skills of one discipline needed to be utilized more than others. For instance, the writers played an integral role in drafting revisions of the script, while the teachers knew precisely what material would be acceptable in the schools where we would eventually tour. The actors and performers in the group could lead improvisations and later help facilitate the touring production. There were also individuals involved beyond theatre and education disciplines, such as a clinical psychologist/counselor and a specialist in transgender issues. These disciplines provided detailed information about the issues we were exploring and offered support to other participants. Each discipline had something active and vital to contribute to the Institute. Moreover, the deliberate inclusion of each discipline seemed to aid the development of the "harmonious relationship" that Douglas Kaufman, David M. Moss, and Terry A. Osborn define as a key facet of interdisciplinary work (6).

However, in situations like this, there will inevitably be "moments in which identities or agendas come into conflict" as participants attempt to assert their own knowledge over others' (Armstrong and Juhl 284). For example, at one point in the script, Ryan, a straight, homophobic character, labels his friend "pussy-whipped."[9] One of the teachers present did not think the phrase would be considered appropriate by school authorities. However, a writer countered her argument by suggesting that the phrase was not only dramatically suitable but also a perfect example of the gender issues we were exploring within the play. The matter was eventually resolved through a process of debate and voting, and the line remained in the script. Although this dispute created only a minor problem, it does underline the difficulties of attempting to solve a specific concern when those in separate disciplines believe they have the "correct" answer.

What/Who Is a Discipline?

Describing the disciplines involved becomes mildly problematic when considering that a number of participants were included in the project by virtue of the fact that they were youth who identified as LGBT and/or queer, not because of their formal background in a particular discipline. However, these individuals were integral to the Institute and to the creation of the final product. As Bowles indicates, the participation of "community members" is vital because their stories generate the basis of the script and "their knowledge about the issues guides the decision-making process" (qtd. in Armstrong and Juhl 297). Although it is complex to classify identity as a discipline, the key is in Bowles's use of the word "knowledge." As Julie Klein states, it is the boundaries of knowledge that form and inform a discipline (19). Without disregarding each individual's complete life experience, perhaps we can assert that the young people involved were part of a shared queer community and, as such, a shared discipline. Lisa Lattuca emphasizes that "disciplines are more than canisters of subject matter. . . . They are social groupings of people who . . . share assumptions, behavior patterns and beliefs" (34). By using their personal/political knowledge as a contribution to the process, these participants took on the role of "expert" as discipline. Importantly, three of the young LGBTQ people involved, two of whom had never acted before, went on to join the cast and tour, which extended the interdisciplinarity of the work and enriched the quality of the tour group's interactions with audiences. The Institute had inspired these LGBTQ youth to interact with and within new disciplines, proving the process itself has just as much transformative potential as its finished outcome, with disciplines informing and enriching one another.

Norma as an Amalgam of Disciplines

As a facilitator, teacher, artist, activist, and participant within the collaborative process, Norma Bowles might be described as an individual who utilizes an interdisciplinary approach *within herself*. In blending the boundaries between her various disciplines, she seems to have created an entirely new methodology that activates the processes of Fringe Benefits. She identifies this combination of disciplines as a cross between the American icons of Richard Simmons and Martha Stewart, individuals who might be described as authorities in their own "disciplines," a vivacious and playful fitness personality and a composed and methodical "lifestyle" entrepreneur, respectively. Bowles indicates that her exuberant Simmons persona is an embodiment of her teaching, "the one who makes everyone feel like they can . . . take some risks" (qtd. in Armstrong and Juhl 292). Conversely, the rigorous Stewart persona focuses her as an activism-led facilitator.

Bowles describes her Martha/Richard, facilitator/teacher dialectic as a "schizophrenic lurching from one extreme to the other"; however, I would suggest that these two disciplines inform and influence one another, ceasing to be distinctly separate (qtd. in Armstrong and Juhl 292). As Ann Elizabeth Armstrong indicates, "Martha's rules create the safe space for Richard to allow everyone to get crazy," suggesting that by utilizing this interdisciplinary approach, participants get the best of both fields, allowing them to feel "safe" and able to take creative risks (qtd. in Armstrong and Juhl 293). Each discipline begins to permeate into the other, creating a hybrid of knowledge, her teaching oozing into her "activist facilitating" (291). From observing Bowles, it becomes clear that she does not snap from teacher to facilitator; rather, these disciplines have merged into one methodology where she can be both authoritarian and encouraging all in one breath. Furthermore, by integrating her artistry and her activism knowledge into this hybrid, Bowles has forged an interdisciplinary process within herself, creating what we might call "facili-teach-art-ivism." Although an impractical label for this new discipline, we see how an "interdisciplined self" could provide new methodologies for creative fields and assist with facilitation on any level.

Frameworks That Bolster Interdisciplinary Work

The Institutes themselves are clearly defined by rules and a precise schedule. Although this could be seen as a block to creativity, it ensures that each participant involved has a clear understanding of how to engage with the process and with each other while also ensuring there is a completed product. Project coordinator and participant Catherine McNamara suggests the process had to "'house' everyone, rather than bend to accommodate."[10] Perhaps by using an interdisciplinary and democratic approach, Fringe Benefits creates a safe space—a feeling of "home" or community in which participants can begin to "bend" to each other, respecting and appropriating different disciplines—rather than bending the process to accommodate individuals. This means individuals cannot view their own discipline as infallible. Housing individuals within the rules-based Institute might not please everyone, but it provides a place for each individual to bring his or her expertise into the room and to offer it toward a final product. As Joe Moran suggests, interdisciplinary relationships encourage disciplines to recognize that "their most basic assumptions can always be challenged and reinvigorated by new ways of thinking from elsewhere" (181).

"The Yanks are coming!" Transposing and Sharing Cultural Methodologies

Having discussed some of the methods Fringe Benefits uses, I would now like to evaluate the possible difficulties of transposing a methodology that has been developed within American communities and using it with a British (London-based) community. In particular, was there anything we, as a British community, could give to or take from the process, and, simply, would it work? Furthermore, if communities such as LGBTQ youth can be considered as disciplines within this process, can cultures also?

Although both communities spoke English, inevitably the vernacular used both in the script and in the workshops did highlight some differences. As we edited the script, the Fringe Benefits facilitators insisted on amending all Americanisms to ensure the characters were speaking with local dialects. Ironically, we often found the script "over-Anglicized," for instance with the word "hiya." Amused by the word's quintessentially British flavor, the American facilitators would often write it several times in one scene. However, the London participants believed that the continual repetition of the word sounded parodic. Most of these greetings were eventually replaced with the more Americanized "hi." Furthermore, the play was originally titled *Shifting Gears*, but participants thought this too culturally unfamiliar,

British vernacular preferring "changing gear" rather than "shifting gears" and "gear stick" over "gear shift." Amusingly, the final title is *Brief Encounters*, due to the "encounters" between characters and a plot device involving boxer shorts, but it is also undeniably a reference to Noël Coward's very British screenplay.

Our cultural differences also became apparent at the close of each workshop when the Fringe Benefits facilitators would gather us in a circle and ask us to evaluate the day's work or articulate a hope for the project. Although this was a pleasant moment for all involved, it struck me that in British workshops, I had never experienced something so ritualistic and positive. This difference was made even more evident when participants were encouraged to shout, "Go team!" This in itself has strong connotations of American sporting functions, and I couldn't suppress the urge to adopt a sarcastic Anglo-American accent for the cry.[11] It was in moments like these that the cultural difference seemed palpable, but due to the facilitators' good humor, it was embraced and enjoyed. In typically British style, we insisted on shouting, "Hip, hip, hooray!" at the close of the final workshop, a fitting good-bye to our American facilitators.

While the adopting of British or American dialects could be considered mockery, it indicates that there was an understanding and a friendship between the two cultures. Through our work, we began to use words from each other's terminology and vocabulary, creating a hybrid of activist language from both the United Kingdom and the United States. Significantly, there was a consistent positive energy in the room, and this underlying optimism supported the methods of the Institute. Although positivity is not exclusive to American techniques, I believe it was in part responsible for the success of the project in a British context. This attitude allowed the participants to relax their "stiff upper lips" and actively enjoy the process, despite its serious components. Additionally, the democratic method opened up space for a dialogue between not only the varied cultures present but also the wide-ranging disciplines. Using this liberating method, the two cultures could debate, share, and develop a collective language to address the issues of the Institute and create the script. The transposing of an American methodology into a British context was not at all problematic, because the Institute process itself creates a space where "points of difference" can be addressed and resolved quickly and affably. Within the Institute process, each culture offered divergent terminology, attitudes, and methods, making it relevant to suggest that these separate cultures might also be considered as disciplines. Thus, it can be said that the process opened up space for a dialogue among varied cultures as well as among diverse disciplines.

Brief Encounters has had many positive reviews in the course of a three-year tour, and the show seems to have been successful in challenging young people's views of homophobic bullying. Questionnaires completed after the first tour revealed a 16 percent increase in the number of students who said they would intervene to stop anti-LGBT behavior after having seen the show and participating in the post-show workshop.[12] I think this impressive upsurge provides further evidence that Fringe Benefits' methodology worked extremely well in a London-based context, that the intercultural transposition of this process was both embraced and effective.

How Did It All Work?

The Fringe Benefits Institute not only endeavors to affect sociopolitical change in a community but also provides a space for participants to unite collectively to achieve this goal. The Institute requires a diverse range of cultures and disciplines in order to produce an effective product and relies on a structured system of democracy to shape the final creation, ensuring every participant has a fair chance to be heard, recognized, and included. By trusting in the process of democracy and, importantly, by sharing disciplines, cultures, and autobiographical histories, an inclusive and safe space is formed, which, in turn, helps facilitate an interdisciplinary approach. Within the site of the Institute, participants can even begin to appropriate and use disciplines other than their own. As such, I believe interdisciplinarity is key to this process, and it is appropriate to label it as such.

During this London-based Institute, the unified group seemed to create a "blended methodology," one that was unique to that space and time, although developed from a methodology that is used in diverse locations and to address a wide range of issues. We shaped our own "language," discovering new ways to talk and interact with each other, in order to create a final product that integrated each participant's voice in some way. Although our individual disciplines did not leave the process modified in any way, in our shared space they melded and adapted to each other. Although at times individuals had to resolve problems in smaller groups or singularly, the democratic process maintained the integrity of the interdisciplinary process. Inevitably, the "whole" gets the final say.

Ultimately, the combination of shared stories, shared responsibility, and shared disciplines creates a safe space. This is what leads to a successful interdisciplinary Institute. Although transposing a methodology created and developed in North America into a British context was a possible gamble, the Institute detailed above was an unmitigated success, creating a hybrid of possibilities for future social activism. As Bowles writes, "If we can work together, we stand a better chance of being heard and heeded" (21).[13] Go team!

Notes

1. Stonewall, "The School Report," 2007, http://www.stonewall.org.uk/education_for_all/research/1790.asp. The School Report survey included over 1,100 LGB youth.

2. On November 28, 2012, Central was awarded the Royal Title; the new, full name of the institution is "The Royal Central School of Speech and Drama" (http://www.cssd.ac.uk/events/news/royal-central-school-speech-and-drama-your-questions-answered).

3. Alice Field and Jay Stewart, Theatre for Social Justice advertisement, May 2008. This advertisement was sent out to Central students' e-mail accounts and through Gendered Intelligence. Gendered Intelligence is a London-based company dedicated to educating about gender. A workshop to accompany the play was also developed and toured.

4. Here I am using Joe Moran's definition of "discipline" as "a particular branch of learning or body of knowledge" (2).

5. The quote is from a personal, pre-published copy of Bowles's "Why Devise?" article.

6. The process detailed here is based on the London Institute, which closely followed Fringe Benefits' standard method.

7. Anonymous participant quoted in Sara Saddington, *Brief Encounters* information pack, 2008 (unpublished).

8. See later in this article for some figures on *Brief Encounters*.

9. This line first appeared in draft 4.5.

10. Catherine McNamara, email message to author, June 10, 2008.

11. Sarcasm itself might be considered a defining feature of "British-ness"!

12. Saddington, *Brief Encounters* information pack, 2008.

13. The quote is from a personal, pre-published copy of Bowles's "Why Devise?" article.

Bibliography

Armstrong, Ann Elizabeth, and Kathleen Juhl, eds. *Radical Acts: Theatre and Feminist Pedagogies of Change.* San Francisco, CA: Aunt Lute Books, 2007.

Bowles, Norma. "Why Devise? Why Now? 'Houston, we have a problem.'" *Theatre Topics* 15, no. 1 (2005): 15–21.

Cocke, Dudley. "Art in a Democracy." *TDR: The Drama Review* 48 (Fall 2004): 165–73.

Epton, S. R., R. L. Payne, and A. W. Pearson, eds. *Managing Interdisciplinary Research.* New York: John Wiley, 1983.

Kaufman, Douglas, David M. Moss, and Terry A. Osborn, eds. *Beyond the Boundaries: A Transdisciplinary Approach to Learning and Teaching.* Westport, CT: Greenwood, 2003.

Klein, Julie. *Interdisciplinarity: History, Theory and Practice.* Detroit, MI: Wayne State University Press, 1990.

Lattuca, Lisa. *Creating Interdisciplinarity: Interdisciplinary Research and Teaching among College and University Faculty.* Nashville: Vanderbilt University Press, 2001.

Moran, Joe. *Interdisciplinarity.* 2nd ed. New York: Routledge, 2010.

Oddey, Alison. *Devising Theatre: A Practical and Theoretical Handbook.* New York: Routledge, 2004.

Are You an Inmate? Collective Decision Making in the Development of *If Yes, Please Explain...*

MEGAN HANLEY

"It *has* to be 'inmate,'" Sandra announced firmly, and the rest of the group fell silent. About thirty of us were gathered to read through a draft of *If Yes, Please Explain...*, a play to promote hiring equality for formerly incarcerated people. Many of the group's members, myself included, were anxious to begin rehearsals; we had only a few weeks to cast, design, and rehearse the play, which would be performed at a launch party for Turning Point Staffing Services, an employment agency for formerly incarcerated women. Yet as we tried to edit the script together, we couldn't get past the word "inmate." We had spent forty-five minutes of our workshop (*forty-five precious minutes*, I remember thinking in an over-caffeinated haze) discussing the issue. On one side, several collaborators objected to the word on an ideological level, finding it dehumanizing and offensive. On the other hand, many other collaborators—especially some of the women who had been incarcerated—saw the word as essential, the most accurate representation of how guards and outsiders refer to people in prison. Even after a lengthy discussion, we could not come to consensus.

If Yes, Please Explain... was developed through the Claremont Theatre for Social Justice Institute, a collaboration between Crossroads, a transitional home for formerly incarcerated women; the Intercollegiate Women's Studies Department of the Claremont Colleges; Fringe Benefits; and the Pomona College Department of Theatre and Dance. As a member of a class at Pomona on theatre and social change, I joined our professor, Norma Bowles, and eight other students in the behind-the-scenes preparations for the project. In the course of four months of collaborative work in 2007, more than fifty people helped create

If Yes, Please Explain. . . . It was a diverse group, made up of people from the community who had heard about the project from friends; students, staff, and professors from the Claremont Colleges who were interested in theatre or activism or both; local Rotarians whom we had recruited; and women who lived or worked at Crossroads. Together, we established three goals for our project: we wanted to break down negative stereotypes about formerly incarcerated people, to convince employers to sign up for Turning Point Staffing Services, and to encourage them to give serious consideration to job applicants who had been incarcerated.

The play follows three formerly incarcerated women and three potential employers through the hiring process. As audiences get to know our three job applicants, they see the effects of incarceration on the individual level and learn that when a person who is released from prison cannot find employment, he or she is much more likely to return to prison than a formerly incarcerated person who is employed (Workforce Solutions). While the employers in the play wrestle with assumptions about formerly incarcerated people, viewers learn about federal incentives that promote equitable hiring practices, including the Work Opportunity Tax Credit, which provides a federal tax credit to businesses that hire a formerly incarcerated person within one year of his or her release (US Department of Labor), and the Federal Bonding Program, which provides fidelity bonds to businesses for certain "at-risk" job seekers, including formerly incarcerated individuals (McLaughlin Company). Through the course of the play, a chorus of employers forms and emerges from the audience to ask questions until their fears are eventually assuaged. (In fact, the chorus is so convinced by our brilliant arguments that they enthusiastically break into song, declaring to the tune of "New York, New York," "Start spreading the news: I'm hiring today! / I want to give a chance to this Work Force! Work Force!") Our hope was that potential employers in the audience could identify with the characters onstage, recognizing the moral, financial, and practical reasons for giving formerly incarcerated people fair consideration for job opportunities, and would be inspired to follow suit.

All of this brings us back to the discussion—let's be honest and call it an argument—over whether to refer to people in prison as "inmates" in our play. We couldn't just delete the line: it was central to a scene about a job applicant's history and was a subtle way to point out the tacit assumptions that potential employers might hold about incarcerated people. In this scene, inspired by a collaborator's personal experience, a visitor to a prison is very impressed by a woman running an event and is shocked to learn that the woman is neither an official of the prison nor a support network volunteer. She asks in surprise whether the woman is . . . what? An incarcerated person? A resident of the prison? A criminal, felon, or inmate?! All of the options made me feel uncomfortable. As we continued debating the line and many people (myself included) grew noticeably frustrated, I became intensely aware of the tensions already present in our workshop: this disagreement was not simply about word choice or so-called political correctness but also about whose opinion mattered. After almost an hour of discussion, when we finally fell silent, I still was not sure what we had decided.

Sandra Davis Lawrence, founder of Giving a Voice to Charities, saw the debate within the context of her and other collaborators' recent experiences of incarceration. She told me:

> I was a proponent of using "inmate" because we were so fresh out of the institution. And that's what we had become, and it was the beginning of the exile, so "inmate" was appropriate as far as I was concerned because it was a truth thing: that's what we were called, that's how we were seen by the public. . . . The play was the reality of the moment; it was THE moment; we were telling our story from yesterday, not yesteryear. It was right now; we'd just gotten out. That's what we were called; it was still embedded in me that this is what we were called. Those people didn't call us "ex-incarcerated people." It was raw. It was down and dirty and ugly, and that's what I thought we were trying to portray: the ugly side . . . our reality, and the people's reality. If that has changed or not, I don't know. I don't know what they are being called now; I don't know any of that. I am a free American citizen.[1]

Sandra's new nonprofit is working to support communities affected by the 2011 tornadoes and storms in Alabama.[2]

Marirose Lescher, a lawyer, PhD student in women's studies and religion, and collaborator on the project, associated the word "inmate" with the ugly history of the prison-industrial complex in the United States and saw in the word an erasure, a denial of the individuality of an imprisoned person. She shared with me her reasons for objecting to the word:

In areas beyond re-entry, the term "inmate" operates to fore-close as it conceals other operative conditions of imprisonment. There is a disparate application of the law to the rich and the poor, making it more likely for the poor to end up in prison. The societal failure to alleviate enduring poverty, racism, sexism and classism is often at the crux of illegal activity. The privatization of the prison industry for profit and the use of prisoners for slave labor mean an increasing prison population is good for business. Thus, a significant number of non-violent persons are impris-oned for relatively minor drug infractions, while the techniques of power that maintain the military-prison industrial complex remain obfuscated and incoherent. For these reasons, I find the term "inmate" more pejorative than useful.[3]

Some members of our group, however, saw the word as the most accurate option available to us. Mallory Scarritt, a member of the theatre and social change class, shared that she remembers feeling uncomfortable with the discussion:

I knew that the politically correct term was "formerly incarcer-ated," but I felt like we should use the term "inmate." I remem-bered some of the women saying that that is what they were called and that no one in a jail would say "incarcerated person." I felt really awkward about the whole conversation. I felt like I didn't really have a right to say anything because I had never been in jail. [Some members of the group] seemed very adamant but it seemed to me to be a very clear example of when political cor-rectness directly contrasts [with] the lived reality of the situation.[4]

Norma Bowles, the director of *If Yes, Please Explain...*, remembers hearing consensus in the silence at the end of the discussion:

After considering the participants' diverse points of view and pro-posals for alternative wordings, I thought the line should be, "Oh, so you're an inmate?!" That is what Sandra had told us the visitor had said to her and, perhaps more importantly, it seemed to be the clearest, most succinct and funniest way to convey the point of the scene. I remember that we had a lengthy, passionate, but respectful discussion that concluded with a long silence—which I read as the group's concession—following Sandra's adamant

"It has to be 'inmate'!" Nevertheless, I should not have made this assumption; I should have asked for a show of hands and/ or I should have asked if Sandra considered hers to be a moral stance on the issue. (Our protocol dictates that moral, ethical or legal concerns take precedence over all other democratically determined dramaturgical options.) . . . I often still find myself ruminating over the issues raised by this discussion, especially whether or not it's okay to use a term that has problematic, though little-known, origins, even though the term is generally thought to be . . . value-neutral.[5]

So we moved ahead with rehearsals without much further debate— or, notably, consensus—over whether to use the word "inmate" in the piece. Only after one of our collaborators, who worked in advocacy and services for formerly incarcerated people, shared that she could not support the use of "inmate" in our play and another collaborator expressed concern that the word referred to an ugly history of abuse and sexual assault of imprisoned people (a history that I have been unable to verify) did Norma make the decision to change the script on the basis that using the word would be unethical. The line was changed to, "Are you . . . incarcerated here?!" Elsewhere in the script, "inmate" was replaced with "resident."

A cast of women from Crossroads and students from the Claremont Colleges rehearsed *If Yes, Please Explain . . .* in the living room at Crossroads and in spaces around Pomona College, and we performed the play in December 2007 to a full house of members of local Rotary Clubs and Chambers of Commerce. The launch party for Crossroads' Turning Points Staffing Services received positive press, including a piece in the *Claremont Courier* that asked prospective employers, "With more than 600,000 people being released from prison every year in the United States, don't you think at least one of them would be qualified to work with you?" and urged readers to contact the employment agency (JamesCourie). In the first three years following our show and launch party, Turning Point Staffing Services offered an employment-readiness program to 147 women, and 121 found employment (Crossroads, Inc., 2).

Given the successes of the project, why does this one disagreement matter? Was it simply an argument over semantics, an exercise in political correctness? I remember walking home late at night with a friend after the long debate. I complained that we had spent so much time talking about the word "inmate" that we had not managed to edit the whole script, and she asked me, "But you understand why that discussion was important, don't you?" In truth, at the time, I didn't understand. I was focused on the end result, the play, more than on the tenuous community that we were attempting to build. I hadn't grasped how essential it was that everyone who wanted to be heard had a chance to speak.

Although I did not understand at the time why the discussion mattered, I think I have a better idea now. The debate over our word choice was also one about the politics of our project, about the unaddressed privileges that shaped our interactions. Our workshops took place on a college campus, and it was hard to create a neutral space within a space of privilege. Surely our collaborators from Crossroads felt the effects of discrimination as they came onto campus, and certainly they heard from some of us students (once more, myself included) a naïveté about the realities of life in prison, about what it felt like to be treated as an "inmate." In this sense, that almost hour-long discussion may have been the most important moment in the entire workshop: it represented a real, if imperfect, attempt to understand each other's experiences, to make decisions collectively, and to respect the opinions of everyone involved. In the end, the choice to remove the word "inmate" from the script represented a shift in our project's tactics. We were not going to focus on—in Sandra Davis Lawrence's words—"the ugly side" of the treatment of incarcerated people. Instead, we would model the shift in thinking and language we were asking our audience to make.

I learned from my collaborators throughout the entire process of creating *If Yes, Please Explain...*, but this discussion was, for me, a particularly transformative moment. If I as an educator hope to answer accusations of political correctness with an insistence that language matters, that words do, in fact, change the way that we think about people, then I must welcome these very long debates. More important, if I purport to work as an ally and collaborator in anti-oppression organizing, I must be eager to listen. This is why solidarity work takes time. This is why it matters.

Notes

1. Sandra Davis Lawrence, conversation with the author, April 30, 2011.

2. To learn more about Sandra Davis Lawrence's organization or to contribute, please visit www.givingvoicetocharities.org.

3. Marirose Lescher, email correspondence, April 12, 2011.

4. Mallory Scarritt, email correspondence, April 21, 2011.

5. Norma Bowles, email correspondence, April 17, 2011.

Bibliography

Crossroads, Inc. December 2010 newsletter. http://www.crossroadswomen.org/index.php/newsletter.

JamesCourie, Rebecca. "My Side of the Line." *Claremont Courier*, December 15, 2007.

The McLaughlin Company. "Highlights of the Federal Bonding Program." http://www.bonds4jobs.com/highlights.html. Accessed May 28, 2011.

US Department of Labor. "Work Opportunity Tax Credit." http://www.doleta.gov. Accessed May 11, 2011.

Workforce Solutions South Plains. "Job Seeker-Services-Services for Ex-Offenders/Project Rio." http://www.spworkforce.org. Accessed May 28, 2011.

Writing Conflict Out of Schools

CRISTINA PIPPA

Creating theatre for social justice is as much about portraying instances of oppression within a community as it is about finding ways to inspire an audience to take action. In 2005, the Theatre for Social Justice Institute team at the University of Iowa wrote a play depicting the discrimination against and abuse of LGBT students in Iowa City high schools. The target audience consisted of area high school teachers, coaches, and staff attending a district-wide professional development day.

We gathered in a large movement studio in the theatre building at the University of Iowa. Darwin Turner Action Theatre members, undergraduate and graduate student playwrights and actors, and professors and staff were joined by members of United Action for Youth and local teenagers. From the beginning of the process, discussions in this diverse group were candid and personal. Everyone had a story about witnessing or suffering anti-LGBT discrimination, and we were united by the common purpose of using theatre as a catalyst for behavioral and policy change within the schools.

One story came up again and again in our discussions. Two young men had wished to attend a dance at an Iowa City high school as a couple, but a parent volunteer refused to sell them tickets at the couples' rate. They went to the dance together anyway, where they were brutally assaulted by their peers. We believed that these acts of violence could have been prevented had the high school community recognized and quelled prior instances of prejudice and discrimination. As shown in the "Pyramid of Hate,"[1] a tool developed by the Anti-Defamation League, prejudiced attitudes can lead to acts of bias, discrimination, violence, and even genocide. We decided to present the chain of events that took place at the local high school, consciously following their progression up the Pyramid of Hate, which mirrors the arc of the typical linear plot structure, including an inciting incident, rising action, and climactic moment.

We also decided to use a Boalian "Joker" to serve as a master of ceremonies and to draw the audience into the world of the play.[2] In her opening prologue, our Joker piles bunches of figurative apples on our audience of teachers' desks:

> JOKER: How can we teach a teacher? You're the ones who helped us puzzle out Calculus and Geometry. You're the ones who taught us to fall in love with History, and introduced us to our favorite book. You're the ones who encouraged us to grow stronger, more creative, more analytical, and more just. You taught us to learn . . .[3]

At the end of the play, we planned for the Joker to invite audience members onto the stage to participate in Forum Theatre improvisations to explore how they might handle the situations presented in the play.

Then, to keep the audience's attention, we looked for a style or genre that would provide a fitting and entertaining approach to adapting the story for the stage. As most Americans are more accustomed to watching television than attending the theatre, and as our audience was sure to include Iowa sports fans, we decided to incorporate elements from a then-popular TV talk show/comedy program called *The Best Damn Sports Show Period*. The structure of the sports show also provided us with an opportunity to use such devices as close-ups, playbacks, interjections of commentary and commercials, and, most important, humor. Imagining that some of the harder-to-reach members of our audience might include straight, male coaches and other sports enthusiasts, we hoped that the sports show concept would help them feel as if they were in their own arena and ultimately more receptive to the social change that we aimed to effect. We chose the title *Welcome to the Game!*, but the game in the play is not football or basketball. Instead, the game is high school, where there are also winners and losers, scores and fouls, and where injury, psychological as well as physical, is a real possibility.

In order to approach issues of harassment and discrimination from multiple perspectives, we featured three "sports" commentators who act as friendly adversaries: Amelia Grand Prix, Teresa Tremblay, and Sugar Ray Bob. Amelia is an extreme social conservative, Teresa serves as an advocate for LGBT students, and Sugar is in the middle, undecided. The commentators' zany names and clashing discourse may be a bit tongue-in-cheek, but their dialogue provides an opportunity to air a broad spectrum of commonly held opinions and to arrive, in the end, at a compelling argument for tolerance. We were confident that this would be the best way to reach the "Sugars," or "Movable Middle," in the audience.[4]

The commentators set the stage by informing the audience that they are "reporting live from the sidelines" at the fictional Iowa Village High School on Homecoming Day. The action of the play then moves to the choir room, where students practice "America the Beautiful" for the homecoming game. The choir director instructs them to line up and give each other shoulder massages to release tension before proceeding with the rehearsal. While the director's back is turned, the students reposition themselves so as to avoid being touched by Bethany, whom they believe is a lesbian. The scene ends with Bethany leaving the classroom as the other students snicker and the oblivious teacher continues on with rehearsal.

Sports commentator Teresa interrupts the scene, exclaiming, "Those girls were being downright cruel to that girl Bethany!" Amelia defends them, arguing, "They're teenagers with natural body awkwardness. Cut them a little slack." Sugar suggests that they replay the scene. This time we hear one girl whisper, "I don't want that lesbian to touch me," and another adds, "Oh my God, I know. Yuck!" Hearing this, Sugar determines that the girls' behavior was not only cruel but also discriminatory. He adds, "Seems like a classic case of 'Whispers, Gossip, Rumors . . . Avoidance'—chapter and verse from the 'Pyramid of Hate.'" At this point, the commentators invite Jim, a member of a local LGBT speakers' bureau, to tell the audience about the "Pyramid of Hate." Equipped with a flip chart and diagram, Jim explains how spreading rumors, name-calling, and social avoidance can quickly progress to violence. Again, our playwriting team demonstrated this by showing an escalation of discriminatory behavior as the play progresses, culminating in physical violence in the final scene.

In the next scene, we find a group of boys in a hallway, trash-talking their homecoming rivals: "What fairies!! I bet they all sleep with each other on away trips." A thuggish character named Ricky adds, "We are so going to beat those faggots into the ground!!!" unwittingly foreshadowing his own actions at the dance that night. A girl walking down the hall overhears the boys and attempts to stop their homophobic "joking" and boasting by reporting them to a teacher. The teacher explains that he cannot intervene, as the derogatory statements did not directly address another student.

An argument ensues among the commentators over whether or not to sympathize with the teacher. Their quarrel is interrupted by a commercial in which pep band music plays as a pageant-winning Ms. Iowa advertises Iowa Village High School, followed by a sobering surgeon general's warning that Iowa Village students hear "over twenty-five anti-LGBT epithets daily. Most of the time there is no teacher response." The warning concludes, "This often results in a higher rate of absenteeism, decreased academic performance, attempted suicide, homelessness of LGBT youth, and risky sexual behavior, resulting in unwanted pregnancy or rape."

Returning from the commercial break, the commentators take us to the lunchroom, where students are buying their tickets to the homecoming dance. When two young men, Tremaine and Carlos, try to buy their tickets, the parent volunteer refuses to offer them the couples' rate, even when they tell her that they have been together for six months. At this point, the conflict in the play has ratcheted up from acts of bias to outright discrimination. When the two young men ask the principal to rectify the ticket price policy, she gives them a free ticket, bargaining, "You're gonna get your immediate needs met, and you're gonna give me some time to work on this. Okay? Trust me on this." Tremaine questions how the principal's short-term solution can lead to any real change.

The commentators wrestle with this question even more vehemently. Teresa feels that the principal is "squashing the issue altogether," while Sugar advocates that she is "just trying to keep the peace." Amelia brings up religious concerns and compares selling a teenage "homosexual" couple dance tickets to promoting gay marriage, which, she claims, "our state law is certainly not in favor of."[5]

The final in-school scene prior to the dance takes place in American history class. When a student gives a brief report about Katharine Lee Bates, the poet who wrote "America the Beautiful," the teacher adds that the writer "was inspired not only by the beautiful Colorado landscape, but by her partner, Katharine Coman." The class erupts, hurling a barrage of homophobic epithets at Bethany and fighting about the appropriateness of introducing LGBT subject matter in the classroom. The teacher ends the class by encouraging the students to question their assumptions.

Teresa launches the next scene with the passion of a sports show host, insisting that the players invest more in the game: "It's important as teachers, and as parents and as citizens of this country, that we make sure that all of our students feel comfortable and included in the classroom, not just the majority . . . ALL of our students!" Egged on by the opposing views of her fellow commentators, she insists, "All students can benefit from hearing about contributions made throughout history by *diverse* individuals! If people knew that some of the individuals they most admire from history were lesbian or gay . . . they might stop discriminating against their gay peers."

Sugar Ray Bob interrupts the scene to announce the entrance of Carlos and Tremaine into the dance hall as if he is giving a play-by-play at the Super Bowl. The students immediately begin ridiculing the gay couple. One girl exclaims, "If they kiss, I'm gonna vomit! I'm gonna vomit all over my new Jessica McClintock dress!" Ricky yells, "Freaks!" Other students follow suit, telling Carlos and Tremaine that they are "gross" and "queer" and that they should go back into the closet. Two parent chaperones inform the principal that they never would have allowed their daughter to attend had they known that "homosexuals" would be admitted. While the principal attempts to calm the parents, the conflict between the students escalates. Ricky attacks Carlos, shoving him to the ground, saying, "Are you looking at my ass? You sick faggot!" Tremaine is the only one who tells Ricky to back off, as other students yell, "Fight! Fight! Fight!!!!" He is also the only one to help Carlos get up and to lead him out of the crowd. At the door, the principal asks Carlos if he is okay, but then she seems to suggest that the couple invited an assault when she adds, "This is what I was worried about! I told you this would take time."

In his final commentary, Sugar no longer sides with the principal: "She knew it might get ugly at the dance. But instead of doing something to address the prejudicial atmosphere in the school, she just tried to avoid . . . to circumvent the problem." Even Amelia, the commentator who was most reticent to admit that prejudice and discrimination were a problem at the school, agrees, "We can't wait until things get violent to intervene." At the end of the play, the commentators turn the stage over to the Joker, who asks the audience when they would have stepped in. Would they have stopped the whispers and gossip in choir class or the hate speech outside Spanish class? Would they have stepped up to the plate and devoted part of their class to LGBT history? Or would they have implemented a policy change to allow same-sex couples to buy tickets to the school dance, thereby making them feel welcome and setting a tone that harassment would not be tolerated? Finally, the Joker invites audience members onto the stage to participate in Forum Theatre improvisations to explore how they might handle the situations presented in the play.

Bryan Moore, the director of Darwin Turner Action Theatre when the play was presented for the Martin Luther King, Jr. Professional Development Day, says that *Welcome to the Game!* was very well received and that numerous educators participated in the Forum Theatre improvisations.[6] Moreover, the Iowa City Community School District invited Darwin Turner Action Theatre to return and present another Forum Theatre piece as the keynote presentation for the following year's professional development day, evidence that the interactive presentation had had a positive impact.

Our dramaturgical approach of combining the use of the Pyramid of Hate and a televised sports show as theatrical devices to structure and set the tone of the play and concluding with Forum Theatre interactions succeeded in creating a highly effective piece of social justice theatre. Using the Pyramid of Hate, the play breaks down the immense problem of a discriminatory atmosphere within a school into recognizable, manageable components. Interacting with the Joker at the end, teachers attending our MLK, Jr. Professional Development Day performance felt inspired to get on their feet and explore strategies for handling instances of discrimination that they might later face in their own hallways and classrooms. The sports fans in the audience may have been accustomed to calling out plays from the bleachers or their couches, but how often had they been given the opportunity to jump in and take over for a player? *Welcome to the Game!* actually invites the audience to become active spectators, to change the events that they have just witnessed, and to take a stand in their own arena. As the Joker reminds us, "In life we rarely get to do things over. So this is our chance."

Notes

1. Please refer to the Anti-Defamation League's "Pyramid of Hate" in appendix E.

2. With Teatro de Arena, Boal "introduced the figure of the Joker, both a narrator who addresses the audience directly and a wild card able to jump in and out of any role in the play at any time" (Schutzman 133).

3. This and other quotations in the essay are gleaned from the unpublished Institute play titled *Welcome to the Game!*

4. For more on the concept of the "Movable Middle," see appendix A.

5. On April 3, 2009, the Supreme Court of Iowa legalized same-sex marriage for the state by affirming "defendant appeals from district court summary judgment ruling holding state statute limiting civil marriage to a union between a man and a woman unconstitutional." See http://www.iowacourtsonline.org/Supreme_Court/Recent_Opinions/20090403/07-1499.pdf.

6. Bryan Moore, email messages to author, March 13 and March 24, 2011.

Bibliography

Schutzman, Mady. "Joker Runs Wild." In *A Boal Companion*, edited by Jan Cohen-Cruz and Mady Schutzman New York: Routledge, 2006. 133–45.

2

Marketing the Revolution: Aesthetics and Impact of Activist Theatre

In this chapter, we explore if, how, and to what extent activist theatre can change hearts and minds and inspire people to become allies for social justice. Fringe Benefits' approach to activist theatre borrows a bit from diverse theories and practices in the areas of anti-bias and diversity training, marketing, political science, education, cultural competency, communications, and, of course, activism. Early in the planning stage for a collaboration, Fringe Benefits Institute facilitators work with our project partners to help them determine the social justice issue they want to address, their activist goals, and the target audience they think it is important to reach in order to achieve those goals. We ask our partners to use our "Measurable Outcomes Worksheet" (appendix B) to flesh out these ideas and to specify how their outcome goals can be measured through post-show audience surveys or with some other evaluation instrument. During the second day of the Theatre for Social Justice Institute, we ask the participants to consider who might be in the "Movable Middle"[1] of their target audience and then to keep an image of that person—and his or her values, concerns, likes, and dislikes—foremost in their minds as we make dramaturgical and marketing decisions. The essays in this chapter discuss these concepts and some of the aesthetic and strategic approaches that Institute participants have developed and employed to change hearts, minds, and behavior among their target audiences and to effect sociopolitical and, sometimes, institutional change. These articles also present anecdotal and statistical evidence about the impact of diverse Institute projects and productions.

David Kaye, associate professor of theatre at the University of New Hampshire, Durham, sets the stage for this discussion with "Moving beyond the Comfort Zone: The Quest for Theatre for Social Justice Impact." Through witty theatrical spoofs of pre-Institute planning sessions, Kaye paints a vivid picture of the rigorous and exhilarating strategizing that led to a statewide Rotary Club tour of a play promoting marriage equality. His inclusion of dialogue segments that "capture" some of the complex negotiations involved in the writing process make this essay a particularly appropriate and cunning addition to an anthology about collaboratively devised activist theatre. Kaye goes on to describe some impressive indicators of the play's success. Several months after the tour, New Hampshire became the first state to enact civil union legislation without being ordered to by the state's courts. Although it is not possible to determine exactly how the show contributed to this remarkable legislative change of attitude, it did have a direct and quantifiable impact on its target audience of business and community leaders and thus, quite possibly, helped change the sociopolitical climate of the state.

In her "Inspiring Change and Action: Measuring the Impact of Theatre for Social Justice," Susan V. Iverson, assistant professor of higher education administration and student personnel at Kent State University, evaluates responses to the pre- and post-show surveys she distributed to first-year students who attended an Institute play. Her findings not only affirm the play's positive impact but also suggest that theatre holds greater potential to motivate attitudinal and/or behavioral change than do discussions or lectures as it evokes empathy and models action, agency, and alternatives. Anthology coeditor and Kent State associate professor of theatre and LGBT studies Daniel-Raymond Nadon considers the same project from a different angle in "Sympathy vs. Stigma: Writing the 'Victim.'" Nadon's essay chronicles the impact of the Institute group's decision to include a story about a local hate crime in their play, despite concerns that depicting minority students as victims might further the negative stigma attached to them.

In "Do Not Try This at Home!," Michael Ellison, associate professor of theatre at Bowling Green State University, explores concerns about offending people and encouraging "bad behavior" when portraying incidents of social injustice onstage. While Ellison offers more questions to ponder than solutions to employ, he tickles the reader with a number of clever ideas about how one might design productions to include humorous disclaimers, Brechtian commentaries, or thought-provoking questions to encourage the audience to grapple with, rather than unconsciously absorb, the offensive behavior that is portrayed.

Many other accounts of aesthetic strategies and activist impact are woven throughout this anthology, providing strong evidence—both quantitative and qualitative—that theatre can be a powerful tool for promoting social justice. Although Institute plays are not usually performed for commercial audiences and, as such, are rarely reviewed, sometimes evidence of their impact is documented by the media. For example, in 2008, a Queensland newspaper printed an enthusiastic audience member's letter to the editor in which she shared, "I am writing after experiencing a wonderful piece of theatre and a truly enlightening moment. . . . There wasn't a dry eye in the house. . . . This is heart-wrenching stuff that I think everyone needs to see to understand how big discrimination is in our community" (Pisani). Two years later, the *NewsMail* printed "Gay Play Helped Destroy Barriers," an article describing some of the continuing impact of the same show (Emery).[2]

Often letters, articles, and advertisements about theatre activist projects can help augment the impact of the work, carrying the message of the shows to readers who did not attend the performances. Sometimes, too, the plays can inspire journalists to spread the word themselves, as was the case with *If Yes, Please Explain…*, the Institute play created to encourage employers to hire formerly incarcerated women. After seeing the show, *Claremont Courier* editor-in-chief Rebecca JamesCourie exhorted her readers: "Right here in Claremont we have an opportunity to give a chance to women formerly incarcerated. . . . Helping others is a no-brainer. Giving people another chance is a part of life. With more than 600,000 people being released from prison every year in the United States, don't you think at least one of them would be qualified to work with you? A formerly incarcerated person who is unemployed is 3 times more likely to return to prison than a formerly incarcerated person with employment. We can change that statistic." JamesCourie concluded her article by providing readers with the phone number for the staffing service we were helping launch through our production.[3] There are countless additional post-show survey results, personal anecdotes, and journalistic responses in our archives that further bolster the claim that theatre can be a powerful tool for promoting social justice.

Notes

1. To read more about how Fringe Benefits participants use the concept of the "Movable Middle" in their work, refer to appendix A.

2. To read more about this Institute play, refer to the essays by Grills and Ainsworth and Pippen in this volume.

3. To read more about this Institute play, refer to the essay by Hanley in this volume.

Bibliography

Emery, Lea. "Gay Play Helped Destroy Barriers." *NewsMail*, November 19, 2010.

JamesCourie, Rebecca. "My Side of the Line." *Claremont Courier*, December 15, 2007.

Pisani, Shelley. "Prejudice Plays Out." *NewsMail*, July 24, 2008.

Moving beyond the Comfort Zone:
The Quest for Theatre for Social Justice Impact

DAVID KAYE

In the fall of 2004, the University of New Hampshire (UNH) joined forces with Seacoast Outright, an LGBT youth support organization that serves the Southern Maine/New Hampshire Seacoast region, to host a Theatre for Social Justice Institute (TSJI). UNH has had a student Theatre for Social Justice troupe, WildActs, since 1999. Though the group had been very active since its inception, the ability for WildActs to have a meaningful impact on issues related to social justice had always been in question. The experience of working with the TSJI brought this critical matter into sharp focus. What became the short play *Caught in the Middle* and the overall program "Drawing a Bigger Circle" was the result of a powerful process that forced all those who took part to create theatre that would have a measurable impact on sociopolitical change.

Developing Issues

Nearly two years passed between receiving word that the TSJI would be coming to UNH and the actual arrival of the Institute's facilitators, Norma Bowles and Natalya Brusilovsky. The political landscape changed a great deal during that time. Our initial proposal was to focus the TSJI on the collaborative creation of a play addressing the issue of discrimination against LGBT individuals. As the time arrived to actually begin the workshop, the subject of marriage equality surfaced as a major issue in New Hampshire.

The struggle for marriage equality came to the forefront in New England with the enactment of Vermont's civil union legislation in 2000. The issue became more heated when, in November 2003, the

Massachusetts Supreme Judicial Court ruled that barring same-sex couples from civil marriage was unconstitutional. The court confirmed that "segregating same-sex unions from opposite-sex unions cannot possibly be held rationally to advance or preserve the governmental aim of encouraging stable adult relationships for the good of the individual and of the community, especially its children."[1] As a result, the state of Massachusetts began issuing marriage licenses to same-sex couples in May 2004. Despite these legislative victories, there was defiant opposition. In Vermont in 2000, a "Take Back Vermont" campaign sought to remove all legislators who voted in favor of the civil union law.

Though the Massachusetts Supreme Court ruling was a major victory in the fight for marriage equality, the step from the concept of "civil union" to "marriage" brought about intense, unabashed opposition throughout the nation. As reported in a 2003 *Slate Magazine* article, Gary Bauer, the former presidential candidate and leader of the conservative Family Research Council, declared that the Massachusetts Supreme Court ruling had taken the "cultural wars nuclear." In the same piece, Brian Fahling of the American Family Association said it was "on an order of magnitude that is beyond the capacity of words. The court has tampered with society's DNA, and the consequent mutation will reap unimaginable consequences for Massachusetts and our nation."[2] These statements, and many similar, stoked the fires of irrational fear and overt intolerance toward the LGBT community.

In New Hampshire, the push to defeat any attempt to establish marriage equality or even civil unions was quickly underway following the Massachusetts ruling. New Hampshire Republican governor Craig Benson established a special commission to seek out statewide opinions concerning "gay marriage." Benson filled the committee with mostly conservative opponents of marriage equality. It was against this backdrop that the stakeholders in the UNH Institute met and decided that marriage equality would be the subject of our work. We soon discovered, however, how much had to be done before we really knew where we were going.

Learning to Ask the Tough Questions

Through my own experience as a cofounder of WildActs, I have come to realize just how often we neglect to address two simple yet crucial questions:

- For whom specifically are we creating this theatrical work?
- Exactly what do we want to happen as a result of performing this piece?

During the planning stages, we thought we had addressed these two points. The Institute facilitators, however, through probing and prodding, revealed that we really had not. What we had done was to fall into models of past projects and performances that were known and comfortable for us. We had created plays, sketches, and interactive theatre models for numerous topics, from sexual harassment to gender bias. But in virtually all these cases, we had failed to really dig deep into these two vital questions. As a result, our work, though interesting, and even at times artful, had limited impact. Why? Because in most cases, this lack of inquiry had led us to devise theatre that ultimately was created for the "choir."

Either consciously or subconsciously, we were keeping the work tucked nicely away in a secure place where we knew we could feel good about what we were doing. We all love performing for those who already support us, people who will confirm that what we are doing is noble and good. Although we thought we were being very courageous, in reality, we were creating and performing work in a zone of safety and comfort. But what is the goal if you perform a piece of sociopolitical theatre for an audience whose views and attitudes you already share? We were in the early stages of the creative process when the Institute facilitators forced us to acknowledge and confront this large "elephant" that had been sitting so quietly in the room.

Scene One

(A phone call with Norma Bowles and project organizers Michele Holt-Shannon [UNH Office of Student Life/WildActs cofounder], David Kaye [UNH theatre faculty/WildActs cofounder], and Tawnee Walling [executive director of Seacoast Outright])[3]

> DAVID: We have all agreed that we want to create a piece that deals with marriage equality.
> NORMA: Wonderful. What does that mean, exactly?
> MICHELE: You know . . . with everything that is happening as a result of the Massachusetts ruling, there is quite a backlash developing here in New Hampshire. It's an issue that needs to be addressed.

NORMA: Great. I agree. What do you want to achieve?

DAVID: Well . . . awareness. Get the information out there. Start people thinking about this.

NORMA: Which people do you really want to reach?

TAWNEE: Well, there are a number of places we can perform on campus. Maybe also in Portsmouth at Seacoast Outright.

DAVID: For students . . . parents . . .

NORMA: Can you narrow it down any further?

MICHELE: This is going to take some more thought. We'll get back to you.

Those of us organizing the workshop were fighting a simple truth: it was so much easier to be general, to not make any hard choices *before* we began. Right from the start, I was coming to realize that we were perfectly willing to hop into an important issue and to begin the process of creating a piece before we really came to terms with whom we hoped to reach and what we hoped to achieve. After a few days, we were ready to continue the discussion.

Scene Two

MICHELE: All right—we've got it. We want to do a piece that will help people be more effective as advocates for marriage equality.

NORMA: Cool. And the audience?

DAVID: People in our region who are passionate about the issue.

NORMA: Do you all feel strongly that this is the most important audience?

TAWNEE: It's one important audience!

NORMA: Is this the BEST way you can achieve a quantifiable step toward promoting marriage equality at this time?

(All three workshop organizers let out a long sigh.)

DAVID: I have to confess that this does feel like a default. I am amazed at how hard it has been for us to really define what needs to be done and how we can honestly evaluate the end result.

NORMA: I've found that once a measurable outcome expectation has been established, it's a great deal easier to determine what really needs to be done, for whom, and how.

TAWNEE: Grrrrr. We'll get back to you.

And so we went back to the drawing board. The proposal we had made focused on people who already supported marriage equality, with the objective of energizing this audience and making them more effective at speaking to other people about this issue. We could evaluate the outcome through a questionnaire that asked audience members in what ways the play made them feel more committed to and prepared to fight for marriage equality. The project organizers, however, concluded that this outcome was still too vague. We all wanted to take concrete steps toward the goal of legislation that would give gay and lesbian couples the right to marry. We finally determined that the measurable outcome we really wanted to see was how many people who opposed or were indifferent to marriage equality we could persuade to be supporters. We all agreed that this would give us the clearest basis to measure the actual impact of our efforts. This thinking led us immediately to a formidable obstacle. How in the world could we get such an audience to actually come and see such a play?

We still had a lot of work ahead of us, but we all could feel the logjam coming loose. Focusing on identifying a specific audience and establishing measurable outcomes helped clarify our vision. Suddenly it came to us: what we really wanted to do was to find a way to bring our play into what we saw as "the lion's den." But how? Time was running out. The TSJI facilitators were about to arrive.

Scene Three

(The TSJI facilitators and the project coordinators have their first face-to-face meeting. The opening session with over forty eager participants is scheduled to begin in just a few hours.)

NORMA: So you want to create a play for people who are not likely to be marriage equality supporters?

DAVID: You've got it. We really want to play a role in bringing marriage equality to this state.

MICHELE: We thought UNH sororities and fraternities might be a good place to start.

NORMA: Will this group have the potential to impact the state?

TAWNEE: Well . . . no, probably not.

MICHELE: AUGH!!!!

DAVID: The marriage equality issue is coming to a head. From what I've been hearing, the move for a state constitutional amendment banning same-sex marriage is already underway.

TAWNEE: They might be laying the groundwork to block legislation for civil unions as well.

NATALYA: Could you perform for the state legislature?!

DAVID: I think it'd be tough to attract an audience of legislators who aren't already supportive of marriage equality.

MICHELE: Wait! I've been hearing about a state commission researching same-sex marriage. They're gathering opinions from people throughout the state. Then they're going to make a recommendation to the legislators in a couple months.

NATALYA: Perfect.

TAWNEE: Actually, not perfect. I've heard about this group. I don't think they'll meet with us.

NORMA: Why not?

TAWNEE: It is pretty well stacked with marriage equality opponents.

MICHELE: There must be some way we can get an invitation to perform for them.

NORMA: How can you gain access to these people?

DAVID: Ah! I have an idea.

TAWNEE: What?

DAVID: Rotarians!

(The room goes silent.)

DAVID: There are a lot of political movers and shakers in that group . . .

MICHELE: Interesting. They always have a guest speaker or presentation at their meetings.

DAVID: We can create a play that will fit right into their format.

TAWNEE: They're pretty conservative, aren't they?

DAVID: They can be. But because they draw largely from the business community, they can also be very pragmatic. And if we can present a pragmatic argument for supporting marriage equality . . .

TAWNEE: . . . they could help take us right to the commission!

NORMA: Do you think you can get the Rotarians to invite you?

MICHELE: (*tapping away on her laptop*) I've got their website up. Rotary International has a series of guiding principles . . . one is called the "Four-Way Test": Is it the truth? Is it fair to all concerned? Will it build goodwill and better friendships? Will it be beneficial to all concerned?[4]

TAWNEE: Marriage equality is essentially a civil rights issue. It's right in line with their guiding principles. I think we can use this to open the door for some invitations.

NORMA: Can we get some Rotarians to work with us on shaping and marketing the play?

DAVID: I'm sure a number of people planning to participate in the Institute have connections to Rotary Club members.

NATALYA: Sweet!

TAWNEE: Finally!

NORMA: Woo-hoo! Looks like we're ready to start!

Where It All Led

What followed was an intensive collaboration with twenty-six youth and sixteen adult participants. Because we now knew exactly who our audience was and what we hoped to achieve, we set out to create a short play that was specifically designed to have maximum impact on this very specific group. Two members of area Rotary Clubs volunteered to help us. After a great deal of exploration using TSJI techniques for play development, we concluded that the best plan of action would be to create a play wherein a person modeled after a Rotarian would be the central character. Several other key questions quickly surfaced that once again brought back the issue of target audience and desired outcome. For example, should the play revolve around a gay couple or a lesbian couple who are facing the marriage issue? The group, with the help of the Rotary participants, concluded that our goal might be harder to achieve if we focused on a male couple. This was not an easy decision, as some participants found it disturbing that the heavily male membership would find two men in love "harder to take" than two women. But our goal was to put forth a rational argument to convince our audience that the current laws pertaining to marriage in the state of New Hampshire were blatantly unfair. Taking a chance on having members "tune out" the play before we could make this point due to their own homophobic feelings about gay men would be counterproductive. If we could make the case against the backdrop of a lesbian couple's story, the thought was that the Rotarians' "Four-Way Test" would help the more conservative members move beyond their limited views concerning male couples.

What evolved was a play we called *Caught in the Middle*. Based on a true story, it involves a medical doctor ("Charles") who, over the years, has developed a close friendship with a lesbian couple. Near the beginning of the play, one of the two women in this couple ("Jill") is brought to Charles's hospital; she is in critical condition and unconscious following a terrible car accident. When the victim's partner ("Gail") arrives, she says she is Jill's domestic partner and asks to see her. She is denied access. She then learns that a critical medical decision must be made. The hospital, having been sued recently under similar circumstances, holds the line that only a "relative" can be allowed to make this decision. Although the couple had already made power of attorney arrangements, the paperwork is with their lawyer, and the lawyer's office is closed for the weekend. Charles now faces a dilemma. He wants to honor and move forward with Gail's wishes, but he is possibly breaking the law and certainly the rules of the hospital if he takes action without the approval of a "relative." This could make him vulnerable to a lawsuit and/or dismissal from his position at the hospital. He is caught in the middle.

The climax of the play was designed to have our audience of Rotarians apply the organization's guiding principles to the plights of both Gail and the doctor. Was it fair that Gail could not have the same rights as any other spouse who found herself in a similar situation? Why should this doctor be faced with such an unreasonable predicament? We had decided that it would be best to make the doctor someone with whom our audience could easily identify, though not specifically a Rotarian. He did, however, begin the process of applying the basic questions found in the Four-Way Test as the basis of his rational evaluation of how to handle the situation.

With a total of only twenty minutes for the entire presentation, we had to be extremely economical with our time. The play we created was ten minutes long. This did not leave us with an adequate amount of time for a talkback session. Michele Holt-Shannon therefore devised a ten-minute program posing the fundamental questions raised by the play, the most important being "Is a more inclusive community a better community?" Our pre- and post-show surveys addressed questions of inclusiveness and fairness in relation to the issue of marriage equality.

Ten Rotary Clubs were contacted about hosting the program. Our first invitation came from the club in Rochester, New Hampshire. This became a critical performance because several of the clubs had a "wait and see" response. If word got out from the Rochester meeting that the program was unacceptable for any reason, the chances of gaining access to the other clubs would be in jeopardy. Fortunately, before our presentation we were able to confer with some members of the Rochester Rotary who gave us invaluable insight into how to make our program work for this very important first audience. Happily, the premiere was well received. We now had a club that the various program directors could contact to address their concerns. Eventually, five additional clubs accepted our offer to perform. Three of these groups were quite enthusiastic about the presentation. The program coordinators of the remaining two voiced concern about the subject matter, but after contacting the Rochester club, they were eager to host the performances. The four clubs that did not invite our group to perform offered a variety of reasons ranging from "No openings for presentations for the next year" to "This is not a program that would be of interest to our members."

Although one Rotarian refused to watch the play, leaving before the presentation began, and three written responses dismissed the play as "left-handed," overall, the results from the surveys and the talkbacks gave us quantifiable evidence that we had indeed had a positive impact on the Rotary Club audiences. More Rotarians than we expected—80 percent of those who took the pre-show survey—were already supportive of marriage equality. But after seeing the performance, *90 percent* of the members registered that they were in favor of marriage equality.[5] In a brief twenty minutes, we had succeeded in swaying 10 percent of our audience to support our cause!

The play was also presented for public audiences at UNH in Durham and at Seacoast Outright in Portsmouth; surveys were also filled out at these performances. Because these audiences tended already to be strong supporters of marriage equality, the post-show surveys revealed less pronounced changes in attitudes. This information was useful, however, as it confirmed that by making Rotarians our target audience, we had given ourselves a greater opportunity to have an impact. Still, we had hoped that the well-received Rotary Club presentations would eventually lead to a chance to present our work before

Governor Benson's commission on the issue of same-sex marriage. Unfortunately, the commission continued to refuse our requests to host a show.

On May 31, 2007, despite the commission's recommendation for a constitutional amendment banning same-sex marriage[6] and several repeated attempts to keep civil union legislation from being proposed, New Hampshire became the first state to enact civil union legislation without being ordered to by the state's courts.[7] In the final analysis, we cannot know exactly what impact WildActs and the TSJI had on this remarkable legislative change. We can, however, take away from this experience the knowledge that we did have a direct, positive, and quantifiable impact on a large audience of well-connected community leaders who were likely to be politically active. Perhaps some of the Rotarian audience members who were influenced by our program spread the word to their state legislators. Perhaps our show had an indirect influence on those legislators' historic vote. In any event, all of us who took part in this TSJI project have taken pride in the knowledge that by working past our generalized thinking concerning the goals, audience, and the play's content, we maximized our ability to help pass HB-437.[8] On June 3, 2009, Governor John Lynch signed legislation making New Hampshire the sixth state to legalize same-sex marriage.[9]

Since working on the "Drawing a Bigger Circle" program, I have continued to take what I learned from planning, devising, marketing, and touring the show and to apply this knowledge and these strategies to many other projects. This includes my current efforts using theatre to address issues related to sustainability. In every case, I find myself asking all the questions that the TSJI facilitators insisted we ask: Who exactly is this for? What is the desired outcome? What is the best way to achieve that outcome? How can we truly assess our effectiveness? When I refuse to accept general answers to these specific questions, I find myself creating theatre that I feel is stronger and clearer in purpose. I am more committed to moving beyond safe, comfortable places in order to explore new ways of thinking and to using art to impact social change.

Notes

1. Commonwealth of Massachusetts, "Hillary Goodridge and others vs. Department of Public Health and another," http://masscases.com/cases/sjc/440/440mass309.html.

2. The Slate Group, "A Common Missed Conception: Why Religious People are Against Gay Marriage," November 19, 2003, http://www.slate.com/id/2091413/.

3. A consolidated account of many meetings and phone calls, as recalled by the author with the support and permission of the participants.

4. Rotary International, "Guiding Principles," http://www.rotary.org/en/About Us/RotaryInternational/GuidingPrinciples/Pages/ridefault.aspx.

5. Based on post-show survey responses (unpublished).

6. Iowa Christian Alliance Education Fund, "Commission to Study All Aspects of Same Sex Civil Marriage and the Legal Equivalents Thereof, Whether Chapter 100:2, Laws of 2004, Executive Summary of Final Report," http://www.marriagefactsmaine.org/mf_me/report/Executive_Summary.pdf, report officially released October 31, 2005.

7. "NH Poised to Become 4th State to OK Gay Civil Unions," *Christian Post*, April 27, 2007, http://www.christianpost.com/news/nh-poised-to-become-4th-state-to-ok-gay-civil-unions-27117/.

8. New Hampshire General Court, "Chapter 58, HB 437, FN Local Final Version," http://www.gencourt.state.nh.us/legislation/2007/HB0437.html.

9. Abby Goodnaugh, "New Hampshire Legalizes Same-Sex Marriage," *New York Times*, June 3, 2009, http://www.nytimes.com/2009/06/04/us/04marriage.html.

Inspiring Change and Action: Measuring the Impact of Theatre for Social Justice

SUSAN V. IVERSON

In *Friendly Fire*, Norma Bowles asks, "Wouldn't it be great if we could hook up all our audience members to those elaborate machines they use in hospitals to monitor people's vital signs?!" (154). In this way, she continues, we could measure the impact of the show, distinguish particular characters with which the audience identifies, and determine if the show had a positive effect on their lives.

What does happen with audience members when they watch social justice theatre? This essay describes the process of measuring the impact of the play *True Lives: I'm a Kent State Freshman* on Kent State college students' attitudes toward lesbian, gay, bisexual, and transgender (LGBT) persons and issues and shares findings from pre- and post-show surveys. These findings illuminate the impact of this play on audience members' attitudes toward LGBT people. Further, responses to a question about what audience members had done before watching the show and will do after watching the show regarding LGBT issues in the community illustrate the power of the performance to inspire action.

Performing Change

Theatre is a powerful medium. Audience members are invited to consider other points of view as they watch the actors perform various roles, and this can promote feelings of empathy (Wesley). Performances can also teach about difference and serve as a catalyst for discussion about social issues (Paul). Awareness of this potential has contributed to an increased use of theatre in US higher education, often presented to new students during orientation to educate and inform students about social problems (Iverson 548).

In April 2007, members of the Kent State University (KSU) community participated in a Theatre for Social Justice Institute and collaboratively developed a play titled *True Lives: I'm a Kent State Freshman*. The script emerged from ideas, stories, and improvisations contributed primarily by KSU students but also by some faculty and staff. The purpose of the play was to address issues of anti-LGBT discrimination on the KSU campus. More specifically, the *True Lives* project was initiated to address the problem of homophobic language and behavior among students. The goal of the production was to raise awareness about how instances of homophobic speech and behavior (for example, saying to a friend, "That's so gay!") exist on a continuum of behaviors leading to incidents of hate crimes.

Through the performance of dramatized real stories, the project sought to raise awareness about LGBT issues and anti-LGBT incidents on campus, influence attitudes toward LGBT people, model interventions that could diffuse homophobic situations on campus, and promote possibilities of taking pro-LGBT action on campus. In particular, the participants identified white, straight, first-year males as the primary target for these project goals. Research shows that first-year students are significantly more negative toward LGBT persons and issues than are students in other classes, and that women—across all age categories and class standing—are generally more tolerant than men toward gay men and lesbians (Engstrom and Sedlacek; Herek, "Heterosexuals' Attitudes"; Liang and Alimo; Mohr and Sedlacek).

In August and September 2007, KSU students performed *True Lives* several times on Kent campuses, reaching more than 550 students. The production was performed during new student orientation, for classes at regional campuses, and for a general audience of undergraduate students. Audience members largely reflected the demographics of the institution: predominantly white and more than 50 percent female.

Measuring Change

Research has shown that interactive educational experiences, such as a workshop on LGBT issues or a LGBT peer panel, can effect positive change in participants' attitudes and behavior regarding the LGBT population and possibly decrease homophobia on college campuses (Guth, Lopez, and Fisher; Nelson and Krieger). Gregory Herek hypothesizes that positive attitudes are likely to develop toward gays, lesbians, and bisexuals when straight people are placed in situations in which their personal values of equality, justice, or compassion are elicited; when significant others encourage and support affirmative attitudes; or when experiences help individuals resolve conflicts they may have about gays, lesbians, and bisexuals ("On Heterosexual Masculinity" 574). While Herek was not setting out to describe the potential of theatre to effect attitude change, his criteria can easily be applied to this medium and further reveals its potential.

So I, as post-show survey chair, assisted by Alison Murphy, a graduate student from higher education administration and student personnel, and Ashley McKee, an undergraduate student in psychology, set out to measure the impact of this play on audience members' attitudes toward LGBT people. First, we needed to identify an instrument. After a review of LGBT attitude scales, we selected and adapted (with permission) Herek's Attitudes Toward Lesbians and Gay Men (ATLG) Scale. The ATLG Scale presents "sets of parallel statements that are highly indicative of a respondent's attitudes toward homosexuality" (Herek, "Sexual Prejudice" 256). The full ATLG consists of twenty items: ten about gay men (ATG subscale) and ten about lesbians (ATL subscale). Herek notes that these subscales consist of different items; however, "researchers wishing to compare subject population's attitudes toward gay men with their attitudes toward lesbians are advised to use parallel forms" of subscale items, "with each presented twice, once in reference to gay men and once in reference to lesbians" ("Attitudes" 392). The short versions have proved sufficiently reliable and valid. Herek reports that "with college student samples completing a written version of the ATLG or its short forms, alpha levels are typically greater than .85 for the subscales and .90 for the full scale" (392).

The *True Lives* survey, administered pre- and post-show, consisted of twenty items: eight about lesbians (ATL subscale), eight about gay men (ATG subscale), and four designed to measure general attitudes toward lesbians and gay men (GA). Of the eight respective subscale items, six were structured using parallel form. For instance, an ATL subscale item (with gay male wording in brackets), "Sex between two women [men] is just plain wrong," was also on the ATG subscale. One item on the scale was adapted in order to correspond with the issues presented in the play. For this instance, the Herek scale, which includes the item "I would not be too upset if I learned that my son were a homosexual," was modified to read, "I would not be too upset to learn my sister was lesbian," and a parallel item, "I would not be too upset to learn my brother was gay," to be consistent with a story line in the play about an undergraduate male, John, who learns that his sister, Megan, is a lesbian. Participants indicated their responses along a 5-point Likert scale, ranging from 1 (strongly disagree) to 5 (strongly agree). Additionally, as part of the post-show survey, audience members were asked open-ended questions such as "What did you like about the play?," "What part(s) of the play did you like least?," and "What can you do regarding LGBT issues in your community?"

As audience members arrived and took their seats, they were given the survey and asked by the play's facilitator to complete page 1 of the four-page survey. This pre-show survey consisted of the twenty-item attitude scale (described above) and one open-ended question: "What have you done in the past to help stop anti-LGBT jokes, put-downs, assaults or other forms of discrimination?"

Following the performance, as audience members engaged in a post-show discussion with the cast, they were asked, again by the facilitator, to complete the post-show survey (pages 2–4 of the instrument). This consisted of the same twenty-item attitude scale they completed pre-show along with questions about characters and issues developed in the play and an open-ended question, "What can you do regarding LGBT issues in your community?"

Scoring was accomplished by summing the numerical values (for example, 1 = strongly disagree, 5 = strongly agree) across items for each subscale. The total score for the ATL and ATG subscales can range from 10 (extremely negative attitudes) to 50 (extremely positive attitudes), and the GA subscale can range from 4 (negative) to 20 (positive).

Changing Attitudes

Quantitative analysis of the survey data revealed that after viewing a performance of *True Lives*, students made significant gains in awareness and changes in attitudes toward LGBT persons and issues on campus. Notable differences were related to gender and age and to items that were directly evident in the play.

Gender

Participants' responses to the Attitudes Toward Lesbians subscale, when analyzed by gender, revealed that women had a lower ATL pre-show score ($x = 30.90$) than did men ($x = 31.08$), but women made greater post-show gains along the ATL subscale than did men ($x = 32.12$ and 31.87, respectively). Respondents' attitudes, as measured by the Attitude Toward Gay Men subscale, also showed significant pre- and post-show changes for men ($x = 29.20$ and 30.03) and women ($x = 30.47$ and 32.01). Finally, regarding participants' general attitudes, women started with more positive attitudes ($x = 14.57$) than did men ($x = 13.88$), but both women and men made significant gains ($x = 15.19$ and 14.30, respectively). Notably, men did not achieve the general attitude levels after the show that women held before the show. These results suggest that the participants' attitude change was less dramatic toward gay men than it was toward lesbians. Scholars agree with this data point: "Heterosexuals' attitudes towards lesbians differ from their attitudes toward gay men in overall intensity" (Herek, "Sexual Prejudice" 262; Liang and Alimo 240). Further, the gender analysis of ATL and ATG subscales are consistent with Laura Louderback and Bernard Whitley's finding that straight males express more negative attitudes toward gay men than toward lesbians, while straight females express more negative attitudes toward lesbians than toward gay men (175).

Age

The three subscales (ATL, ATG, and GA) were each analyzed according to respondents' ages. Significant change was reported within the two age categories representing the majority of audience members (20 and under, and 21–35). For the ATL subscale, individuals age 20 and under had pre-show attitudes below that of individuals age 21–35 ($x = 30.82$ and 31.07). Post-show attitudes improved for both age categories and were equivalent ($x = 32.00$). For the ATG subscale, both age categories made significant gains, and the post-show score for individuals age 20 and under exceeded the pre-show attitude score for the 21–35 age category. Finally, on the GA subscale, both age categories again made significant gains. Of note, the post-show score for individuals age 21–35 barely exceeded the pre-show general attitude score for the 20 and under age category.

Selected Items

I will now focus on two items that were directly related to the script. As noted above, one thread in the play illustrates how "John," a popular, straight college male, responds when he learns that his sister, "Megan," a high school senior, is a lesbian. Many respondents identified the relationship between John and Megan to be the most poignant part of the play and indicated they have found themselves in similar situations.

- "I liked when John accepted Megan for her decision. Nothing is better than support from someone you love."
- "I liked when John said he loved his sister, Megan, no matter what."

Quantitatively, a relationship between this aspect of the play and attitude change was also evident in responses to ATL item 4, "I would not be too upset if I learned my sister was a lesbian," and ATG item 6, "I would not be too upset if I learned my brother was homosexual."

Another thread in the play focused on "Anton," a closeted gay male who is in the Reserve Officers' Training Corps (ROTC). Among other things, this thread was used to convey how policy (for example, the military's former policy of "Don't Ask, Don't Tell" or DADT)[1] can contribute to closeting one's true sexual identity. As exemplified by one respondent's surprise at "ROTC's unacceptance of homosexuality," many audience members did not seem aware of this policy or its potential impact on campus climate. In response to General Attitude subscale item 1, "ROTC 'Don't Ask, Don't Tell' policies should be abolished," respondents showed a significant positive change in attitude (from 3.30 on the pre-survey to 3.53 on the post-survey). These results, although not conclusive, point to a meaningful relationship between the material covered in the play and changes in student attitudes regarding LGBT issues on college campuses.

Inspiring Action

I now turn to individuals' responses to a survey question about what audience members had done before watching the show and what they felt they could do after watching the show regarding LGBT issues in the community. Their responses illuminate the power of the performance to inspire action.

On the pre-show survey, audience members were asked, "What have you done in the past to help stop anti-LGBT jokes, put-downs, assaults and other forms of discrimination?" Of all the surveys returned, 375 individuals responded to this open-ended question. Of those responses, 36 percent indicated they had done nothing. These responses ranged from "never really seen any such situations" to "nothing; I think homosexuality is wrong," "I don't really know; not a lot I guess," and "nothing, until today." Other responses, articulating what individuals had done, conveyed a range of actions, including participating in a Day of Silence, marching in a Pride Parade, signing petitions, organizing educational programs, political organizing, and holding positions in LGBT school organizations. The most common response (after "nothing"), however, was by 66 respondents who indicated they did not make derogatory jokes or did not laugh when homophobic comments were made; they had "told people to stop using hurtful language" and "asked people not to be too quick to judge" or just "ignored it [homophobic comment] to show disapproval."

On the post-show survey, audience members were asked a related question: "What can you do regarding LGBT issues in your community? (This can range from interrupting a joke to attending a rally, from voting in favor of LGBT-friendly policies to joining a student group.)" Of all the surveys returned, 282 individuals responded to this open-ended question and only 2 respondents wrote "nothing." These 2 (or less than 1 percent of respondents) represent a dramatic decrease from the 135 respondents (36 percent) on the pre-show survey who indicated they had done nothing before the show. The post-show responses articulated an increased desire to take some type of action in response to the LGBT issues portrayed in the *True Lives* performance. Post-show, respondents expressed increased motivation to educate themselves and others or to serve as allies for LGBT persons. These data excerpts illustrate this emphasis:

- "I can speak up and allow people to know the wrong issues with this."
- "Educating friends, family and even strangers on how to take efforts to improve the gay community."
- "Correcting others, joining groups on campus, becoming more independent/active in the community."
- "I am willing to do whatever it takes for a safer more open-minded community."

Finally, regarding the project's goal to address the problem of homophobic language and behavior among students, audience members' post-show responses suggest this goal was achieved. Many in their open-ended responses indicated they were surprised and even put off by the free use of slurs and derogatory language in the play, but as many indicated the strong language was powerful in conveying the story. In post-show responses, many expressed they would "stop using 'gay' in my sentences," "stop stereotyping," "stop making jokes," "stop saying 'fags' and 'gay' because it's negative toward gay people," "stop saying 'that's so gay,'" "try to stop people from saying 'gay,'" and "be more aware of jokes and try to put a stop to it." This analysis of the pre- and post-show responses reveals that after watching the performance, students wanted to take a more active role in preventing harassment and abuse of LGBT students. Consistent with findings from a recent study into the development of social justice allies, Ellen Broido noted that "gaining information was a precursor to advocating for social justice" (qtd. in Evans and Herriott 330).

Discussion

The results of my research suggest that using theatre to educate, inform, and change student attitudes and behavior can be a powerful tool for individuals seeking to raise awareness and change attitudes. More specifically, my research suggests that many of the respondents' changes in attitudes and intended behavior occurred in response to situations that were dramatized in the *True Lives* vignettes. For example, positive changes in student attitudes were evident in responses to the ROTC post-show survey question. These attitude changes reveal a correlation with the ROTC vignette that involved the struggle a young man faced in making a decision as to whether he could or should "come out" to his peers and risk consequences with his supervisors in the ROTC. Herek reminds us that positive attitude change is likely to occur when people are placed in situations in which their personal values of equality, justice, or compassion are elicited ("On Heterosexual Masculinity" 574). Theatre provides a powerful way for eliciting such emotions and values and to encourage empathy (Weems).

Similarly, noticeable changes in students' attitudes were evident in response to the questions related to having a gay brother or sister. As noted above, one of the vignettes in the *True Lives* performance told the story of an older brother who learned that his sister was a lesbian. The sister had been afraid to tell him because she thought he would reject her. The vignette shows the love the brother has for his sister, his subsequent change in attitude toward lesbians, and his desire to protect his sister. Viewing interactions, such as this vignette, can help individuals resolve conflicts they may have about LGBT people or issues (Herek, "On Heterosexual Masculinity" 574). And Augusto Boal tells us that theatre allows individuals to create a safe space and explore the interactions that make up their lives. Philip Auslander adds that theatre is a "laboratory for social experimentation" (104), and through this space individuals can explore possibilities for social relations (Weems 7).

In addition to the positive relationship between student attitude changes and theatrical vignettes that dramatize particular topics of interest, results suggest that theatre can be used as a catalyst to promote positive social change on college campuses. Audience members' post-show responses revealed a heightened commitment to ally with LGBT individuals and advocate for their rights. Further research is warranted regarding the permanence of these attitude changes as well as the extent to which individuals enact their intention to take action.

Note

1. On September 20, 2011, the DADT policy officially ended. See http://www.nytimes.com/2011/09/20/us/after-toiling-in-shadows-to-end-dont-ask-dont-tell-1st-lt-josh-seefried-greets-a-new-era.html?pagewanted=all.

Bibliography

Auslander, Philip, ed. *From Acting to Performance: Essays in Modernism and Postmodernism*. London: Routledge, 1997.

Boal, Augusto. *Theatre of the Oppressed*. Translated by Charles A. and Maria-Odilia Leal McBride. 1979. New York: Theatre Communications Group, 1985.

Bowles, Norma, ed. *Friendly Fire: An Anthology of 3 Plays by Queer Street Youth*. Los Angeles: A.S.K. Theatre Projects, 1997.

Engstrom, Catherine, and William Sedlacek. "Attitudes of Heterosexual Students toward their Gay Male and Lesbian Peers." *Journal of College Student Development* 38, no. 6 (1997): 565–76.

Evans, Nancy, and Todd Herriott. "Freshmen Impressions: How Investigating the Campus Climate for LGBT Students Affected Four Freshman Students." *Journal of College Student Development* 45, no. 3 (2004): 316–32.

Guth, Lorraine, David Lopez, Kimberly Clements, and Julio Rojas. "Student Attitudes toward Lesbian, Gay and Bisexual Issues: Analysis of Self-talk Categories." *Journal of Homosexuality* 41, no. 1 (2001): 137–56.

Guth, Lorraine, David Lopez, and Manda Fisher. "In-person versus Internet Training: A Comparison of Student Attitudes toward Homosexuality." *NASPA Journal* 40, no. 1 (2002): 145–64.

Herek, Gregory. "Attitudes toward Lesbians and Gay Men Scale." In *Handbook of Sexuality-Related Measures*, edited by Clive Davis, William Yarber, Robert Bauserman, George Schreer, and Sandra Davis. Thousand Oaks, CA: Sage, 1998. 392–94.

———. "Heterosexuals' Attitudes toward Lesbians and Gay Men: Correlates and Gender Differences." *Journal of Sex Research* 25 (1988): 451–77.

———. "On Heterosexual Masculinity: Some Psychical Consequences of the Social Construction of Gender and Sexuality." *American Behavioral Scientist* 29 (1986): 563–77.

———. "Sexual Prejudice and Gender: Do Homosexuals' Attitudes toward Lesbians and Gay Men Differ?" *Journal of Social Issues* 56, no. 2 (2000): 251–66.

Iverson, Susan V. "Performing Gender: A Discourse Analysis of Theatre-Based Sexual Violence Programs." *NASPA Journal* 43, no. 3 (2006): 547–77.

LaMar, Lisa, and Mary Kite. "Sex Differences in Attitudes toward Gay Men and Lesbians: A Multidimensional Perspective." *Journal of Sex Research* 35, no. 2 (1998): 189–96.

Liang, Christopher, and Craig Alimo. "The Impact of White Heterosexual Students' Interactions on Attitudes toward Lesbian, Gay, and Bisexual People: A Longitudinal Study." *Journal of College Student Development* 46, no. 3 (2005): 237–50.

Louderback, Laura, and Bernard Whitley Jr. "Perceived Erotic Value of Homosexuality and Sex Role Attitudes as Mediators of Sex Differences in Heterosexual College Students' Attitudes toward Lesbians and Gay Men." *Journal of Sex Research* 34, no. 2 (1997): 175–82.

Mohr, Jonathan, and William Sedlacek. "Perceived Barriers to Friendship with Lesbians and Gay Men among University Students." *Journal of College Student Development* 41, no. 1 (2000): 70–80.

Nelson, Eileen, and Shirley Krieger. "Changes in Attitudes toward Homosexuality in College Students: Implementation of a Gay Men and Lesbian Peer Panel." *Journal of Homosexuality* 33, no. 2 (1997): 63–81.

Paul, John Steven. "Body of Work: Sexuality in Recent American Drama." *Annual Review of Sex Research* 17 (2006): 200–214.

Weems, Mary E. *Public Education and the Imagination-Intellect*. New York: Peter Lang, 2003.

Wesley, Sherre. "Multicultural Diversity: Learning through the Arts." *New Directions in Adult and Continuing Education* 116 (2007): 13–23.

Sympathy vs. Stigma: Writing the "Victim"

DANIEL-RAYMOND NADON

Kent State University partnered with Fringe Benefits in 2007 to develop a play addressing the homophobic climate on the Kent campuses. While Kent has a reputation as a progressive institution and is home to the first LGBT minor program in the state of Ohio, the local political climate in 2007 had led to a number of homophobic incidents on and around campus. Most notably, a violent act was perpetrated against a young lesbian student.

Stories about these incidents revealed themselves quickly on the second day of the Theatre for Social Justice Institute, when the Fringe Benefits facilitators asked the students and other participants to share stories about anti-LGBT discrimination on campus. While the discussion included a barrage of name-calling incidents, as well as some mentions of vandalism, intimidation, and institutional homophobia, the focus of the discussion returned frequently to the single aforementioned violent act. The story is that of a young lesbian activist who was heading home late one night from a gathering of friends. She happened upon a duo of intoxicated young men, assumed to be "townies," near campus. They noticed the androgynous look of the woman and mistook her for a gay man. During the ensuing savage attack, the student tried to conceal the fact that she was a woman for fear that, if the men made this discovery, the attack would escalate into a sexual assault. The crime received little notice from the campus community or the campus newspapers but was well known in the campus LGBT community.

Among the shared stories, this was seen as the most powerful, and an overwhelming majority voted to include it as one of the three central stories in *True Lives: I'm a Kent State Freshman*. There was, however, a small dissenting minority that remained silent during the

Institute process. After the Institute, a discussion ensued in my LGBT studies class; most of the students had also been participants in the Institute. Many of these students had experienced heterosexist discrimination on campus firsthand, and some had known the gay-bashing victim personally. The following questions were asked:

1. Does presenting LGBTQ individuals in the role of victim combat or exacerbate the discrimination they face?
2. Will the portrayals of LGBTQ victims present LGBTQ students as "poor me" and "whiney" and cause non-LGBTQ students to react more negatively toward them, blaming them for their own victimization?
3. Could the Institute play "stir up a hornets' nest" by further stigmatizing LGBTQ students as hated and isolated individuals and by depicting them as being at odds with campus traditions, mores, and values?
4. Instead of focusing on discrimination, might it not be better to look through another lens at well-adjusted, "normalized" LGBTQ families? Could that make a more powerful and positive statement?

The students began to question the entire approach of the Institute. While many questions were raised, none were answered during class time. They did, however, prompt some research on my part.

The concerns voiced by the class were in line with those articulated in Christopher J. Lyons's essay "Stigma or Sympathy? Attributions of Fault to Hate Crime Victims and Offenders." In his study, using data from the 1990s, Lyons examines two competing viewpoints with regard to the blaming of and prejudice against minority victims of discrimination and hate crimes. He points out that "stigma associated with the status of typical hate crime victims may induce prejudiced or ambivalent evaluations of the victim and less negative reactions to the offender" (40). In other words, according to Lyons's "stigma perspective," the public often derides minority victims and offenders because of their marginal status. But then he points out: "In contrast, what I call the 'sympathy perspective' predicts that the public will be especially sensitive to imbalances of power, viewing attacks against minorities as deserving greater public sympathy than similar attacks against members of nonminority groups" (40).

Using data from a decade later, Samantha Reis and Brian Martin presented a second theoretical matrix in their article "Psychological Dynamics of Outrage against Injustice," in which they discuss how an individual develops emotional "outrage" to his or her perception of social injustice (6). This outrage can manifest in social action, which they refer to as "backfire." In this model, powerful perpetrators of perceived injustice will try to maximize what Lyons calls "stigma" by limiting the effects of outrage and thereby mitigating the responses to a hate crime. This is done by implementing five important strategies: covering up the action, devaluing the target, reinterpreting the events, using official channels to give an appearance of justice, and employing corresponding counter tactics (10).

A comparison of the two studies, implemented a decade apart, is enlightening. The results of Lyons's study, undertaken in the 1990s, support the "stigma" perspective. While acknowledging the changing nature of American society, he finds that a majority of people in the general public still believe that LGBT victims are at fault for attacks against them and that prejudice toward them may be valid. Lyons posits that the reason for this is the common belief that we live in a just world. In such a world, people tend to get what they deserve (Lerner). Lyons was the first theorist to look specifically at the instances and statistics of anti-LGBT prejudice and hate crimes.

Lyons summarizes the works of J. L. Fernald and Hope Landrine and their colleagues by stating: "Considerable research confirms that the stigma of homosexuality is correlated with discriminatory be-havioral outcomes; therefore we have reason to believe that a vic-tim's sexual orientation also will influence third-person evaluations of victimization" (41). At the time of his study, there continued to be heightened stigmatization of members of the LGBT community: "Victims' and offenders' statuses, however, influence attributions of fault; respondents appear to be more sympathetic to victims of racial hate crimes than to victims of other types of hate crime, including gays and lesbians" (56). These findings seem to support the fears and concerns of my LGBT studies students.

However, Lyons sees some positive data in his research. He believes that American society may be undergoing a paradigm shift with re-gard to attitudes toward minority victims and perpetrators of violent crimes: as time passes, LGBT individuals will be more accepted, less stigmatized. According to Valerie Jenness and Kendal Broad in their study *Hate Crimes: New Social Movements and the Politics of Violence*, a major goal of the antiviolence movement has been to change the way violence against minorities is perceived in hopes of achieving greater sympathy for victims and condemnation of offenders (Lyons 40). This goal matches the goals set forth by Fringe Benefits and other community-based activist theatres. Reis and Martin did not specifically deal with sexual orientation but created their study with an acute awareness of homophobia. With regard to changes in the importance/dominance of "stigma," they agree with Lyons, stating that this shift may be due to the successful mitigation of outrage, but they hold an even more optimistic view, contending that blame is now more often assigned to the attacker than to the victim (11). This could signal a tipping point with regard to the dominance of "outrage" and the consequent social action driven by "backfire."

In support of this paradigm shift, Lyons points out that the adoption and support of hate crime legislation has begun to chip away at the stigmatization of victims and of homosexuality: "Discourse surrounding hate crime legislation paints 'new portraits of victimization' that encourage particular social reaction. Hate crime legislation also categorizes hate offenses as deserving increased punishment and condemnation as an emphatic message to society and potential offenders that such activities are no longer tolerated" (42). He further posits that "one goal of hate crime legislation has been to alter normative structures that stigmatize certain constituencies and affect public reactions to victims and offenders" (56). The emergence of discourse in favor of hate crime legislation, in short, may parallel overall reactions to victims and offenders. From 1999 to 2009, for example, support of hate crime legislation in the United States moved well past the 50 percent mark and was adopted on a federal level in 2010.[1] In Canada, where Reis and Martin published their essay, hate crime legislation was enacted at the national level in 2004. Therefore, hate crime legislation had been settled law for four years when they conducted their study.[2]

Lyons focuses on the challenges in overcoming the stigmatization of minorities. Reis and Martin, however, also suggest a strategy for implementing this change. This strategy attacks a variety of mitigating factors of "outrage." First, they suggest diligence in foiling any plot to cover up the details of any violent act with lies, deceit, or other spin. Next, they cite the need to combat the "moral disengagement"—usually applied to perpetrators but also applicable to citizen observers—that comes from the understanding that the victim's conduct has somehow caused his or her own ill-treatment. In short, the victim needs to be, through education, humanized in the eyes of society. Fringe Benefits attempts to strategize in these ways—educating, revealing the truth, and humanizing.

In order to fully understand how Fringe Benefits aims to serve as a catalyst for this paradigm shift, however, we need to be cognizant of where it is currently taking place and with whom. The younger, "post-Ellen" generation is gaining awareness of heterosexism and is propelling this paradigm shift forward. While Lyons's study and article sample a diverse cross-section of the population, our collaborating team selected freshmen as our target audience, focusing, thereby, on reaching a younger, educated audience and assuming a degree of open-mindedness and flexibility of thinking even among the more resistant. In short, our play aimed to create positive change where it is already occurring, in our youth. Kent State University rests in a fairly progressive (by Ohio standards) college town. Many students do, however, come from the surrounding rural and urban areas. The impact of the play, then, potentially could extend from the progressive college environment to the entire region.

As we considered the impact we hoped our play would have on our young university audience, we decided to give primary focus to the story about the recent hate crime perpetrated against a lesbian student. All three stories lead up to the beating of the character we named "Dani." This story became the climactic moment of the play and the springboard for the epilogue in which each character reacts to reports of the bashing and responds to the incident by becoming more aware, more understanding, and more activist. In the post-show discussion, the audience is asked to do the same.

The show was performed six times on three different Kent campuses; of these performances, two occurred during the Week of Welcome. The post-show discussion following each performance revealed that Dani's story was the most compelling to the audience, which consisted primarily of freshmen experiencing their first weeks of classes. During some post-show discussions, I took copious notes. In these discussions, roughly 60 percent of the verbal questions and comments addressed the story or attempted to secure more information about the woman who inspired Dani's character. The comments fell into two categories. In the first, the compassionate response, approximately two-thirds of the audience demonstrated sincere empathy for Dani. It seemed inconceivable to most of the students that such a crime had been committed near the Kent campus. Further, they indicated that it was her story that inspired them to move toward participating in and/or encouraging activist efforts to stop anti-LGBT discrimination. In the second category, the fearful response, the remaining one-third showed concern that violence, any violence, had taken place on the Kent campus. They exhibited fear that we had an ineffectual safety service department, bands of violent marauders, and an unconcerned or uninformed student body. The first group of responses, by far the larger group, showed concern for Dani and the LGBT community on campus. The second group showed a more personal concern for their own campus experience. While it is impossible to identify which of the respondents were members of the LGBT community, such information would be valuable to this analysis.

My distinguished colleague Susan Iverson's pre- and post-show surveys invited audience members to share their reactions to the show. While the surveys did not include questions about the post-show discussions, they did include specific questions about the play itself, providing us with an additional opportunity to examine the play's impact on the audience.

The story that audience members "liked least," as well as the one that they found most surprising, was Dani's story. Many students remarked that this story "shocked" them, made them feel "sad," and made them "uncomfortable."[3] Of those audience members who mentioned a particular story in their answer, over 85 percent noted that Dani's was the most surprising, and over 75 percent liked it the least. The audience was genuinely repulsed by the violence and hateful language hurled at Dani. They did not "like" to feel uncomfortable or upset. One explained her surprise: "That just wasn't something that I would expect at Kent." Others described their aversion: "The ending was brutal"; "I was repulsed by it." In spite of their discomfort, audience members showed compassion for Dani. One stated, "This is something that happens too often." Another said, "Whether she was straight, gay, boy, or girl, nobody deserves that." Others remarked, "It was just wrong," "It wasn't fair," "It was really heartbreaking," and "It's so unfair—no one should have to feel afraid. It's sad, it makes me really sad." The audience was outraged by what happens to Dani in the play and in the true story on which those dramatic events are based.

The compassion displayed by the majority of the audience exemplifies their outrage. Dani's story, the depiction of an anti-LGBT hate crime, had provoked a "sympathy response" as opposed to a "stigma response." Iverson's analysis of the survey responses underscores this. In her essay in this volume, "Inspiring Change and Action," she reports that, following the show, there was a quantifiable, statistically significant attitude "movement" in the audience's perception of LGBT persons and lives and that this "movement" was toward compassion and understanding. Although long-term change has not been quantified, the short-term surveys support the presence of Reis and Martin's notion of "outrage" and Lyons's definition of a "sympathy response."

A large number of students from my LGBT studies class attended the performances of *True Lives*. They were all abuzz over the culmination of the process that they had begun a year prior. Their commentary focused on the quality and believability of the performances, the structure of the text, and the audience members' responses, most notably their outrage.[4] They also talked about how they had paid especially close attention to Dani's story and to the audience's comments about it. None of them seemed to think that telling Dani's story had stigmatized the LGBT community. They seemed relieved by the performance, happy that it had happened and that it had been included in the Week of Welcome. They felt the outrage of their fellow students. They noticed the sympathetic responses to the play even as they saw the potential for backlash and felt called, again, to social action. I asked one student how she felt about the inclusion of Dani's story now that it was done. She shrugged. Then she asked me what I thought about it. I had never voiced my opinion during the Institute or during the show. I replied, simply: "It is true life. It is one of our stories. Of course, it needs to be told."

We must battle fiercely against silence. We must use our voices and our stories to deconstruct and eliminate the stigma against LGBT people. Everyone's story—including, *perhaps especially*, anti-LGBT discrimination and hate crime stories—needs to be told truthfully, honestly, and loudly if we are going to win this battle.

Notes

1. "The Matthew Shepard and James Byrd, Jr. Hate Crimes Prevention Act" is an American act of Congress, passed on October 22, 2009, and signed into law by President Barack Obama on October 28, 2009, as a rider to the "National Defense Authorization Act for 2010" (HR 2647).

2. In December 2001, the Canadian Hate Crimes law was amended under the Anti-Terrorism Act. "Hate" is defined as a crime under two parts of Canada's criminal code: sections 318 and 319.

3. These quotations were extracted from audience responses to post-show surveys (unpublished).

4. These comments were gleaned from responses articulated by students during classroom and post-show discussions and as they left the theatre, as well as in their post-show surveys.

Bibliography

Fernald, J. L. "Interpersonal Heterosexism." In *The Social Psychology of Interpersonal Discrimination*, edited by Bernice Lott and Diane Maluso. New York: Guilford, 1995. 80–117.

Harry, Joseph. "Conceptualizing Anti-gay Violence." *Journal of Interpersonal Violence* 5, no. 3 (1990): 350–58.

Jenness, Valerie, and Kendal Broad. *Hate Crimes: New Social Movements and the Politics of Violence*. New York: Aldine, 1997.

Kwong, Dan. "Beyond Victimization." *High Performance* 72 (1996). http://www.dankwong.com/printables/beyond_essay.html.

Landrine, Hope, Elizabeth A. Klonof, Roxanna Alcaraz, Judyth Scott, and Phyllis Wilkins. *Multiple Status Variables in Discrimination*. New York: Guilford, 1995.

Lerner, Melvin. *The Belief in a Just World: A Fundamental Delusion*. New York: Plenum, 1980.

Lyons, Christopher J. "Stigma or Sympathy? Attributions of Fault to Hate Crime Victims and Offenders." *Social Psychology Quarterly* 69, no. 1 (2006): 39–59.

Reis, Samantha, and Brian Martin. "Psychological Dynamics of Outrage against Injustice." *Journal of Peace Research* 40, no. 1 (2008): 5–23.

Do Not Try This at Home!

Dealing with socially charged topics, one is often drawn into a world of prejudice, narrow-mindedness, and invective. These elements are a part of our world, and in Theatre for Social Justice (TSJ), they cannot be ignored. On the contrary, it is (in part) the very presence of behavior that might be viewed as "bad" that makes TSJ so necessary. For the purposes of this essay, what constitutes "bad behavior" is behavior that is potentially offensive or even destructive—which might include, but is not limited to, catcalls, sexist behavior, racial slurs, derogatory statements, and/or violent actions. If addressing "bad behavior," as so defined, is intrinsic to the work we do as purveyors of TSJ, how do we find healthy ways to do so?

This question continued to arise throughout the creation and performances of *Changing Channels*, our Theatre for Social Justice Institute piece addressing sexism at Bowling Green State University, created in the fall of 2005. Utilizing that show as a case study, I will examine in this essay healthy strategies for interfacing with bad behavior.

While the work of Augusto Boal[1] is often used as a model for Theatre for Social Change, *Changing Channels* is not Boalian in two regards: (1) the script does not lend itself to audience intervention strategies, and (2) the fact that the primary actors are "watching television" with "programming" that is fixed means that they, like the audience, are situated as reactors rather than as what Boal terms "spect-actors"[2] (audience members empowered not only to comment on but also to change the action they witness onstage).

In *Changing Channels*, a heterosexual couple views a number of television programs, each of which calls up a different aspect of sexism. Many of the "programs" they encounter in their channel surfing are takeoffs on familiar programs or commercials, always with a twist. A few brief examples:

1. *CSI* Barbie and Ken dolls investigate the aftermath of a wild college party and the "Walk of Shame."
2. "Martha Stewheart" shares her recipe for "The Thursday Night Homerun"—"for a night *you'll* never forget . . . but *your date* will never remember!"[3]
3. *Girls Gone Crazy* segments include a girl who is willing to flash the camera only if the commentator and cameraman will flash as well and a second sequence wherein the girl hands the commentator her prosthetic breasts, proclaiming she had "a double mastectomy—cancer."

Various sequences of the show are connected through the convention of channel surfing, as the viewing couple keeps changing channels only to find yet another demonstration of sexist behavior. While the show culminates with a longer, more serious sequence concerning date rape, it is easy to see how portions of these sequences noted above could be considered offensive by some people as they either exhibit or, in the case of the Martha Stewheart segment, even seem to promote bad behavior.

Many questions then arise. Is it possible to address charged issues of sexism or prejudice without putting bad behavior on display? Even if the answer is yes, is that strategy the most effective in all cases? Is exposing bad behavior—putting it on display for scrutiny—enough to shift the consciousness of the audience? Or is it acceptable only to present bad behavior in this context if it is immediately critiqued as unacceptable? These loaded questions lead to a plethora of attendant questions around the central query: What do we do with bad behavior in shows promoting social justice?

1. *Deride it?* Do we then become the "behavior police"?
2. *Ignore it?* Does that set us up to pretend it doesn't exist, ensuring we only present acceptable behavior? Not only is that very likely to be less theatrically engaging, but it is not true to life.
3. *Instruct how to avoid it?* How? By simply avoiding people who encourage us to behave badly? By strategizing different ways of responding when confronted with bad behavior?

4. *Demonstrate it?* Do we simply bring it up for discussion and leave it to the facilitator to utilize it as a reference point from which to inspire and promote change?
5. *Exploit it?* If so, how? Use it to prove that we are hip and real? Use it, then blow the whistle on it to subvert it?
6. *Make fun of it?* Use it to poke fun at those who behave badly, making them look ridiculous?

There are no simple answers to any of the questions I am posing here. I am bringing them up for consideration because these issues arise frequently in the creation and performance of TSJ. I believe it is vital that we continue to reexamine our processes and our texts concerning how bad behavior is addressed, because the interrogation of bad behavior is primary for theatre created to promote social change.

Here I will address, briefly, four possible tools for dealing with bad behavior in TSJ: humor, disclaimers, calling "bad behavior" into question within the piece itself, and facilitation.

Humor

This issue is especially loaded: bad behavior and humor. Bad behavior as a source of humor is a part of our society, like it or not—witness *America's Funniest Home Videos, Saturday Night Live,* or *The Simpsons.* The list is truly endless. How many cruel acts are perpetrated—from tripping someone to humiliating someone even to the point of suicide—in the name of humor? If bad behavior is utilized in this manner for humor, is it being subverted? Or is it actually being reinforced—touted as acceptable or simply as "the way things are"? Do we perhaps even run the danger of featuring bad behavior in a way that is so entertaining that we unwittingly present it as a model for people to follow (exactly the opposite of the effect we might hope to have)? For example, there may be people who justify their bad behavior, be it rudeness, drunkenness, or sexist banter, by saying, "I guess we're just two wild and crazy guys!"[4]

Humor is a potent tool that must be utilized consciously. In the creation of *Changing Channels*, we found it useful to include humor in order to draw in the audience. A male audience member, responding to one of our earliest showings of *Changing Channels*, remarked that he really appreciated the humor of the play. It reassured him that our intention was not to preach, which allowed him to relax and get involved, so that when the piece turned more serious at the end, he was both surprised and moved.

Still, given the plethora of examples merely touched on earlier, we cannot simply assume that humor automatically "blows the whistle" on bad behavior. What marks the difference between humor that exposes bad behavior and humor that justifies, exploits, or (consciously or unconsciously) reinforces it? I believe the primary issue is consciousness.

Humor is often based on stereotypes, but exploiting a stereotype and calling stereotypical assumptions up for consideration promote vastly different agendas. Often it is the jokester's facial/physical response to what he or she has just said that either underscores or subverts the behavior and calls it into question. If humor is utilized to help audience members be more conscious about an assumption they themselves or segments of society make, then it would be fair to say that to represent bad behavior onstage is not simply to exploit it but rather to use it as a tool to raise consciousness and promote understanding.

Brechtian tools[5] may be useful here as they pull the audience out of the emotional flow of a moment and call attention to the behavior as a choice. The simple technique of adding "he said" to behavior you want the audience to question brings a perspective that calls the behavior up for consideration. Similarly, a double take by either the perpetrator of the bad behavior (that might suggest "Did I really just say/do that?") or by his or her onstage partner(s) (as if to say, "I can't believe he just said that!" or "I can't believe she just did that!") can subvert the bad behavior. Distancing techniques such as these call the choice of the bad behavior up for conscious consideration rather than allow it to be regarded as simply "acceptable." Humor is a powerful force, often used to create "winners" and "losers." It is vital that we use it consciously, creating connection rather than division, thus leading not only to a humor that is conscious but perhaps to a humor with a conscience, or a "humor of consciousness." TSJ is perfectly situated to help society shift into a "humor of consciousness."[6]

Disclaimers

Often, shows that exploit the exhibition of bad behavior solely for the purpose of entertainment begin with a disclaimer: "The content of this program does not necessarily represent the views of this station" or "These are paid professionals; DO NOT TRY THIS AT HOME!" The producers of the television program *Jackass* went even further, proclaiming that not only were they not encouraging the behaviors exhibited, but they would not view any videotapes that were sent to them, as watching their show often seemed to encourage some viewers to create their own dangerous stunts. Are disclaimers effective? Do they really create any kind of distance between the actor and the act? Do they help discourage viewers from imitating the bad behavior presented? Or are they merely intended to exonerate the producer from any culpability, should the show "inspire" viewers to demonstrate similar bad behavior? Might it nevertheless be helpful to create, as part of our script, a disclaimer, hopefully humorous, to remind audience members of their ability to make conscious choices about their behavior?

In January 2009, the Humanities Troupe[7] at Bowling Green State University created a disclaimer that was recorded and used in a total of sixteen performances, primarily with student audiences. An attendant feedback sheet monitored the disclaimer's and the show's effectiveness. The disclaimer concluded: "We know that we do not need to remind you—as the mature audience member that you now claim to be—that you are responsible for YOUR OWN behavior (yes, drunk or sober, until you have officially been declared legally insane by a court official). The fact that you may witness behavior on this stage that is less than respectful of others does not in any way condone your offensive behavior in real life. Thank you and enjoy the show."

From performances where this disclaimer was read, the Humanities Troupe gathered feedback forms from 352 respondents. Of those responding, 78.7 percent felt that disclaimers in general "work," while 5.7 percent thought they work sometimes and 15.6 percent not at all.[8] Asked to describe their reaction to this particular disclaimer (with multiple responses allowed), 186 (52.8 percent) checked "useful," 198 (56.3 percent) checked "informative," 137 (39 percent) "thought-provoking," 196 (55.7 percent) "amusing," and 46 (13 percent) "pointless." While a majority (55 percent) of those surveyed felt this particular disclaimer did not affect how they viewed the show, the fact that large numbers of the respondents found the disclaimer by turns useful, informative, and amusing while more than one-third found it thought-provoking suggests that disclaimers can prove effective in preparing an audience for potentially controversial subject matter and behavior.

Of course, what is controversial for one audience might seem tame to another. It is vital that the intended audience is considered for each performance. The Theatre for Social Justice Institute emphasizes that any show must be written with the specific target audience in mind. Not surprisingly, the Humanities Troupe discovered that shows presented to college students are considered pristine and unreal if the language is too clean and we avoid all curse words, while some members of the faculty and staff may be offended and put off by the same "colorful language." We have to face the fact that we cannot please everyone, so the best we can do in that regard is know our audience, pick our battles, and not get carried away with colorful language for its own sake. The notion of knowing your audience, of course, becomes more complicated when the audience is not homogeneous, which is often the case. In such instances, clarifying the intended audience as well as addressing the issue of "What did you find offensive?" with the audience may help to foreground the fact that offensive behavior is often in the eye of the beholder and that ignoring someone else's point of view can often, even unintentionally, lead to hurtful behavior.

Calling "Bad Behavior" into Question within the Piece Itself

For a fully scripted piece that is not designed for Boalian intervention, one way of subverting bad behavior is to find ways to be sure the behavior is not simply accepted but rather acknowledged as a potentially destructive choice. As we performed *Changing Channels* and received feedback, we discovered that in earlier versions of the script, the couple watching the television shows often simply responded to a program or commercial with a physical gesture or facial expression before changing channels rather than by verbally calling the issue or behavior out for interrogation. In numerous rewrites, we kept extending and deepening the responses of the two characters to what they were viewing. This not only gave them more dimension and deepened their relationship but also made the texture of the piece much richer, as they often related what they were viewing to their own experience. For example, following the Martha Stewheart sequence about the "date rape potion," the two respond in this way:

> MIKE: *(indicating the screen)* Somebody did that to Rick's girl-friend, Emily. They went to this kegger . . . and after one beer, she was wasted.
> CYNTHIA: Oh, she's a lightweight.

MIKE: No, it normally takes, like . . . 4 or 5 beers for her to even feel buzzed. Someone slipped something in her drink when she wasn't looking.

CYNTHIA: That's messed up! Is she okay?

MIKE: Yeah . . . Rick took care of her.

CYNTHIA: What if she'd been alone!? Did they ever find out who did it?

MIKE: Rick went up to the guys who were throwing the party, and they were like, "Man, if we knew you were dating her, we never would've done it."

CYNTHIA: Bastards. I'm never putting a drink down again.

MIKE: Yeah. Me neither.

CYNTHIA: What?

MIKE: Yeah, it doesn't just happen to women. Last week Abby's little brother went to this bar, had one drink, and the next morning, he came-to in a cornfield.

CYNTHIA: Creepy! I don't want to think about it. *(grabs the remote & turns the TV back on)*

By having Mike and Cynthia respond with compassion and insight to what they are viewing, the bad behavior does not go unexamined; rather, it is referenced as something that is not only all too real but also unacceptable.

Facilitation

Facilitation is crucial in TSJ. In shows dealing with potentially inflammatory social issues, how the show is mediated is a huge component of its effectiveness. Is it enough to simply call the bad behavior into question through facilitated discussion? Can discussion override the power of the image? Or, as Boal suggests, is it vital to exemplify the transformation by having the actors or spect-actors act out the new behavior? In a more interactive format, the audience can call specific behavior into question, and Boal's Joker[9] can even stop the action and invite the audience to replay it a different way. *Changing Channels* was not designed to create opportunities for such interventions. This decision sprang from a concern that Forum interactions on this sensitive subject matter could become problematic with regard both to the settings of performances (which we assumed would most likely be the student union and residence halls) and to the limited time allotted for facilitation.

One of our goals was to encourage the audience to question what they see in the media. Consequently, part of the facilitation involves questioning the behaviors encouraged by the media and helping audience members strategize what they as viewers can do to call behaviors they witness into question. It is crucial for the mediation to encourage audience members to think about how what they have viewed might inform and apply to their own lives. In addition, it is important to challenge audience members to look beyond the specifics of the show they are viewing and consider how the ideas presented might connect to other issues that might be more applicable to their own experiences. Thus, the Humanities Troupe finds it important to include in post-show discussions not only questions such as "How can the events you have witnessed here help you think about other people's or even your own behavior?" and "What can we do if we see someone being sexist or racist or making a joke at someone else's expense?" but also questions like "What other situations have you witnessed or encountered where someone was treated badly for any reason? What did you do? What could you do?"

In Conclusion

There are many ways that TSJ may choose to examine, utilize, and subvert bad behavior. What we cannot afford to do is ignore it or shy away from showing it onstage for fear of offending someone who would prefer to pretend such behavior does not exist or who believes that putting bad behavior onstage promotes or even valorizes it. It is vital that we address bad behavior as an issue to be discussed, confronted, and transformed. Utilizing "humor of consciousness," including disclaimers that are informed rather than perfunctory, threading in framing devices and/or responses within the piece itself that call bad behavior into question, and employing insightful facilitation are a few tools that can assure that bad behavior in TSJ does not go unexamined, unquestioned, or unmediated.

Notes

1. Augusto Boal (1931–2009) was a Brazilian cultural activist, politician, and theatre practitioner whose theories and practices surrounding what he termed "Theatre of the Oppressed" have served as a foundation for a worldwide movement in Theatre for Social Change. One aspect of his work centers around Forum Theatre, in which audience members are able to intervene in the onstage action.

2. For more information about the spect-actor, see Doug Paterson's "A Brief Biography of Augusto Boal" at http://www.ptoweb.org/boal.html.

3. This and all *Changing Channels* script excerpts quoted in this article are from play draft 15, April 16, 2007 (unpublished).

4. In *Saturday Night Live*'s "Two Wild and Crazy Guys" sketches, Steve Martin and Dan Aykroyd portrayed the Festrunk brothers, who were always trying to "pick up chicks." See http://snltranscripts.jt.org/77/77afestrunks.phtml.

5. Bertolt Brecht (1898–1956) was a German dramatist-director who coined the term *Verfremdungseffekt*, which translates as "alienation effect." "It involves the use of techniques designed to distance the audience from emotional involvement in the play through jolting reminders of the artificiality of the theatrical performance." See http://www.britannica.com/EBchecked/topic/15423/alienation-effect.

6. This concept is aligned with Paulo Freire's term *conscientização* (conscientization): "the process of developing a critical awareness of one's social reality through reflection and action." See http://www.freire.org/conscientization/.

7. The Humanities Troupe was started in 2005 in the Department of Theatre and Film at Bowling Green State University by the author and a handful of graduate students with the support of the Diversity Liaison Committee. The troupe uses theatrical tools to provoke and promote dialogue about controversial issues. The troupe's first major project was *Changing Channels*.

8. These numbers were drawn from feedback sheets collected by the Humanities Troupe from performances between January 2009 and February 2011. Bowling Green State University Human Subjects Review Board Project H09P175FX2 (unpublished).

9. With Teatro de Arena, Boal "introduced the figure of the Joker, both a narrator who addresses the audience directly and a wild card able to jump in and out of any role in the play at any time" (Schutzman 133).

Bibliography

Boal, Augusto. *Theatre of the Oppressed.* Translated by Charles A. and Maria-Odilia Leal McBride. New York: Theatre Communications Group, 1993.

Schutzman, Mady. "Joker Runs Wild." In *A Boal Companion*, edited by Jan Cohen-Cruz and Mady Schutzman. New York: Routledge, 2006. 133–45.

A Few More Thoughts about Aesthetics

NORMA BOWLES

As mentioned in the introduction, humor is frequently employed as a strategy in Institute plays, perhaps most often when the subject matter is serious. The use of comedy to promote social change has a long tradition. Throughout the world, since long before Aristophanes sent his protagonist Trygaeus to heaven on a dung beetle to bring Peace back to Earth, theatre artists and comedians (as well as jesters, clowns, bouffons, satirists, and the like) have used humor to raise our awareness, to tweak our consciences, and to spur us to act, to rebel, to transform ourselves and the world around us.

But, as Michael Ellison just elucidated so eloquently, comedy is a mercenary creature: it can be enlisted to create and maintain social inequities as easily as it can be employed to disrupt or destroy them. Actually, and unfortunately, it's a lot easier for those in power to use humor, and/or any other tool they might choose, to maintain the status quo than it is for those whom they are oppressing to "dismantle the master's house" (Lorde), regardless of how perfectly suited their tools are to the task. In fact, oppressive individuals and organizations of all stripes, from schoolyard bullies to Fox News to Goebbels, often use jokes and caricatures to dehumanize and dominate others.

As several writers have pointed out, the Anti-Defamation League's "Pyramid of Hate" (appendix E) illustrates how the proliferation of humor rooted in stereotypes can create a toxic climate in which increasingly destructive discriminatory behavior is more likely to occur. The hate crimes perpetrated against Matthew Shepard and James Byrd Jr. did not occur in a vacuum. Homophobic and racist misconceptions perpetuated by unchallenged comments, jokes, and media portrayals effectively dehumanized these two men in the eyes of their murderers.

Nazi propaganda machine–generated cartoon caricatures of Jews as rats, wolves, poisonous mushrooms, and bloodthirsty vultures helped create an environment in which people stopped seeing their Jewish neighbors as fellow human beings and instead tolerated, sometimes even colluded with, the systematic killing of six million Jews.

Still, as derogatory, stereotype-based "humor" can lay the foundation for a pyramid of increasingly destructive, hateful behavior, perhaps other kinds of humor—such as the consciousness-raising humor Ellison just described in his essay—might provide an ideal tool with which to dismantle, to topple, that Pyramid of Hate. It is interesting to note that all twenty-five Institute collaborating teams mentioned in this anthology decided to include comic elements in their plays. Some used these elements very sparingly, either to provide a little "comic relief" for the audience or to dramatize the impact of derogatory joking. Many of the play-devising teams, however, employed comic devices quite liberally: peppering dialogue with humor, satirizing discriminatory behavior, and/or parodying biased media representations.

Bibliography

Bowles, Norma. "Running the Gauntlet: Battling Sexism in Academia with Greasepaint, Bed Sheets and Mardi Gras Beads." In *Feminist Activism in the Academy: Essays on Personal, Political and Professional Change*, edited by Ellen C. Mayock and Domnica Radulescu. Jefferson, NC: McFarland, 2010. 61–77.

Lorde, Audre. "The Master's Tools Will Never Dismantle the Master's House." In *Sister Outsider: Essays and Speeches by Audrey Lorde*. Berkeley: Crossing Press Feminist Series, 1984. 110–13.

Community and Coalition Building:
Reaching beyond the Choir

The essays in this chapter focus on strategies for bringing diverse people, ideas, and talents together and for cultivating environments that foster creative and constructive dialogue about difficult issues. To achieve their activist goals, our Theatre for Social Justice Institute partners generally present their plays to target audiences of people who are not already "on board" with their ideas. In order to help ensure that their plays reach these audiences (both literally and figuratively), they work to include members of their target audience in the Institute play-development process. This chapter covers various outreach strategies that have been used to bring together Institute playwriting teams, to reach target audiences, and to promote constructive dialogue. This chapter also includes several different perspectives about how effective various Institutes have been in terms of community and coalition building.

Diane Finnerty, a faculty member in the School of Social Work at the University of Iowa, Iowa City, opens the chapter with her exploration of our Institute process as a step toward creating utopia in "Creating Space for Intergenerational LGBT Community and Movement Building." Finnerty examines how the Theatre for Social Justice Institute creates a context that fosters vital, mutually respectful connections among youth and adults and helps build social change movements. She describes some of the ways the Institute process decenters adult paternalism, nurtures youth leadership, and allows all participants to bring their full selves—intellectual, imaginative, and physical—to the work while maintaining appropriate boundaries. Finnerty also speaks to the crucial role Intergenerational Space can play for and in all oppressed communities.

The next two essays present strategies for effectively connecting with target audiences as a way to build bridges among and within diverse communities. Both were written by the project directors of the Miami University (Ohio) Institute through which we developed a play promoting marriage equality, which enjoyed a highly successful, multiyear tour of their campus and beyond. Chicago-based theatre artists/educators Amanda Dunne Acevedo and Lindsey Barlag Thornton were both Miami University undergraduates when they coordinated the Institute and subsequent play tour. Their coauthored "What Comes Next? A Guide to Organizing, Activating, and Rallying the College Campus" gives us a roadmap for planning, outreach, and coalition building. Ann Elizabeth Armstrong, feminist theatre scholar and coeditor of *Radical Acts: Theatre and Feminist Pedagogies of Change*, hosted this marriage equality–focused Institute, and mentored Acevedo and Thornton and their peers, as they worked on the project at Miami University, where she serves as an associate professor. Armstrong offers invaluable advice and strategies for training students to develop and facilitate post-show discussions in "Rehearsing for Dialogue: Facilitation Training and Miami University's *A More Perfect Union*."

Next, in "Pushing without Shoving: Ethics of and Emphasis on Target Participation in TSJ Institutes," Bryan C. Moore considers some of the advantages and dangers of setting "quotas" to ensure the diversity and balance of voices in Institute collaborations. Moore grounds his arguments in his experiences coleading two Institutes and serving as the project coordinator for a third while pursuing an MFA in dramaturgy at the University of Iowa, Iowa City.

High school English teacher and Gay-Straight Alliance sponsor Tracey Calhoun concludes this chapter with "We Are Who We Are: Theatre to Confront Homophobia and Transform Education into Social Praxis," in which she examines how the process of creating and performing a play about homophobia helped a group of high school students understand how to live the Freirian link between "right thinking" and "right doing." Calhoun elegantly supports her arguments with a combination of extensive scholarship, participant and audience survey responses, and her own firsthand observations of participants before, during, and after the project. Her article takes a comprehensive look at how programs such as the Theatre for Social Justice Institute can serve as powerful examples of praxis and create opportunities for oppressed individuals and their allies to work together to transform their communities.

Creating Space for Intergenerational LGBT Community and Movement Building

DIANE FINNERTY

I was a Girl Scout leader throughout my daughter's elementary school years—an out lesbian Girl Scout leader in a public school in Iowa. My motivations for leading the troop were many and included my desire to share time with my daughter and her friends, to temper any stigma she might experience as a child of lesbian moms, and to act on my general belief about the importance of parents' involvement in their children's education. Who knew that years later I would be participating in a Theatre for Social Justice Institute designed to address homophobia and heterosexism in schools with one of my former Girl Scouts—who was then in high school and an "out" lesbian herself.

But this essay isn't about the role of lesbian Girl Scout leaders mentoring the next generation of lesbians (although a massive volume could surely be written on that topic, if it hasn't been already); it is about the need for intergenerational movement building within the lesbian, gay, bisexual, and transgender (LGBT) community and my belief in the power of Theatre for Social Justice to facilitate that work.

Intergenerational LGBT Space

As pointed out by Dan Berger and Andy Cornell, author of and contributor to, respectively, *Letters from Young Activists: Today's Rebels Speak Out* (see Berger, Boudin, and Farrow), intergenerational communities "are not simply about people of various ages being in the same room. Instead, they are about building respectful relationships of mutual learning and teaching based on a long-haul approach to movement-building" (Berger and Cornell). Intentional focus on creating intergenerational community is needed in all social movements and, given several unique challenges, especially within the LGBT community. For example, LGBT youth rarely interact in families of origin with adults or elders who share their social identity. Further, cross-generational interactions within the LGBT community are stigmatized due to societal homophobia equating adult/youth interactions with pedophilia. This hateful stigma was clearly communicated to me by a fundamentalist minister whom I debated in front of a high school class several years ago. In an attempt to make an argument against lesbian and gay parenting, he asserted that because "the gays" could not (pro)create our "race," we had to recruit youth to our "lifestyle" by "turning them gay" through sexual molestation.[1] To expose the hatred and lack of logic in his argument, I coolly responded that I did not appreciate being accused of raping my daughter. And while I was not alarmed by his tired and erroneous assertion, I am deeply saddened by my perception that this very stigma has been internalized by older LGBT people, especially gay men, making it difficult to build intergenerational community. I was reminded of this a few weeks ago when I asked a fifty-year-old gay friend to attend an event with the local LGBTQ&A[2] youth group and he declined, *half*-jokingly saying, "Sure, and then it would be all over town that I'm a 'chicken hawk.'"[3]

It is not surprising, then, that Glenda M. Russell and Janis S. Bohan note in their essay "The Gay Generation Gap" that interactions within the LGBT community tend to be age-segregated. "Out" youth gather in their local high school Gay-Straight Alliance (GSA), in online communities, and in friendship circles, but they rarely socialize with adult LGBT folks in the community. This age segregation requires that "any contacts across generations must be arranged with the explicit intent of creating cross-generational interaction" (Russell and Bohan 2). When my daughter was young, I attempted to bring the local same-sex parents group and the high school GSAs into closer contact but achieved little success. I wrongly assumed lesbian and gay parents would form natural connections with LGBT youth, but the adults were already saturated with "kid-centered" activities and sought "adult time" with other queer parents. I live in a college town where multiple generations of LGBT people coexist with one another, but intentional intergenerational community is rare to find outside of interactions in which roles are professionally fixed (for example, faculty/student, adult-facilitated youth groups); intergenerational LGBT groups with an express commitment to social justice are even rarer. People of various ages may share the same space, but adult perspectives dominate. For example, local high school youth were recently involved in organizing the annual community-wide Pride Month activities but reported that they were disheartened by the number of events being planned around alcohol consumption and felt excluded from after-meeting socializing when the older committee members headed to a bar for drinks.

In spite of (and because of) these and other challenges, LGBT people committed to the "long-haul" approach to movement building must find authentic methods that honor our common experiences and also our unique generational differences. Young activists caution against adults using intergenerational interactions to "focus on their glory days or on lecturing 'the youngens'" (Berger and Cornell). Nor should we, as adults, set ourselves up as one-way mentors of youth while concurrently refusing to acknowledge and learn from youth leadership. I received an example of this paternalistic approach when a respected adult leader in the local LGBT community responded to the following post on my Facebook page: "Diane is thinking about what it takes to connect intergenerationally for movement-building." She half-jokingly responded: "Bring chocolate and let them think they are in control! Works for me! lol." True intergenerational space requires eliminating adultism[4] and embracing what seventy-one-year-old lesbian activist Suzanne Pharr calls "co-mentorship," a relationship in which we "mentor each other through this moment, this present day, and which requires complex understanding and skills. Here's what I know, tell me what you know—how can we figure this out together?" The type of intergenerational space needed is one in which adults can pass on to the next generation, paraphrasing Ella Baker, that which was passed on to us,[5] but also one that enables youth to pass *up* to adults the questions of the day and new ways of being.

Russell and Bohan make a convincing appeal for the need to improve intergenerational communication within the LGBT community by applying Margaret Mead's concept of "prefigurative cultures" in which societal change occurs so rapidly that envisioning the future is not possible using lessons only from the past or present but rather requires intentional cross-generational communication to co-create the world that is to come. For example, I was born in 1960, coming out and coming into radical lesbianism in the early 1980s. Same-sex parenting was taboo, assisted conception was science fiction, and legal same-sex marriage was inconceivable. This vantage point provides me with insight about struggle and change that might be of use in co-creating the future, but it also carries internalized baggage that could easily limit the vision of what is possible for the generations ahead.

> [LGBT] elders cannot always know the answers, but they can convey the importance of seeking answers. They cannot know what values will serve one well, but they can encourage the careful articulation of one's values. Youth, on the other hand, become the bellwether for the community's future. They are on the front edge of change, unhindered by ties to the past. They are more likely to envision a future that is radically different, where new questions are central and old answers are not wrong, but rather no longer relevant. Yet, youth lack the resources and the wisdom of life experience to find and enact answers on their own. In this circumstance, adults must be prepared to follow the lead of youth and to learn from youth; while youth must be prepared to rely on the mentoring of adults and on their experience with solving problems, if not on their access to ultimate answers. (Russell and Bohan 3–4)

But theorizing about the need to nurture intergenerational connections within the LGBT community and actually *doing* it are quite different matters. I found my words and my deeds coming together in profound ways through participating in a Theatre for Social Justice project.

Fringe Benefits and the Theatre for Social Justice Institute

On February 25, 2005, an intergenerational group of eighteen people gathered in the Theatre Arts Building at the University of Iowa for a five-day Theatre for Social Justice Institute (TSJI) facilitated by Norma Bowles and Cynthia Ruffin from Fringe Benefits. Fringe Benefits was founded by Bowles in 1991 and uses "theatre as a tool to create a context within which people can engage in constructive dialogue about controversial/divisive issues" (Bowles 16). Fringe Benefits holds an esteemed place within the tradition of the Theatre for Social Justice movement. Theatre for Social Justice is rooted in the concept of "Theatre of the Oppressed," developed in the early 1970s by Augusto Boal and "practiced *by, about* and *for* the oppressed, to help them fight against their oppressions and to transform the society that engenders those oppressions" (Boal as cited by International Theatre of the Oppressed Organisation, "Techniques"). This type of theatre is grounded in the tradition of liberatory education, which promotes "learning for critical consciousness and collective action. Such education seeks to transform power relations in society, relations between teacher and learner, and among learners. It strives to be 'radically democratic'" (Arnold et al. 22). Toward this end, Fringe Benefits created a "radically democratic" play development process, the "Dramaturgical Quilting Bee," as a methodology for creating transformational theatre (Bowles 16).

The UI Theatre Arts Department, under the leadership of Tisch Jones, brought Fringe Benefits to campus to facilitate an Institute focused on issues related to youth and homophobia. I was invited to participate because of the LGBT-related work I had done on campus and in the community. Other participants in the Institute included high school students in a local LGBTQ&A group, undergraduate and graduate students, and others from the broader community. The group included lesbian, gay, bisexual, and heterosexual people of various ages and racial/ethnic identities.

I entered the Institute space the first evening, and imagine my surprise when I was greeted by a young woman who was *my* former Girl Scout (emphasis added to challenge the paternalism of my own adultism). I was excited to see her but, quite honestly, a bit unnerved. While I had enjoyed knowing this young woman as a girl in my troop, I had not yet known her as an adult nor established (and this was especially relevant in that moment) a queer-identified relationship with her. I was "out" as a Girl Scout leader and school parent and had heard through the grapevine that she had "come out," but we had not yet openly acknowledged our shared identity as lesbians. I once heard Urvashi Vaid, executive director of the National Gay and Lesbian Task Force from 1989 to 1992, say that a role model in the closet is no role model at all.[6] I had taken her words to heart and intentionally shattered closet walls as an "out" parent in the school. I have since heard from youth who later "came out" that knowing an "out" parent in their early years was significant for their development. But sharing *community* with a young "out" lesbian who was my daughter's age—now *that* was a different matter and required a whole different type of courage.

The transformation began for me on the first evening as we gathered in a circle and were led in "Games of the Oppressed" warm-up activities. These warm-up activities are crucial to the community-building process in that "all our senses, our perception of reality, and our capacity of feeling and reasoning tend to become mechanical by everyday repetition. We tend to become less creative, accepting reality as it is, instead of transforming it. Games of the Oppressed is a system of Games that help us 'to feel what we touch,' 'to listen to what we hear,' 'to see what we look at,' 'to stimulate all senses,' and 'to understand what we say and hear'" (Boal as cited by International Theatre of the Oppressed Organisation, "Games of the Oppressed"). Norma and Cynthia served as open, generous, and joyful facilitators of the group's process. The opening energizer activities enabled each of us to bring our whole selves into the circle. Because I was always rushing in from either a work or parental responsibility, the warm-up activities played an essential role in helping me to de-clutter my adult "mechanical" mind and ready my authentic self to be more present with my coconspirators. These games also drew upon the youths' strength of spontaneity and were a natural fit with the LGBT community's cultural value of playfulness. (See Reed for an exploration of creativity in queer protests.) Additionally, these physical exercises brought the queer body into the room. Others have written profoundly and thoroughly about the targeting of LGBT peoples through the oppression of all things physical and sexual in our lives (see Miller; Johnson and Henderson; and Sedgwick and Frank); to create healthy intergenerational LGBT space, we must integrate intentional activities designed to enliven our senses and mitigate the societally imposed shame that resides in too many of us.

After ample time dedicated to warm-up and community building, we were led in Fringe Benefits' "Dramaturgical Quilting Bee" process. We sorted through ideas contributed by all members of the group and eventually chose to develop a play to address the harassment of lesbian and gay students in high school, with the goal of increasing the awareness and skills of teachers and administrators to intervene and enforce nondiscrimination policies. We collectively came to this conclusion through storytelling, sorting the many narratives, and then agreeing to a common theme. The creation of a final draft of a script was the desired outcome, but the script development also served as a vehicle, a means to the end of creating intergenerational dialogue and community. In one of the high school classroom scenes we improvised, I found myself acting in the role of a teacher across from several youth acting as students, including the young woman who was my former Girl Scout (identified as "Bethany" in the final script). While the teacher/student roles we enacted were similar to the ones we inhabited in our day-to-day lives, the space and process offered us the opportunity to experience these roles in a dynamic way that felt more akin to co-mentorship than what would have occurred in these roles in the general society. In those moments, I forged a new connection with "Bethany"—not just as adult/youth but as lesbian activists of different ages.

The script, *Welcome to the Game!,* depicts a day in the life of high school students, including a lesbian student experiencing peer harassment and a same-sex couple wanting to attend a high school dance. The piece educates about the myriad ways anti-LGBT discrimination is infused throughout everyday high school experiences and presents choices that adults can make to serve as allies to LGBT students. It also portrays the resilience of the "gay community" by educating about LGBT people in history as well as by featuring youth who possess tenacity and unabashed self-esteem.

The process of developing the piece offered participants the opportunity to dissect the anatomy of a specific social injustice and to search out actions that would bring about change. The group used the Anti-Defamation League's "Pyramid of Hate," which demonstrates how micro-aggressions can escalate, if unchallenged, to discrimination, overt violence, and genocide.[7] As a group, we addressed issues relevant to youth and also included actions that youth could take as agents of change in their own lives. This is significant for intergenerational movement building given that so much of what passes for the national "gay rights movement" impels LGBT people to focus on single-issue policy campaigns (for example, same-sex marriage and employment nondiscrimination). These campaigns emphasize voting and making financial contributions as key political strategies—both of which are only remotely possible for youth—and narrowly focus on legislative battles rather than on the broader movement or a full re-visioning of society. As the organization Queer to the Left states, "Stonewall didn't happen at the ballot box." The Institute empowered people in an intergenerational LGBT space to critically explore oppression and devise actions drawing upon the many and varied forms of power we hold in our own hands.

Lowering/Raising the Curtain: Moving Forward

I have kept in touch with "Bethany" since the 2005 Institute. A few months after the Institute, I wrote a letter recommending her for a scholarship honoring out-and-active LGBT high school students in Iowa. Shortly after that, I received an invitation to and attended her high school graduation party in her family's home. In 2009, after Iowa's state supreme court ruled that it was unconstitutional to deny same-sex couples the right to marry, my partner of twenty years and I exchanged vows in a hand-fasting and were legally married in front of several hundred friends and family members at a neighborhood block party/wedding; "Bethany" and her girlfriend were there. And now, of course, we keep in touch through Facebook as "friends" in intergenerational cyberspace.

Lessons learned from the Institute stayed with me as I went on to work with LGBTQ&A youth through a local youth-serving organization. I hosted a fund-raiser for the group and met regularly with youth to develop a cookbook as a community fund-raiser. As with the *Welcome to the Game!* script, the cookbook served as an organizing vehicle to bring youth and adults together to co-create a product. We gave ourselves the name "Generations of Change," and the cookbook and its essential ingredient, food, served as great organizing themes to build intergenerational LGBT community. We found that the topic of food was relevant to all of us as eaters, as food holds the potential to nourish the body and bring pleasure. We also discovered that the local LGBT community boasts many great cooks and, thus, opportunities for connections. Exploring the politics of food production offered opportunities for critical reflection and political analysis. And of course the subject of food provided many opportunities for playfulness. Just the process of naming the book generated a great deal of laughter as we played with double entendres in titles, such as *Everything Fruits and Nuts* and *The GLTBQ&A Alphabet Soup.* The waffle art developed during our "Generations of Change Waffle Retreat" was memorable, if not edible.

Youth leadership took on many roles in the cookbook project: youth initiated interviews of LGBT adults engaged in the local food movement (for example, fair trade and organic farmers, locavore chefs and bread bakers); youth coordinated distribution of the call for recipes; and youth artwork was solicited. We planned to sell the cookbook as a fund-raiser for the youth group during the June Pride Month activities and to hold a culminating multigenerational "Queer Iowa City Cook-Off" featuring multigenerational teams competing in a youth-friendly environment.

The process of creating our plans took us in many great directions, but I am sad to say that, as of this writing, the cookbook has not yet materialized. The collaboration experienced several challenges that included being housed in a nonprofit organization with its own agenda, having difficulty recruiting adult participants, and, of course, limited funding. In retrospect, I would do several things differently, but the process carried us through many months of positive intergenerational interaction and resulted in other positive outcomes, such as an intentional community-wide discussion of the need for local intergenerational LGBT connections and a youth-led public panel presentation on this topic.

My participation in Fringe Benefits' TSJI solidified my understanding of the importance of intergenerational organizing among LGBT youth and adults and also strengthened my commitment to intergenerational movement building in my other activism. For example, I carried this commitment into an immigrant justice project I co-coordinated just months after the Institute. We developed a vibrant multigenerational, multinational organizing team as a result of our collective efforts. I have miles to go in developing my co-mentoring skills, and, as with all forms of social privilege, I need to stay ever vigilant as to how I perpetuate adultism in my everyday life, but the Institute awakened in me a deeper commitment to do the work and be a worthy adult ally.

While few of us will choose the path to become Theatre for Social Justice facilitators, those of us committed to social justice for LGBT peoples can build upon the following intentional practices to bring adults and youth together.

- *Create intentional intergenerational space.* Decenter adult paternalism and draw upon the strengths, norms, and lived realities of both youth and adults. Use interactive exercises to open up possibilities for bringing our full selves to the circle.
- *Identify a short-term-focused outcome.* Use a concrete project (for example, a script, a cookbook) as a mutual focusing point and vehicle for the group's collaboration.
- *Focus from the beginning on co-mentoring.* Introduce concepts that give a name to youth-adult dynamics (for example, co-mentoring, adultism, paternalism) and interrupt oppressive behaviors if and when they occur.
- *Nurture the queer body.* Focus on enlivening the senses and challenging internalized shame and detachment; name this as an intentional political strategy.

- *Focus on the long haul and sustainability.* Ask how the current short-term project contributes to a longer-term vision of social change. Focus on the development of youth leadership and the continued growth of adults as co-creators of change.

Intergenerational movement building is essential within all communities committed to social justice. While spaces such as the Girl Scouts, college classrooms, and issue-based campaigns may find youth and adults sharing the same location, the need for intergenerational community committed to social justice calls us—in very intentional ways—to build community that enables co-mentoring for the long haul. Done well, it holds the potential to lead, in Suzanne Pharr's words, "toward the sometimes illusive dream of equality and justice—which can contain all our best ideas without requiring an age i.d." There will be no Girl Scout badge awarded for this lesson, but it is certainly the one that will sustain our movement into the future.

Notes

1. These quoted words, and those from other personal communications, have been reproduced to the best of my recollection. Names have been omitted, where appropriate, to protect privacy.

2. LGBTQ&A is shorthand for lesbian, gay, bisexual, transgender, questioning, and allied. I have used various versions of the acronym throughout the essay but do so only for expediency's sake since I believe grouping all of these varied identities into one alphabetic expression is problematic.

3. "Chicken hawk" is a slang term in the gay community for an older gay man who prefers sex with younger men.

4. Adultism refers to "behaviors and attitudes based on the assumption that adults are better than young people, and entitled to act upon young people without their agreement. This mistreatment is reinforced by social institutions, laws, customs, and attitudes" (Bell 540–46).

5. From "Ella Baker" on the *Civil Unrest* website. See http://www.heroism.org/class/1960/cu-unknown.htm.

6. Loosely quoted from a speech presented by Urvashi Vaid at Drake University in Des Moines, Iowa, in 1996 (unpublished).

7. See the "Pyramid of Hate" diagram in appendix E.

Bibliography

Anti-Defamation League. "Responding to Bigotry and Intergroup Strife on Campus: A Guide for College Presidents and Senior Administrators," 2008. http://www.adl.org/campus/guide/guide.pdf.

Arnold, Rick, Bev Burke, Carl James, D'Arcy Martin, and Barb Thomas. *Educating for a Change*. Toronto: Between the Lines, 1991.

Bell, John. "Understanding Adultism: A Key to Developing Positive Youth-Adult Relationships." In *Readings for Diversity and Social Justice,* edited by Maurianne Adams, Warren J. Blumenfeld, Carmelita Castañeda, Heather W. Hackman, Madeline L. Peters, and Ximena Zúñiga. 2nd ed. New York: Routledge, 2010. 540–46.

Berger, Dan, Chesa Boudin, and Kenyon Farrow, eds. *Letters from Young Activists: Today's Rebels Speak Out*. New York: Nation, 2005.

Berger, Dan, and Andy Cornell. "Ten Questions for Movement Building and Reflection on the Current Period." *Monthly Review Zine*, July 24, 2006. http://mrzine.monthlyreview.org/2006/bc240706.html.

Boal, Augusto. *Games for Actors and Non-Actors*. 2nd ed. New York: Routledge, 2002.

Bowles, Norma. "Why Devise? Why Now? 'Houston, we have a problem.'" *Theatre Topics* 15, no. 1 (2005): 15–21.

Freire, Paulo. *Pedagogy of the Oppressed*. 30th ed. New York: Continuum, 2000.

International Theatre of the Oppressed Organisation. "Games of the Oppressed." http://www.theatreoftheoppressed.org/en/index.php?nodeID=76.

———. "Techniques." http://www.theatreoftheoppressed.org/en/index.php?nodeID=74. Accessed June 16, 2011.

Johnson, E. Patrick, and Mae G. Henderson, eds. *Black Queer Studies: A Critical Anthology*. Durham, NC: Duke University Press, 2005.

Love, B. J., and K. J. Phillips. "Goals, Key Concepts, and Definitions for Module I: Appendix 15B." In *Teaching for Diversity and Social Justice*, edited by M. A. Adams, L. A. Bell, and P. Griffin. 2nd ed. New York: Routledge, 2007. 461–63.

Miller, Tim. *Tim Miller Queer Performer* website. http://timmillerperfomer.blogspot.com/.

Pharr, Suzanne. "Co-mentorship: Working for Equality across the Ages," February 25, 2008. http://suzannepharr.org/2008/02/25/co-mentorship-working-for-equality-across-age/.

Queer to the Left. "Stonewall Didn't Happen at the Ballot Box." *Historical Propaganda Archive*. http://www.queertotheleft.org. Accessed June 16, 2011.

Reed, T. V. *The Art of Protest: Culture and Activism from the Civil Rights Movement to the Streets of Seattle*. Minneapolis: University of Minnesota Press, 2005.

Russell, Glenda M., and Janice S. Bohan. "The Gay Generation Gap: Communicating across the LGBT Generation Divide." *ANGLES: The Policy Journal of the Institute for Gay and Lesbian Strategic Studies* 8, no. 1 (2005): 1–8.

Sedgwick, Eve Kosofsky, and Adam Frank. *Touching Feeling: Affect, Pedagogy, Performativity*. Durham, NC: Duke University Press, 2003.

What Comes Next? A Guide to Organizing, Activating, and Rallying the College Campus

AMANDA DUNNE ACEVEDO AND LINDSEY BARLAG THORNTON

Do you see problems and want to solve them? Do you feel overwhelmed? Stumped? Do you want some easy ways to start tackling an issue you are passionate about? Keep reading.

This is how we did it. From April 15 to April 26, 2005, Fringe Benefits came to Miami University in Oxford, Ohio, to facilitate a Theatre for Social Justice Institute with the Walking Theatre Project, a student-led collective we cofounded to address challenging social and political issues on Miami's campus. We invited Fringe Benefits to help create our first play, which focused on marriage equality. In the course of planning the Institute, collaboratively writing the script, and rehearsing, marketing, and touring the play, we not only increased support for marriage equality among Miami University students and faculty but also helped create and galvanize a network of campus and community groups dedicated to promoting progressive social change.[1] This is how you too can become a progressive organizer!

Use Theatre as a Tool for Social Justice!

> Theatre is a language through which human beings can engage in active dialogue on what is important to them. It allows individuals to create a safe space that they may inhabit in groups and use to explore the interactions that make up their lives.
>
> —Augusto Boal

We have all heard it before: "College students are apathetic! They don't vote, they don't participate in political discourse, and they don't seem to really care about much of anything!" Sentiments such as these do not do justice to the college students across America and around the world who are passionately working to promote social change. College campuses can and frequently do serve as the frontlines for civic debate and social change.

On election night, November 4, 2004, six college students stood together in confusion, fear, and uncertainty. Together with our friends Emily, Jennifer, Cecilia, and Kat, we witnessed the consequences of apathy: Ohio had passed a constitutional amendment banning same-sex marriage, and similar amendments had passed in twelve other states. We were outraged, distraught, and perplexed. How could so many people feel it was right to deny their fellow citizens this basic civil right, this basic human right? How many potential allies had not felt motivated to go to the polls? We made a decision to act. We did not want to be labeled "apathetic college students" any longer. But what was the next step?

Theatre has the potential not only to entertain but also to create a space for constructive intellectual and political dialogue, so we decided to use theatre as a tool to educate and create dialogue around topics that students might otherwise ignore. We founded Walking Theatre Project, a campus theatre collective "that desires to create theatre that provokes thought and provides a space for people of varied perspectives to come together in dialogue."[2]

In December 2004, we began having conversations with our peers at Miami, asking them how they had voted and why. Additionally, through grassroots organizing, we found other campus organizations to partner with on the project. In April 2005, after a semester of research, brainstorming, and discussion, we brought Fringe Benefits to campus to conduct a Theatre for Social Justice Institute. In preparation for the Institute, we partnered with SPECTRUM (Miami's gay-straight alliance), GLBTQ Services, the College Democrats, the Western College of Interdisciplinary Studies, the Marketing School, the Farmer School of Business, and students and faculty from our Department of Theatre. Twenty-eight Institute participants worked together as playwrights, utilizing physical exercises, brainstorming, dialectic reflection, story circles, and improvisation over the course of five workshop sessions. The play that came out of those workshops was reflective of the experiences and shared stories of the participants. After the Institute, we continued to workshop and refine the script, and by September 2005 we were ready to perform for Miami's student body.

On October 11, 2005, National Coming Out Day, we presented a staged reading of our theatre piece, *A More Perfect Union: A Response to Issue 1*, followed by a panel discussion as part of our theatre department's Staged-Reading Series. We then partnered with other student organizations, university academic departments, and community members to continue producing the play and organizing events around campus. In the 2005–06 academic year, Walking Theatre Project toured twenty-one public performances of the piece, reaching an audience of over one thousand. We facilitated workshops and discussions around the issue, organized public rallies, raised over $10,000 to support production costs, and were invited to perform at the 2006 Pedagogy and Theatre of the Oppressed Conference in Chapel Hill, North Carolina. The show stayed in Walking Theatre's repertoire until spring 2009, with continued requests for performances from a diverse range of classes and organizations. It also was performed annually on National Coming Out Day.

How did we create a diverse coalition? What tools and resources did we use? How did we facilitate the outreach and dialogue that took place on campus?

Three Things to Remember

- Not everyone in your organization may identify as a member of the group being discriminated against. Learn to *embrace* and understand the *role of the ally*.
- Remember who your *target audience* is and be able to speak to those people in a vocabulary and in a manner to which they can relate.
- Keep brainstorming *new strategies* for reaching an audience that may not feel an immediate connection to the issue that you are addressing.

Build a Diverse and Strong Group

The role of ally offers young people who are white, male, and in other dominant categories a positive, proactive, and proud identity. Rather than feeling guilty, shameful, and immobilized as the "oppressor," whites and other dominants can assume the important

Amanda Dunne Acevedo and Lindsey Barlag Thornton

and useful role of social change agent. There have been proud allies and change agents throughout the history of this nation, and there are many alive today who can inspire us with their important work.

—Andrea Ayvazian

You are your most important resource. It is imperative that you educate yourself about the issues. Whatever topic you choose to tackle, be ready to answer questions and know the facts. Continue to update yourself, and your group, as new information becomes available. Meet frequently, weekly or biweekly, to talk over current events and project planning.

We recommend finding an advisor to help guide your process. We created a semester-long independent study with our professor and mentor, Dr. Ann Elizabeth Armstrong. Each group member researched and reported on a specific topic associated with our issue during weekly breakfast meetings. After the Institute, we created a Theatre for Social Justice course with Dr. Armstrong through which we collectively explored and trained in facilitation techniques. This education and guidance was vital to our work. Being in a college environment provides you with an abundance of resources, but you have to ask! You have to seek them out. Find professors in your department or at your college who can share their knowledge and expertise.

Share ownership in the project. It's not just about getting people in the room; you have to give them a purpose. As the group grows, it is important to work together to create clear job descriptions, delegate responsibilities, develop a chain of command, establish procedural guidelines, and follow a project timeline. Meet regularly so those in the group can function as each other's source of checks and balances.

Establish an Infrastructure for Your Group

- Our primary positions were: president, secretary, treasurer, marketing director, campus outreach coordinator, and dramaturge.
- We developed clear job descriptions for all of these positions as well as a chain of command.

Including diverse voices within your organization is key. We began working to build alliances right away, in preparation for the Institute. It was important to include not only our friends and theatre majors but also students and faculty from other disciplines who could add their diverse experiences, perspectives, and talents to the project.

How do you get diverse voices in the room? Seek out partnerships with other progressive college and community groups. Such organizations often share compatible messages and can benefit from mutual support. Creating these partnerships will lead to a larger base for all involved organizations.

> **Partnering with a Campus Organization**
>
> Each group should have a member who is required to attend both organizations' meetings. Communication is vital to making any strong alliance grow!

Think outside the box. Reach out to create dialogue with campus and community groups with which you don't suspect you have much in common. Avoid just preaching to the choir and build coalitions with organizations and individuals with a diverse array of viewpoints. Through mutual support of each other's activities, we were able to partner with such organizations as the Center for American and World Cultures, Associated Student Government, and the Student Honors Program.

Maximize Opportunities and Resources

Take things to the next level by organizing events on and around campus. Think about how your organization can use theatre in nontraditional applications. Use theatre techniques when organizing campus rallies, happenings, or public performances that draw attention to your issue. Look for *all* opportunities to bring your issue to a wider audience on campus and in your community.

Example one: If your university is bringing a guest to campus to speak on matters related to your issue, create a rally in support of or in opposition to that speaker. In November 2005, Ohio state representative Tom Brinkman (R-Cincinnati) sued Miami University over the school's domestic partner benefits policy. The Miami College Republicans brought Representative Brinkman to campus to speak. With only two days' notice about his visit, we were able to mobilize all of the campus organizations with which we had developed alliances and held a rally in support of Miami's policy (featuring a special performance of *A More Perfect Union*) before Brinkman's speech. Our collective outreach drew over 250 people who congregated outside before the speech and then filled the student center, outnumbering our opposition. Because there were so many of our supporters in the room, we were able to take over the microphones during the question and answer session and demand that Representative Brinkman respond to our concerns. We also reached out to local papers and news channels about the rally, garnering coverage on the *Cincinnati Nightly News* and in several local papers, including the *Miami Student*, the *Cincinnati Enquirer*, the *Oxford Press*, and the *Hamilton Journal*.

Partner with University and Community Officials

- Find out the protocol necessary to secure approval for your event from university and community officials.
- Obtain documentation of this approval from these officials and keep copies with you at all times. This will help prevent your group and/or event from being compromised when challenged by opposition.

Example two: Use parts of your theatre piece as speeches, stories, or chants to create performances in public spaces to promote your project's primary agenda and/or in support of other related social justice causes. It is especially helpful to do this in conjunction with other pre-existing campus events such as those held on National Coming Out Day or MLK, Jr. Day, during Disability Awareness Week or Women's History Month, or even on Homecoming or Parent and Grandparent Day. In 2005, we decided to partner with the College Democrats of MU to address a recent string of homophobic incidents on campus. During their annual Progressive Week, we spent a day in the central quad performing a section of *A More Perfect Union* that included a slew of homophobic slurs heard around campus and homophobic letters to the editor written by Miami students and published in the *Miami Student*. Several performers carried signs posing questions such as "Is this hate speech?" and "Do you use hate speech?" An important part of this performance was our use of facilitators who walked around the area engaging students in dialogue about what they were hearing and seeing.

Spread the word. There are endless ways for the university and surrounding community to support your work. Sometimes the tricky part is finding these resources and taking advantage of them. A vital step is to connect with an array of professors, local businesses, and community organizations to help get the word out about your events to as many students and community members as possible. Ask your friends to come, and ask them to bring friends. Announce events in classrooms. Post flyers wherever possible. Make a Facebook invitation. Tweet updates through your group's Twitter account.

We were able to reach vast student audiences because we partnered with both academic departments and campus organizations. To initiate partnerships like this, begin by setting up in-person meetings with professors and leaders of campus organizations to discuss opportunities for partnership and engagement. Start this work as early as possible to ensure that potential liaisons feel like stakeholders and have a sense of shared ownership in the endeavor. Walking Theatre Project reached out to other campus organizations and academic departments before bringing Fringe Benefits to Miami, thus affording future stakeholders an opportunity to participate in the creation of the play and strengthening their sense of shared ownership. Come prepared to give a brief, clear verbal description of what you are doing and what you need. Be willing to listen to and incorporate new ideas.

Initially, we reached out to professors in subject areas that seemed like an obvious "fit" for our project, such as women and gender studies and fine arts. But, because we were able to explain how our work was relevant to their disciplines, we were invited to present classroom performances and workshops in a wide range of academic areas, from the business school to the religion department, from physical education to economics, thus ensuring that we reached a broad base of our student body.

Tools to Promote Awareness & Attract Audiences

> **Tools to Promote Awareness & Attract Audiences**
>
> - It is important to have professional-looking brochures and pamphlets that you can distribute to promote awareness about your organization and events. We collaborated with students in Miami's graphic design program to help us design a logo and marketing materials.
> - We used guerrilla marketing to garner student support at rallies and other university-sponsored events.
> - We made and wore T-shirts with information about our group and events. This can be done cheaply with white T-shirts and permanent markers.
> - What attracts people to an event? Volume and food! A megaphone and pizza were our secret ingredients to increasing student attendance.

Find campus organizations that can offer material support. By showing that our work was relevant to campus life, we were able to partner with Miami's Associated Student Government and receive funding. We were also able to rent megaphones, microphones, extension cords, projection screens, and the like from our campus technology center. Inquire how funding and other resources can be obtained at your college and make the most of them!

Find ways the local community can support you. Have a local business sponsor your organization. By printing its name on your flyers, you can receive funding for marketing materials. We were able to cover the majority of our printing costs by having the local bike repair shop sponsor us.

Always call the local papers and tell them about your events. Exposure in the community leads to a steady dialogue on the topic you are addressing. We stayed engaged in the public conversation about the marriage equality issue by consistently writing editorials for our campus newspaper. Several articles in our newspaper further exposed us to a wider campus audience. In 2005, on National Coming Out Day, the *Miami Student* helped promote awareness of our work on campus. "Rather than using a more conventional means of raising awareness of gay issues, a student-initiated theater production offers a fresh medium for education and debate on these critical matters. In addition, it is through efforts like these that Miami will be able to quit talking about improving diversity on this campus and actually begin taking tangible steps toward solving the problem" (Editorial Board).

Foster Dialogue on Campus!

> You want a safe space, but not a comfortable space.
> —Michael Rohd

Have a post-show discussion or workshop after each and every show or event. We created a piece of theatre that could easily be cut down into ten- to fifteen-minute chunks. That way, if time was very limited for a particular presentation (especially in classes), we could still spend significant time discussing the issues. After all, perhaps the most vital part of this work is the dialogue that is fostered.

When working with sensitive subject matter, it is crucial that those moderating the discussion have a solid understanding of the issues being discussed and, more important, good training in facilitation techniques. In order to make sure we had this crucial training, we worked with Dr. Armstrong to create a Theatre for Social Justice class at Miami. By the time we entered a classroom of our peers and began a conversation on the potentially explosive topic of marriage equality, we knew how to handle ourselves in a neutral manner, protect everyone who wanted to be a part of the conversation, and ensure that the dialogue stayed positive and constructive. In her essay in this volume, Dr. Armstrong discusses this training, which was so vital to our campus outreach work.

Preaching to the choir can be useful, in terms of rallying your allies, but your organization should be trying to engage members of the opposition and/or the "Movable Middle" in dialogue.[3] In either case, the goal is to open people up to new ideas so that positive change can begin.

During performances, our facilitators would gauge the atmosphere in order to be prepared to meet each unique audience where it was and lead the conversation in a positive direction.[4] We also made sure that our facilitators did not take sides or provoke but instead asked open-ended questions and gently encouraged the audience to look at the issue from various angles. Initially, it can be hard as a facilitator to leave your opinion at the door and create an open dialogue. In one of the first classroom workshops we co-facilitated, one female student would not stop interrupting others to interject her religious views in an attempt to shut down the conversation. Instead of creating an opportunity for other students to share their thoughts and perhaps challenge her viewpoints, we went on the defensive and started to share our personal views. Once we revealed our personal feelings on the topic, all dialogue closed down. We quickly learned the importance of remaining neutral and allowing the participants to explore their own positions on the issues.

It is your responsibility to help push your peers to go beyond what they already think and know. As college students, you have an advantage in facilitating these dialogues. You can relate to the audience members as peers; neither you nor they are experts on the matter at hand. This can create an atmosphere wherein equal participation is possible and people feel safe entering the conversation. As you continue fostering dialogue on campus, it is imperative to record and document your progress. Obtaining and reflecting on this feedback will help push *you* to go beyond what you already think you know.

Track Your Impact

- Ask each audience member to fill out a survey.
- Use these surveys to record and track your impact. This data can help you strengthen your message and improve the way you communicate. It also can help you prove your track record so that you can obtain support for future endeavors.
- See if your survey has to go through a campus review board. Look into and complete the certification and approval process.

Continue to Spread the Word

Share your work beyond your campus. Find workshops and conferences beyond your school community that your organization can attend and/or where you can present your work, such as the annual Pedagogy and Theatre of the Oppressed (PTO) and Association for Theatre in Higher Education conferences, as well as local and international art and fringe festivals. Research political and grassroots organizations that support your issue. See if the sponsoring organizations have any upcoming events where you can share your work. This not only will give your organization more exposure and leverage but also will provide you with great learning experiences and occasions to receive valuable feedback.

Presenting at PTO not only allowed our work to receive national exposure but also provided us with the opportunity to reconnect with Fringe Benefits. At PTO, we facilitated panel discussions on building coalitions and conducting outreach on our college campus, a step that laid the foundation for this article. Post-college, we now work as Institute facilitators with Fringe Benefits, collaborating with students nationally and internationally. In many ways, our work has come full circle.

There is still so much more that needs to be done! Grassroots organizing is never over, never complete. You may never be fully satisfied with the outcome, so keep going! Be open to critical dialogue about what you have done and are doing. Remember, what you are doing is unique. The issue you are addressing, your strategies for tackling it, and your achievements are worth documenting and sharing with others.

You can always reach more people. You can always improve your outreach strategies and facilitation techniques. You can always strive for something better. Never stop questioning and learning. Use the Institute as a springboard. Find creative ways to reach out to your campus and your community. We hope that this guide will give you a little inspiration, a little structure, and a few ideas. You can become an organizer on your campus and in your community. Good luck!

Notes

1. These assertions are based on data gleaned from audience surveys that Walking Theatre Project distributed after each performance and collected and summarized in a report for Fringe Benefits (unpublished).

2. Walking Theatre Project By-Laws, Mission Statement, 2005 (unpublished). The founding members of Miami's Walking Theatre Project are Lindsey Barlag Thornton, Amanda Dunne Acevedo, Emily Rose Goss, Jennifer Leininger, Cecilia Miller, and Kat Paddock. Our faculty advisor was Dr. Ann Elizabeth Armstrong.

3. For more about the "Movable Middle," see appendix A.

4. We found that it is often helpful to have two co-facilitators leading post-show discussions in order to tag-team back and forth: one primarily responsible for posing and fielding questions, the other for assessing the atmosphere in the room.

Bibliography

Ayvazian, Andrea. "Interrupting the Cycle of Oppression: The Roles of Allies as Agents of Change." In *Race, Class, and Gender in the United States: An Integrated Study*, edited by P. Rothenberg. New York: Worth, 2001. 598–604.

Editorial Board. "Walking Theatre Project Offers Changes for the Better." *Miami Student*, October 11, 2005. http://www.miamistudent.net/2.8194/walking-theatre-offers-changes-for-the-better-1.1155481.

Rohd, Michael. *Theatre for Community, Conflict, and Dialogue: The Hope Is Vital Training Manual*. Portsmouth, NH: Heinemann, 1998.

Rehearsing for Dialogue: Facilitation Training and Miami University's *A More Perfect Union*

ANN ELIZABETH ARMSTRONG

The Theatre for Social Justice (TSJ) Institute play *A More Perfect Union: A Response to Issue 1* succeeded in many of its goals, primarily in fostering dialogue about Ohio's 2004 ban on same-sex marriage, the effect of this ban on our community, and the underlying homophobia within Miami University's student culture. In their essay, Amanda Dunne Acevedo and Lindsey Barlag Thornton describe the trajectory of the Walking Theatre Project, the peer-led student activism theatre company that took a lead role in developing and touring the play and that has continued for seven years, tackling topics such as sexual assault. As we prepared for our 2005 Institute, I realized that a critical component of the project would be training the members of the Walking Theatre Project as facilitators. At a public university with a liberal arts focus, Miami University students have grown weary of administration-led diversity initiatives, so a peer-led theatre company was particularly important. Students know how to reach other students, they know what issues are meaningful to them, and they know the best ways to talk about them. However, the marriage equality issue was a flash point, one that elicited heated debates. Even though we had carefully planned partnerships in order to reach the "Movable Middle," facilitators would be working through a minefield of hot-button issues such as religion, sexual identity, and legal rights.

An independent study preceding the spring 2005 Institute produced dramaturgical research that significantly informed our facilitators' approach. Then, in fall 2005, I taught a class called Performance Techniques for Social Activism. The course focused on the techniques of Augusto Boal's Theatre of the Oppressed, briefly touching on other community-based theatre methods. Acevedo and Thornton were among the students in the class who trained themselves as Theatre of the Oppressed facilitators with an audience talkback approach. Throughout the life of the project, the demand for *A More Perfect Union* grew, and facilitation training became an issue that we needed to address again and again. We needed a trained pool of facilitators who could adapt the performance and post-show discussion for each audience.

In the post-show, the facilitator's goals were to (1) guide an interactive discussion to engage diverse perspectives, (2) help audience members position the problem within their own communities, (3) deepen the engagement with the problem, and (4) suggest future actions, if the first three goals were successful. In "Dialogue in Artistic Practice," Andrea Assaf notes that "participatory arts practice requires skills that dialogue specialists identify as fundamental to productive dialogue, such as creating safe space, listening for meaning, revealing assumptions, and leveling power dynamics" (v). In this essay, I'll explore a few of the challenges we faced in *A More Perfect Union* and propose a kind of facilitator's "boot camp" curriculum. While we didn't use this curriculum, my reflection on the Walking Theatre Project's work has led me to develop it. The curriculum allows a peer-led theatre company to continue to expand its pool of facilitators.

Problems, Theories, and Methods

There are many different ways to conceive the role of the facilitator for community-based theatre. In "The Art of Community Conversation," Anne Ellis describes the post-performance discussion as a catalyst that creates dialogue contextualizing the performance within the audience's frame of reference (92). In referring to the Jokers of the Theatre of the Oppressed, Augusto Boal calls them "difficultators" rather than facilitators (*Rainbow* xix). Like a catalyst, the Joker helps participants see a problem from a new vantage point and acknowledge its complexities. Indeed, as Mady Schutzman writes, the Joker is a trickster clown that is constantly pushing on the boundaries of the community and shining the spotlight on its own contradictions ("Joker Runs Wild" 139). On the other hand, other facilitators privilege the role of listening, reflecting back to the community like a mirror.

No matter how the role of the facilitator is imagined, facilitation requires a complex balancing act between asserting a structure for dialogue and simply acknowledging, affirming, listening. More than anything, facilitators need to adapt to their context, which makes it difficult to pin down a single formula for success. Not every facilitation format will work for every audience. Some groups may thrive with interactive physical games, while others may prefer to engage through intellectual discussion generated by thoughtful questions. Though one can utilize different forms of communication in order to break up habitual scripts, to level power dynamics, and to encourage deep dialogue, sometimes counterproductive audience resistance can test the mettle of even the most adroit facilitator.

One model that inspired our facilitation approach came from Laurie Brooks's "Put a Little Boal in your Talkback." Building upon Boal's Forum Theatre and Dorothy Heathcote's "Process-Drama," Brooks describes her method: "Like a dance performance, it has the feel of an improvisation, but is tightly structured to provide a safety net for audience and performers, while encouraging an exploration of ideas, values and ethics. The [talkback] never has a predictable outcome; it is not lesson-driven but allows audience members to reach their own conclusions" (58). Though Brooks's project aims for values clarification rather than for political activism, her approach combining discussion with interactive theatre techniques offers an excellent model.

Brooks organizes the talkback in three distinct phases—Statements, Exploration, and Reflection—each calling for different methods ("Afterplay"). Brooks's simple structure provides a guide that helps facilitators move through the process. Most of A More Perfect Union's facilitated sessions followed a similar three-part structure. The "Statements" section allows the audience to recall information presented and then to form a relationship with it. Sometimes sociometry techniques can be used to allow the group to make their "statements" visible.[1] These are techniques where the facilitator asks audience members to stand, move across the room, or raise their hands in order to agree, disagree, or respond with "don't know" to the facilitator's statement. Using prompts that relate to situations within the play can provide a safe way for participants to reveal opinions, divisions, and knowledge about the issues.

For A More Perfect Union, after opening with a warm-up—a simple game from Boal's Games for Actors and Non-Actors, which encouraged audience members to open up nonverbal channels of communication—facilitators used prompts such as "I know someone who is LGBTQ," "I know someone who has been affected by the ban on same sex marriage," "I have witnessed discrimination against LGBTQ members of our community," or "I believe marriage is a legal contract (or a spiritual bond or a civil right)." Depending on the composition of the group and the context of the presentation, the facilitator made a choice about whether to frame the prompts as personal or political. In other sessions, this section was more of a conversation with scripted questions, such as "What information was presented that was new to you?" and "How does the ban on same-sex marriage affect our community?" Audience members were also asked to summarize the problems presented, allowing the facilitator to see where their consciousness lay. This conversation was guided to emphasize that the events of the play were based on the real experiences of the Miami University community, offering opportunities to reinforce factual information.

For the "Exploration" section, Brooks proposes different ways to present ethical dilemmas, encouraging the audience to debate character choices and to pose solutions for problems. She suggests ranking characters' culpability in a problem situation, using "hot seat" improvisations to learn more about characters, or exploring the associations audience members made with the play. This section allows the audience to define problems and explore opinions relating to the issue.

For our project, facilitators utilized a variety of methods, some more interactive than others. Some facilitators separated audience members into small groups and invited them to share personal stories based on their experiences of being deprived of rights, feeling they were without a voice, or feeling oppressed. In other situations, students were asked to use Image Theatre to explore experiences of homophobia or ideas about marriage and family by creating static tableaux (with their own bodies) based on prompts. In a few instances, we utilized Boal's Forum Theatre to explore situations implied by the play. For example, in one session, we used the situation of a student coming out to her mother. This allowed students to build empathy as they considered their roles as LGBTQ allies and opened up a conversation about how this coming-out situation could be different if marriage were legal for same-sex couples. The last scene of the play, in which a lesbian character is denied entry to see her partner who has been hospitalized after a car accident, sometimes also was used for Forum Theatre explorations.

The third and final section of the talkback offers an open-ended opportunity for audience members to respond and encourages them to look toward future actions. This section provides closure (at least temporarily) and offers an opportunity to integrate new insights. With our show, this "Reflection" section discussion took varied forms, including such questions as "What should we do next?" and "What resources do we have in our community to address this?" Frequently, the conversation turned toward current events and offered a space to contemplate next steps in taking action. Some sessions, particularly large group sessions, ended with another sociometry-type exercise, this time with prompts including suggestions for the future. Completing the session with some form of ritualized closure is very important. Even if disagreements are not directly engaged, the facilitator plays an important role in reviewing new ideas brought forth, in affirming the identities in the room, and in symbolically restoring the unity of the group.

While Brooks's interactive post-show methodology offers an approach to teaching values clarification, Fringe Benefits' work has a more activist intent emphasizing the relationship between values and action. Unlike Forum Theatre, our project was designed to cultivate new allies rather than to practice solidarity among allies. We were trying to persuade others who had not thought about the issue to consider the injustice of the current law. Each post-show session was facilitated with a different structure based on the context of the presentation and the facilitators' preference. While most of our presentations were for university classes, many were for a variety of campus programs. We did a performance and talkback for the Department of Theatre on National Coming Out Day, another for the Student Affairs "Let's Talk" series, and several similar programs in the residence halls. Each context had a different time limit, different spatial constraints, and different audience expectations. Even in the classroom situations, there were different sizes of classes and different disciplinary ways of thinking about the marriage equality issue. Different instructors had different goals for introducing the issue to their classes.

When we asked, "What parts of the play and/or post-show discussion were the most powerful/effective?," we received many positive responses, such as, "The discussion was the most effective. It was interesting to hear everyone's point of view,"[2] "When we talked about the issues after the play," "It was a great discussion," "The openness of the discussion," and "Great job facilitating and keeping the discussion open and controlled." One respondent noted, "I liked the end [of the play]. I think that it was good for a group discussion." Others enjoyed activities from the "Exploration" section, the improv exercises, and the "audience participation option." One student even commented, "Prior to the play I had more of a neutral stance on Marriage Equality, but now I am against issue one [the ban on same-sex marriage]." This last comment perfectly encapsulated our desired response. Certainly along with these successes, there were miscalculations in our facilitation planning. I will discuss some of these as I walk through the steps in laying a foundation for facilitation and how to proactively plan.

Steps for Laying a Foundation

Understanding the Play's Dramaturgy and the Target Audience

The planning of our post-show discussion began with devising the script. Using Fringe Benefits' dramaturgical approach, we embedded relevant arguments and questions deep into the fabric of the play. In order to bridge the play with the audience, facilitators had to understand the relationships among the core issues within the play. The student facilitators also needed to understand what issues are *not* in the play and why they were left out.

For example, at the end of the play, the lesbian protagonist is denied the opportunity to see her partner in the hospital. This unresolved ending offers the facilitator an opening to ask, "How could marriage rights change this situation?" The inclusion of such characters as the friend who had been divorced multiple times and the cross-racial and cross-religion couples assisted the facilitator in linking issues and posing questions about connections among sexist, heterosexist, racist, and religion-based assumptions, practices, and institutions.

One of our most challenging concerns was how to address religion-based opposition to marriage equality. While we included both heterosexual and homosexual Christian characters, as well as a parent character who expresses disapproval of homosexuality based on religious reasons, we did not deal with religious issues head-on in the play. For many reasons, we also decided not to delve into these thorny issues in our talkbacks. Nevertheless, our facilitators did prepare to address this topic as it is raised, albeit briefly, in the script and as it is a significant factor affecting our target audience's views on marriage equality. In fact, audience members frequently raised the issue. Facilitators need to consider how to pose questions that build upon what's in the script and how to field questions that may be raised by the script.

Research and Current Events

To develop the show and talkback, the students researched such topics as the history of marriage, religious faith and marriage, religious faith and sexuality, family structures, legal rights, and LGBTQ community issues. The play captures much of this research in chorus sections that frame dramatic scenes by filling in legal information or historical anecdotes to broaden the picture. Frequently, audience members contested our portrayal of the subject matter, so it was very important to have factual data to back up our choices. For example, some people protested that "a lesbian partner would never be turned away in a hospital," so it was important to note that, while it doesn't always happen, based on the laws in place, it could happen (and has) (Dwyer). The research process also led to the creation of a research packet and fact sheet that became indispensable to future facilitators.

Throughout the life of our project, battles around the issue of marriage equality continued to break out around the country. As Acevedo and Thornton discuss in their essay in this volume, Representative Tom Brinkman sued our university claiming that our domestic partner benefits violated the statewide ban. Some states passed same-sex marriage laws, other states had their laws revoked, and still others passed more bans. As the project continued, students needed regularly to check websites, such as the Human Rights Campaign site, to stay up-to-date on the issues. This ongoing research also helped the students develop the "Reflection" section of the discussion and helped the audience think about next steps.

Planning and Publicity: Clarifying Expectations

While our presentation was carefully planned as a twenty-five-minute play with a twenty-five-minute talkback, we were not always successful in communicating that our presentation came with a prepared facilitation and trained facilitators. In looking back, we should have asserted this more clearly so that student facilitators would have been given the time, space, and authority they deserved. In some instances, instructors wanted to lead the discussion. One sponsor insisted on providing his own facilitators, who were trained in diversity education but had little knowledge of the issues we were addressing or our theatre methodology. Their facilitation carefully dodged conflict, emphasized personal reflection, and diverted attention away from the engaged dialogue we strove to evoke. Many of these sponsors underestimated our role as theatre artists based on a lack of understanding of the interdisciplinary methodologies of Theatre for Social Justice. We could have addressed these assumptions directly when advertising our presentation by touting the qualifications of facilitators who were trained in techniques of both education and theatre.

Role of the "Expert"

While expertise in legal issues and LGBTQ affairs was indispensable to the process, we had mixed success in incorporating "experts" into post-show discussions. In one situation, we invited a panel of faculty, staff, and community to share their expertise and/or experiences after a performance. While this created an insightful discussion among panelists and faculty in the audience, not one student made a comment during the discussion. However, in another situation, a representative from the student counseling center served as an excellent complement to the student facilitators. Acknowledging the students' authority, he succeeded in providing a broader context to the discussion. Understanding that knowledge equals power, one important precondition to facilitating dialogue is the leveling of power dynamics in the room. This required that we consciously shift the frame of discussions so that students shared authority.

Performing "Neutrality"

Facilitators must appear neutral in order to encourage dialogue, and, yet, they are *not* neutral. This is a conundrum that has haunted many facilitators and requires the most delicate of balancing acts. Certainly this is a difficult issue for any facilitator but even more so for someone seeking to influence his or her own peer social network. Many scholars have debated the ethical issues of a seemingly "neutral" leader, teacher, or facilitator, particularly within the framework of a Freirian critical pedagogy.[3] Clearly, facilitators have an agenda, and even if they do not directly voice that agenda, their position allows them to manipulate the discussion. It can be helpful for facilitators to be transparent about their agenda, but it's important for them to be careful about wording. For example, instead of saying, "I'm here to make sure you change your vote on this issue," the facilitator might explain that he or she is here to "address a problem that deprives others of constitutional rights." For a student peer educator, this might feel dishonest and manipulative. Moreover, it may be particularly challenging for a college student who has just achieved clarity in his or her own consciousness and who may feel uncomfortable with misrepresenting his or her own identity.

In order to create a safe space, it is important for the facilitator to project a sense of openness so that audience members can freely participate, no matter what point of view they hold or what level of knowledge they have. Projecting that openness requires a certain kind of objectivity and an ability to see all points of view as equally worthy of being voiced, presented, and acknowledged. Of course, all points of view are not equal. For this reason, the facilitator must understand the line between fact and opinion. The process of constructing the play circumscribes the common ground upon which "facts" rest and helps facilitators understand how multiple points of view interact along a continuum of consciousness-raising, moving toward social action.

Though facilitators should understand the range of ethical positions on the issues, it is important that they also know how to set clear boundaries and be aware of how their language reflects and/or potentially skews these boundaries. They have to be prepared to contradict misinformation, misleading terminology, or rumors presented by audience members and to clarify that certain ideas presented as facts are actually beliefs or opinions. For example, we began our project with the assumption that Ohio's ban on same-sex marriage deprived LGBTQ individuals of their constitutional rights and directly caused harm to members of the Miami University community. This "fact" was supported by evidence we had carefully gathered and included. However, even within this statement, there is much to debate. For example, should marriage be a legal right or a spiritual or religious commitment? What constitutes "harm," and how does this effect extend beyond individuals to affect communities? Still, we maintained that our audience members would want to become allies of the LGBTQ community once they knew about the harm the laws caused.

In some instances, we encountered individuals who cited religious reasons for supporting the ban. We recognized that many of these positions would be intractable and not receptive to dialogue. We also had to recognize that people had a right to express those beliefs. In order not to turn the discussion into a forum on religious belief or a debate about interpretations of particular Bible verses, we kept the discussion focused on the issue at hand, namely the fact that same-sex couples were deprived of legal rights that other citizens enjoyed, including the ability to adopt children and jointly own property, as well as other hidden privileges embedded within the legal rights of marriage.

When presenting to a group of LGBTQ allies, the facilitators' neutrality allowed them to become "devil's advocates" and channel differing perspectives and arguments to help broaden the discussion. While it is important for facilitators not to emphasize their own personal opinions, I noted instances when student peer educators' use of personal stories had a dramatic, dynamizing impact on the audience. Especially when a group was reticent, peer educators channeled their own outrage, confessed their own ignorance, or shared experiences of how the ban had directly affected their friends or family members. This approach tended to work best with a facilitator who was an LGBTQ ally, the position that we hoped many of our audience members would also come to share.

Performing "neutrality" and finding a firm yet flexible moral stance on the issues at hand can be the most challenging aspect of facilitation. Below, I detail how to begin to rehearse these skills, which are mostly skills of language and phrasing, but it is important to be able to embody and perform this "neutral" role of the facilitator and practice these skills improvisationally.

Writing a Facilitation Script

Though in the end, most experienced facilitators work from an outline, I think creating one's own facilitation script is an invaluable exercise that each facilitator should undertake. It is particularly useful vis-à-vis finding the right language and terminology. Here is a quick approach to conceiving such a script:

Structures of time and space. To assure success, it's critical that the facilitation plan work within the time and space provided by the performance sponsor. For example, if you have only ten minutes for a talkback and fifty people in a room with furniture fixed to the floor, you have some options, but success will depend upon working within those limitations. When time and space are very limited, it is especially important to consider how to get to core issues quickly and to think clearly about transitional moments.

Question-asking. John Borstel's essay "The Art of the Question" from Liz Lerman's website provides an excellent guide for getting beneath the surface to start people talking. How do you articulate open-ended questions? What kinds of questions do people want to answer?

How can you link these questions to the dramaturgical questions of the play? How can you follow up questions with more questions if no one has a response? This is a creative exercise, and the more you practice honing this skill, the better the resulting conversations. Finding the right question that touches upon the audience members' interests is the key. Start with easy questions reviewing the issues and then move toward analyzing contradictions and making judgments about the situations.

Writing sociometry prompts. This exercise quickly reveals differences and common ground to audiences. As with writing questions, it's best to conceive sociometry prompts in relationship to each specific audience and to give specific attention to wording and sequence. Prompts that are too direct or too personal, such as "I am for/against marriage equality" or "I identify as a LGBTQ person or ally," tend to stymie discussion. However, prompts that address issues obliquely, such as "I always/rarely vote in elections" or "In a group situation, I frequently identify with the majority/minority," generate more productive starting places for conversations. It's important to ask participants not to talk during the exercise, then strategically build prompts that will lead toward discussions after the exercise.

Rules and instructions. Safety is always a primary concern, both physically and emotionally; thus, it is important to make assumptions transparent and establish rules of engagement. Rules are always embedded within any cultural group, so consider what may be unwritten practices of a group. Are you maintaining those practices or working against them? For example, one class may have a custom of hand raising during discussion; you might decide to work with that or encourage a more active "jumping in." The way the rules are communicated is part of a facilitator's unique style. I am fond of Liz Lerman's advice on communicating rules: "Tell people what to do, not what *not* to do." By consciously phrasing the rules in your script, you can be clear and proactive.

Active engagement. When outlining activities, consider ways to balance talking with doing. How can you use different forms of dialogue other than talking? How can you make space for others to join the conversation, the ones too shy to jump in? How are you transitioning between times of talking and creative exercises?

Co-facilitation. All of our performances of *A More Perfect Union* were co-facilitated. Students felt more confident with this arrangement and were able to provide support for each other. This also allowed us to pair experienced facilitators with newcomers. By writing a co-facilitation script, you create a tool for communicating with your co-facilitator and can easily divide up activities.

Facilitation "Boot Camp"

As noted above, one of the primary challenges of facilitation rests in how the facilitator adapts moment to moment to the unfolding conversation. Below, I detail a series of exercises designed to train muscles for developing awareness, deep listening, and strategic responses when conflicts emerge. I borrow a three-part concept from one corporate model of facilitation[4] that utilizes three communication strategies:

1. *Pushing.* This style of communication involves persuading and asserting. In situations where the facilitator is correcting factual misinformation or conveying what is at stake in the issue, pushing is particularly important. If overused, however, facilitation can cause audiences to tune out.
2. *Pulling.* This style involves bridging and encouraging participants to envision solutions to problems. These tactics are essential to creating common ground and conveying the values of the group.
3. *Moving away.* This style employs strategies to disengage or avoid. When conflict becomes destructive to dialogue, or when participants go on tangents away from the issue at hand, these strategies become particularly important (Franklin 11).

Knowing Yourself

A key step in facilitation requires that you understand how others perceive you and what experiences inform your facilitation of the topic. To develop this awareness, you might begin by creating a mind map or bubble map of communities and identities that make up your experiences. When facilitating a particular group, some of these may be visible and/or relevant, but some may not be. How can you draw from these different aspects of your own identity to create common ground with the group you are facilitating? Create another bubble map, but this time map out your personal experiences with the issue you are facilitating. Which of these experiences share common ground with the group you will work with? Which would be helpful to reveal and which not?

Active Listening

While true listening is a complex task, there are different ways to practice this skill. It's important to reflect back statements in a post-show discussion to make sure they are clearly heard. Here are a few different exercises to help develop this skill. Working in pairs, one person tells a story. A prompt might be "Tell a story about a time when you had to make a difficult choice." While one person shares his or her story, his or her partner maintains eye contact and simply listens. When the story is completed, the listening partner can do one or all of the following:

1. Simply repeat the story back to the partner with as much detail as possible. Together, compare this version with the original.
2. To practice "pulling" energies, the listening partner asks questions about the story. Can you find out more about the context? How is the story important to this teller's identity? What emotions are latent within the story?
3. Try to condense the teller's story. Can the listener describe what the root problem conveyed in the story was? What it meant to the teller? What emotions the experience evoked? Try to be as objective and concise as possible with one-sentence statements. When facilitating a large group discussion, this skill is particularly important since you may have to reflect back comments that audience members have difficulty hearing, or you may have to quickly summarize and integrate a series of comments.

Shaping Rhythms

The facilitator must be tuned into the rhythms of the group and maintain the right amount of energy and structure in the conversation. This exercise gets facilitators to think about nonverbal communication, rhythm, listening, and structure. Also known as the "Conductor" exercise,[5] one person takes the role of the conductor of the "orchestra." Everyone else in the group becomes the orchestra. To begin with, each person in the orchestra can demonstrate the sound that he or she will make as part of the orchestra. Then the conductor will begin to conduct the group, creating a musical composition. Using only movement, the conductor should guide the group, setting up rhythms and modulating volume. As you repeat this exercise, listen for transition points. How long can instruments sustain a pattern? When do the participants get tired and stop listening to one another? How can you introduce elements of surprise? How can you use your nonverbal gestures to create a clear means of communicating with your instruments? Finally, reflect on analogous situations in the work of the facilitator of a post-show discussion. Can you use these techniques to set the tone and rhythm of a discussion or exercise? How can the facilitator's energy maintain a productive amount of pressure on the conversation?

Facilitator in the Hot Seat: Pushing, Pulling, and Redirecting

Facilitation is a performance, so ultimately you have to rehearse it on your feet. First consider some of the audience behaviors you may encounter. A few common challenges include: someone raises a disagreement based on his or her knowledge, experience, beliefs, or opinion; one person tries to dominate the conversation; participants are reluctant to speak up and participate; a participant puts undue focus on his or her own experiences; a participant says that this discussion makes him or her feel guilty; or a participant belittles the work as being an exercise in "political correctness" (Schmidt). Develop a list of provocative statements you think participants are likely to make. How can you turn audience members' moments of resistance into productive opportunities to engage? Take turns serving as the facilitator to practice strategies for responding to each scenario. When does it work best to use "pushing, pulling, or moving away" strategies?

You can set this exercise up like a game called "Boxing Seconds" (Babbage 130). Half of the group can coach the "unruly" participant; the other half can coach the facilitator. (Experienced facilitators will be best qualified to coach the "unruly" participant in this exercise.) With two actors improvising the imaginary interaction, the teacher/moderator can yell "Stop!" and allow each "team" to huddle up and brainstorm strategies for responding to the "opponent" in the next round of the scene. Do several repetitions of each exchange and rotate facilitators so that you can explore as many strategies as possible. Different student facilitators can take turns responding to the "unruly" participant and compare and contrast the effectiveness of various tactics. Not all strategies will work in every context and for every facilitator, so it's important to have multiple tools in your arsenal.

Another useful formula that can be applied to the "Boxing Seconds" exercise comes from a workshop with the group Nonviolent Peaceforce.[6] Using the acronym CLARA, they break down the recommended response of a facilitator in a conflict situation:

C—Stay *Calm*.

L—*Listen*. Using active listening skills, "listen for something you have in common with the other person." You may have to ask clarifying questions in order to accomplish this.

A—*Affirm*. Say something that "acknowledges what you have in common, perhaps one 'piece of truth' that you recognize in the other's statement." This is perhaps the most difficult of the CLARA stages and a skill that can be practiced as you rehearse confrontational situations in the "Boxing Seconds" exercise. In the "Affirm" stage, practice "pulling" tactics to learn more about the participant and to try to establish that common ground. This stage will be critical for facilitators in rehearsing "performed neutrality" and maintaining an authentic engagement with audiences.

R—If *and only if* you are able to move from C to L to A, then "*Respond* to the concerns the person raised" when you were listening.

A—"*Add* something about the way you see the topic that builds on the connection you've established." Depending on the success of the previous "Affirm" stage, you should either "push" to develop your point of view or "move away" and refocus the conversation or find another ways to diffuse the conflict (Nonviolent Peaceforce 27).

An exercise like "Boxing Seconds" will help student facilitators assess and develop their abilities to engage conflict productively.

In Conclusion

Throughout this discussion, I have explored how facilitation of a post-show workshop inflects the entire process of Theatre for Social Justice. From the beginning, it is important to think about the quality of the conversations you want to evoke and to start planning for them. Post-show discussions can run seamlessly without effort, but they can just as easily fall flat. Consequently, it is important to demystify the qualities of an effective facilitator, prepare for facilitation, and set up a clear structure that is flexible and allows you to create a conversation that gets beneath surfaces and ripples into other productive spaces.

There is no doubt that *A More Perfect Union* created such ripples, ones that have continued to resonate more than eight years later. Those ripples were created and sustained through a complex interaction between our audiences, the facilitators, the play, and the overall context of the work in our community. The success of our student peer educators stemmed from their authentic commitment to the issues and persistence in reflecting upon and improving the facilitation process. While peer leader facilitation might not fit every context, a training structure that engages deep reflection, active listening, and conflict resolution goes a long way toward developing facilitators' skills and creating a satisfying experience for audiences and a deep connection between the work and community.

Notes

1. Sometimes called the "Human Thermometer" or "Vote with Your Feet," sociometry techniques were originated by psychologist Jacob Moreno and are the basis of many studies on group dynamics in education and psychology. See, for example, Chris Hoffman, "Introduction to Sociometry," *The Hoop and the Tree* website, 2001, http://www.hoopandtree.org/sociometry.htm.

2. Audience quotations have been extracted from responses to post-show surveys conducted in 2005 (unpublished).

3. See, for example, Patti Lather, "Critical Pedagogy and Its Complicities," *Educational Theory* 48, no. 4 (1998): 487–98.

4. From Boyce Appel, Appel Associates, Atlanta (as cited in Franklin 11–20).

5. Augusto Boal describes his version of this exercise as "The Orchestra and the Conductor" in *Games for Actors and Non-Actors,* 101. Joseph Chaikin describes a version of this exercise as "Conductor" in Robert Pasolli, *A Book on the Open Theatre* (New York: Avon, 1972), 27.

6. Nonviolent Peaceforce "promote[s], develop[s] and implement[s] unarmed civilian peacekeeping as a tool for reducing violence and protecting civilians in situations of violent conflict." I am borrowing from its workshop materials and exercises, many of which have been influenced by communication scholars and writers like Marshall Rosenberg. For more information, please visit www.nonviolentpeaceforce.org.

Bibliography

Assaf, Andrea. "Dialogue in Artistic Practice." In *Dialogue in Artistic Practice: Case Studies from "Animating Democracy,"* edited by Barbara Schaffer Bacon and Pam Korza. Washington, DC: Americans for the Arts, 2005. v–xi.

Babbage, Frances. *Augusto Boal.* London: Routledge, 2004.

Boal, Augusto. *Games for Actors and Non-Actors.* New York: Routledge, 1992.

———. *Rainbow of Desire.* New York: Routledge, 1995.

Borstel, John. "The Art of the Question." Liz Lerman Dance Exchange Toolbox, 2010. http://danceexchange.org/toolbox/home.htm.

Bowles, Norma. "Why Devise? Why Now? 'Houston, we have a problem.'" *Theatre Topics* 15, no. 1 (2005): 15–21.

Brooks, Laurie. "The Afterplay Interactive Forum: A New Model for Talkbacks," 2008. http://www.lauriebrooks.com/plays/newmodeltalkbacks.html.

———. "Put a Little Boal in Your Talkback." *American Theatre* 22, no. 10 (2005): 58–60.

Dwyer, Devin. "Hospital Visitation Rights for Gays and Lesbians Take Effect." ABC World News, January 19, 2011.

http://abcnews.go.com/Politics/hospital-visitation-rights-gay lesbian-partners -effect/story?id=12642543.

Ellis, Anne. "The Art of Community Conversation." *Theatre Topics* 10, no. 2 (2000): 91–100.

Franklin, James. "Facilitative Skills." Workshop handouts for the American Institute for Architects, 1994, 11–20 (unpublished).

Lerman, Liz. "Foundations." Liz Lerman Dance Exchange Toolbox, 2010. http://danceexchange.org/toolbox/home.htm.

Nonviolent Peaceforce. "Participant Handbook Nonviolent Conflict Intervention One Day Workshop." September 2009 (unpublished).

Schmidt, Sheri Lyn. "Skin Deep Facilitator's Guide: Working with Challenging Situations." Compiled by Hugh Vasquez. *California Newsreel: Film and Video for Social Change since 1968*. http://newsreel.org/guides/skindeep. htm.

Schutzman, Mady. "Guru Clown or Pedagogy of the Carnivalesque." *Theatre Topics* 12, no. 1 (2002): 63–84.

———. "Joker Runs Wild." In *A Boal Companion: Dialogues on Theatre and Cultural Politics*, edited by Jan Cohen-Cruz and Mady Schutzman. New York: Routledge, 2006. 133–45.

Walking Theatre Project and Fringe Benefits. *A More Perfect Union*, 2005–2006 (unpublished).

Pushing without Shoving: Ethics of and Emphasis on Target Participation in TSJ Institutes

BRYAN C. MOORE

The 2006 Theatre for Social Justice Institute with Fringe Benefits, the University of Iowa (UI), and the Iowa City Community School District (ICCSD) focused on issues of cultural competence and racism in local high schools. Participants in the Institute collaborated to create a Forum Theatre play to be performed for faculty, staff, and administrators as the keynote presentation of the ICCSD Martin Luther King, Jr. Professional Development Day 2007. The play presented problematic situations that could arise in a high school setting so that the audience could consider and practice how to resolve or prevent similar problems in the future. Many of the Institute participants, including high school students and staff members, also performed in the play.

Early in the planning stages for an Institute, Fringe Benefits staff members emphasize the need to include participants of diverse genders, ethnicities, ages, cultures, disciplines, fields of expertise, and positions of power, as well as participants who can share personal experiences with the specific discrimination issue that will be addressed in the Institute. They also urge participating organizations to include representatives with diverse viewpoints about that social justice issue. Fringe Benefits asserts that the participation of this kind of diverse coalition of individuals is needed in order to create the most accurate, engaging, and effective theatrical depiction of a situation possible (Norma Bowles, personal communication).

A perfect balance of diverse representation within an Institute is, however, an ideal that is not usually feasible. Moreover, sometimes the specific participant diversity goals that are established and/or the particular recruitment strategy that is implemented for a collaboration can draw in individuals with unworkable, conflicting agendas or insufficient motivation for participating.

Balanced Representation

For their 2006 collaboration, Fringe Benefits, Darwin Turner Action Theatre (DTAT), UI, the Iowa Theatre Department, and the ICCSD Equity Office drafted a project Memorandum of Understanding (MOU), which included participant recruitment targets. The MOU stipulated that the ideal Institute "team" should comprise high school students and teachers, Educational Equity staff, and UI theatre students, as well as the play director, project coordinator/producer, individuals with legal, counseling, and diversity expertise, and allies with experience in education, activism, the arts, and/or parenting.[1] Another important goal identified was diverse racial/ethnic and gender representation. Together, the partners discussed strategies for fulfilling the various diversity targets, or quotas, outlined in the MOU.

In order to help ensure the specified broad and diverse participation, the UI faculty member who served as the project liaison required DTAT members and UI graduate school directing students to participate in the Institute. Additionally, the ICCSD, through its equity director, recruited students, faculty, and staff through general memos and personal contact. The partnering organizations recruited over thirty participants who represented, to varying degrees, the groups of individuals specified in the MOU. While there were a sufficient number of students from UI and the high schools, few ICCSD faculty and staff participated. There were also relatively few white males.

As I reflect on this Institute, which I co-facilitated with Norma Bowles, many questions arise regarding the potential (and actual) obstacles created by establishing quotas: Should there be any participant-diversity goals in the first place? What if the people who might be most willing and able to devote the time and energy needed for an Institute do not fit neatly within the established demographic markers? What other factors play into assembling an effective team? What are some of the possible risks and benefits of mandating participation? In trying to ensure specific target representation, might we risk encouraging or compelling less-than-committed individuals to participate while missing out on the involvement of other interested parties? Might the project suffer as a result? An evaluation of these questions, along with the choices made and their impact, will help support the work already being done by Fringe Benefits and point toward strategies that might more effectively address representation-related issues in future Institutes.

Should Projects Like This Set Participant Diversity Goals?

As many of the Institute plays address cultural oppression, diverse cultural representation is necessary within the Institute, thus creating the need to set quotas. But racial quotas—often used in educational institutions and businesses to promote equal representation and to mitigate the effects of institutional and historical racism—are controversial and are considered by some to be a form of "reverse racism."[2] Setting quotas for participation in community-based theatre projects can also lead to an unfair exclusion of interested individuals. Quotas can present additional challenges when the pool of available volunteers does not provide the necessary diverse representation.

In Iowa City, a predominantly white town, we assumed it would be more difficult to find enough people of color to participate in the Institute. Through dedicated recruitment, however, this turned out to be manageable. We were not, however, able to recruit many white men. And the majority of those who did join the group, especially those who were participating only to fulfill a course requirement, seemed to feel disinterested in and/or uncomfortable with the project. We needed to include their voices—both as theatre artists and as white men—in our work. Still, as they did not seem to feel a compelling motivation to contribute their time and effort to the cause, we were not able to fully benefit from their presence. Was the core issue that they had been forced to be there? Or were they simply not a good "fit" for the project and the project not a good "fit" for them?

Who Is a Good Fit for the Process?

Potential institutional project partners include theatres, universities, high schools, grassroots activist organizations, religious or community centers, and support groups. The way an organization defines its mission and constituency and the way it approaches collaborative/group work may augur well or poorly for a productive and relatively comfortable "fit" with the Institute process. Grassroots activist groups, for example, might be ideal Institute partners as their members tend to be knowledgeable about and highly motivated to address the identified issues; still, they might not have sufficient expertise or resources to produce the play following the Institute. With their diverse populations of youth and adults interested in the arts and humanities and with, potentially, a built-in audience, high schools might seem a perfect fit, and yet they might find the Institute's egalitarian approach to collaboration—with students, faculty, and staff all having an equal voice—challenging.

Fringe Benefits' Institutes consist of five labor-intensive and creatively challenging four-hour workshops. Some groups have difficulty adjusting to the brisk pace of the Institute. One notable example was the support group with which we partnered on another Institute that I co-facilitated. This group was accustomed to taking unlimited time to process the feelings of its members when issues arose. In contrast, the Institute devising process requires facilitators and members to work through difficult moments quickly and efficiently and to keep the work moving forward in order to complete a script in five sessions. The convergence of these incompatible approaches to handling discomfort created an impasse in the above-mentioned Institute. In the end, substantial adjustments were made to the process to accommodate the support group participants and to avoid losing them physically or emotionally. Those accommodations, however, resulted in a significant loss of time, and the script was not finished by the end of the Institute. Upon reflection, it seems that perhaps the Fringe Benefits staff should have described their methodology more thoroughly to this partnering organization before committing to a collaboration. Perhaps the two organizations might have been wiser not to have partnered on an Institute at all.

Fortunately, the majority of the Iowa Institute's participants, especially the members of DTAT and the ICCSD, enthusiastically embraced Fringe Benefits' activist agenda and fast-paced process. Even so, the demands of the Institute challenged our team. Some participants were not able to attend every session but contributed as they could, sharing ideas and topic-related information. Their inconsistent attendance, however, slightly destabilized the ensemble and shortened our work time as we needed to help them get "up to speed." Nevertheless, the participation of several different types of organizations—a university theatre department, a diversity-focused theatre group, an educational equity office, and several high schools—with their diverse missions, methodologies, and memberships, helped create a strong, multitalented team. But we still were missing at least one indispensable perspective.

How to Recruit Participants with Opposing Viewpoints?

Another challenge for Institute organizers is finding people willing to represent the point of view of "the oppressor" during the writing process, especially once they understand that critiquing this point of view is integral to the show. Such individuals are needed to help guide the devising process so that the resulting play can speak effectively to audience members who share their perspective. Moreover, it is likely that the oppressor's point of view will be embodied in at least one character in the play; the input of like-minded participants helps insure that this character will be believable to the target audience.

In the case of our Institute addressing racism in local high schools, our team felt that this character probably would be a white individual, most likely a male teacher. Again, unfortunately, only a few white males joined our Institute, and most of them chose to remain silent through the story sharing and brainstorming. Their limited participation reduced the group's access to perspectives crucial to creating white male characters and to fleshing out our play.

Working around the obstacles presented by the limited input from these men, the participants created more scenes that involved female oppressors and scenes that addressed racial tensions and discriminatory behavior among individuals of diverse races and ethnicities, primarily African American and Latino/Latina. While we were able to address a number of significant issues related to racist discriminatory behavior in our script, and the show was well received, a crucial point of view was not adequately represented.

How Do Apathetic Participants Affect Results?

The opportunity to earn academic credits or volunteer hours or to fulfill a course requirement can tempt or force students to participate in a project in which they are disinterested or that they even resent. Their apathetic or negative attitude can impede constructive collaboration, discourage other members, and cause unproductive conflicts. Resentful participants may tend to criticize others' ideas or the process in general without offering constructive suggestions, thereby crippling group cohesion and impeding the progress of the work. And again, without the input of these disinterested members, crucial issues, plot points, and/or characters may not receive adequate consideration from the playwriting team, which could result in misrepresented characters, implausible situations, or a slanted view of the issues.

Though not ideal, our situation could have been worse. Although some of the UI graduate students were not actively involved in the collaborative process, at least they did not choose to vocalize their discontent. Still, their lack of participation limited the quantity of stories and ideas shared and the complexity of our discussions and improvisations. Fortunately, the number and quality of stories from the other individuals and their high level of engagement helped compensate for the white male grad students' lack of participation and made it possible for us to complete our play successfully.

Alternative Approaches to Recruitment

While it can be counterproductive to require disinterested individuals to participate in collaborative projects such as this, it can also be excessively challenging for some *interested* individuals to participate due to financial and workload obstacles. Many students cannot afford to spend time on extracurricular endeavors without academic or internship credit, community service credit, work-study pay, or some similar compensation. Consequently, the participating team may end up being lopsidedly wealthier and white. One possible solution might be to offer some type of academic incentive, such as the option to participate in the project for extra credit or in lieu of writing a term paper. This approach offers students a fair choice and provides potentially interested students with additional motivation. Another solution is to clarify in the course description if such a project is part of the mandatory curriculum. Yet another option is to collaborate with other community and campus organizations on outreach and recruitment. This third approach can potentially attract broader, more diverse participation in the work.

The success of the TSJ Institutes relies on the representation of a healthy balance of perspectives from a diverse group of people. Still, as we have seen, even if it were possible to assemble a "perfectly" diversified ensemble, it would not be possible to guarantee that everyone would be equally engaged and invested in the work or able to articulate all of the diverse perspectives needed. Fringe Benefits and the partnering organizations of the 2006 Iowa Institute worked hard to gather and maintain an ideal balance of perspectives, but they could not control or overcome all of the individual or societal challenges.

In retrospect, offering incentives for participation instead of requiring it and partnering more on outreach and recruitment might have encouraged more diverse and more enthusiastic participation. The success of the Institute, though, demonstrates that passionate individuals with creativity and theatrical knowledge can compensate for an insufficiently diverse group and/or a group in which some participants are less actively engaged. Ultimately, when the Institute coordinators cannot recruit the desired demographic or cultural quota of fully committed participants, they need to focus on recruiting participants on whom they can rely to collaborate well using the methodology at hand to achieve the project's goals.

Notes

1. "Fringe Benefits, Darwin Turner Action Theatre, University of Iowa Theatre Arts Department, and the ICCSD Equity Office Theatre for Social Justice Institute Memorandum of Understanding," June 26, 2006 (unpublished).

2. Louis P. Pojman, "The Case against Affirmative Action," *International Journal of Applied Philosophy*, Spring 1998, http://www.csus.edu/indiv/g/gaskilld /business_computer_ethics/the%20case%20against%20affirmative%20action.htm.

We Are Who We Are: Theatre to Confront Homophobia and Transform Education into Social Praxis

TRACEY CALHOUN

During my first year teaching at Woodrow Wilson High School, I was asked to sponsor a new club—the Gay-Straight Alliance (GSA). A small group of students had been working to form this club for some time but had been unable to secure faculty support. Being young, progressive, and naive, I immediately agreed to work with these youth, although none of us had much of an idea of who we were or what we wanted to accomplish. When an opportunity arose for our group to work with a local theatre company, we jumped at the chance. I had long been familiar with Fringe Benefits' unique brand of community-based social justice theatre and felt that a collaboration with that group might help my GSA students develop a sense of identity and purpose while inspiring a positive change in attitudes and behavior toward lesbian, gay, bisexual, and transgender (LGBT)[1] issues on campus.

In October, when we began work in the Theatre for Social Justice Institute as part of a semester-long Fringe Benefits residency to create and present an original play about homophobia, I thought our main purpose would be to address homophobia and homophobic behavior on our school campus. However, as the process moved on, I realized how important the residency had become as a space for students to build a strong sense of self and purpose that runs counter to the narrative of the troubled and suicidal LGBT youth, a reality that has been documented in much of the research done on this population.

One student, a young man named Bobby[2] who was also in my first period English class, joined the residency at the very beginning but sat on the outskirts of our storytelling circles in the first two weeks. Then, during the third session, he "came out" to the group and shared a story about his own experience with discrimination. Several weeks earlier, Bobby explained, he had confided in a friend about a crush he had on another male student. Bobby's friend apparently had betrayed his confidence because a few days later, word had spread and students in Bobby's first period class were asking him, "Are you gay? Is it true you're a *fag*?" Although he denied the rumors, Bobby said his peers were persistent and had begun openly heckling him. It hit me then that Bobby was speaking about an incident that had occurred in my classroom. And, I realized with a sinking stomach, I had had no idea this was going on.

I was shocked by Bobby's disclosure, or rather by what his story implied about my teaching practice—my own classroom had been a site of anti-LGBT hate and harassment. After all, I am an openly gay educator. I am the faculty sponsor of the GSA. And I am vigilant about acknowledging and responding to all acts of bias and discrimination in my classroom and do my best to turn these instances into "teachable moments." Considering my personal philosophy of education and my professional experience, I did not want to believe the truths that Bobby's experience unmasked.

Bobby's disclosure highlighted a persistent need to be aware of and confront anti-LGBT bias in the classroom. An emerging body of research vividly demonstrates the prevalence and seriousness of victimization of and violence toward youth who are or are perceived to be LGBT. The National Mental Health Association reported in a survey of twelve- to seventeen-year-olds that 93 percent hear other kids at school or in their neighborhood use words like "fag," "homo," "dyke," "queer," or "gay" at least once in a while, with 51 percent hearing such words every day, and 78 percent reporting that kids who are gay or thought to be gay are teased or bullied in their schools and communities. At Wilson and other area schools, despite the passage of the California Student Safety and Violence Prevention Act of 2000, which amended the state's education code to prohibit harassment and discrimination in public schools on the basis of actual or perceived sexual orientation or gender identity, anti-LGBT harassment and violence remains an embedded part of school life.[3] In its 2001 "Understanding the Social Environment" survey, the Los Angeles Unified School District found that sexual orientation was the second most likely trigger for bias-related harassment in school, after race/ethnicity. Nonconformity to stereotypical gender norms (males thought to be too feminine or females thought to be too masculine) was ranked third as a basis for harassment. Furthermore, the survey found that victims of anti–lesbian, gay, bisexual, transgender, and questioning (LGBTQ) bias made up the only group that did not seek help from school authorities (Gilstrap 9, 13).

As a social justice educator, I am certainly familiar with the need to address anti-LGBTQ bias in schools. However, my experiences with the residency have prompted me to reframe my response to homophobia and heterosexism: in light of Bobby's story, I realize that it is not enough to simply confront and stop acts of anti-LGBTQ bias. A reactive pedagogy falls short of affecting social change. Rather than "teach" social justice from a historical or problem-solving perspective, educators need to be proactive and facilitate opportunities for students to identify issues of concern and to become agents of change.

So how does a social justice educator move beyond simply responding to injustice? How do we create a space for students to conceive of and create their own vision of a just society, in and out of our classrooms? As Paulo Freire has written: "The teacher who really teaches, that is, who really works with contents within the context of methodological exactitude, will deny as false the hypocritical formula, 'do as I say, not as I do.' Whoever is engaged in 'right thinking' knows only too well that words not given body (made flesh) have little or no value. Right thinking is right doing" (*Pedagogy of Freedom* 39). I believe that encouraging "right thinking" and "right doing" not only requires our own thoughtful practice but also demands that educators find ways in which we may inspire "right doing" in our students. Bobby's story suggests a possible solution. Although I believed I had created a classroom environment in which LGBT students felt safe and supported, my classroom had not been a safe space for Bobby. He had not felt comfortable enough in this environment to bring his concerns to me, nor had he felt empowered to respond directly to the harassment he experienced. Instead, he remained silent for weeks until he found a safe space in the residency. In this space, Bobby revealed his sexual orientation out loud, perhaps for the first time, because he realized he was part of a community of individuals committed to taking action to confront homophobia. It was a space in which he could envision his own agency to enact social change.

To truly embody the tenets of education for social justice, one must not only design inclusive, diverse curricula but also be an educator who, through his or her pedagogy, interrogates inequalities and, by example, leads students to understand and critique their own just and unjust assumptions and actions (Bourdieu; Freire, *Pedagogy of Freedom*; Oakes and Lipton). A social justice educator must hold ideologies of equity and justice and must also actively work toward challenging inequities.

Sociocultural education theorists have argued that schools serve as sites for cultural reproduction, including the transfer of inequalities and social stratification (Bourdieu; Giroux). The experiences of LGBT youth in school reflect larger social issues; likewise, cultural inequities are acted out in schools through the experiences of individual students. It is incumbent upon the socially just educator to interrupt such reproduction and create a space within which students and educators can work together to defeat social, cultural, political, and economic obstacles (Diaz and Flores).

Unfortunately, the legislative, pedagogical, and social services responses to anti-LGBT inequality, particularly in regard to youth, have, for the most part, served only to further perpetuate the problem, even when such interventions have been undertaken in the name of social justice. In his book *The New Gay Teenager*, Cornell University professor Ritch Savin-Williams argues that focusing on the archetype of the troubled gay youth both pathologizes the individual and circumvents the root issue:

> Many gay-friendly researchers, professionals, activists, and organizations cite a long litany of ways in which gay teens deviate from their heterosexual brothers and sisters. Perhaps they do this to legitimize the pain of growing up gay, to elicit sympathy for gay youth, or to obtain financial or other resources for prevention and/or intervention programs. The finger-pointing is usually directed at an uncaring mainstream culture; the aim is usually to educate professionals in mainstream institutions (especially schools) about the unique needs of gay teens. These gay "advocates" usually portray young gay people as weak and defenseless in the face of a troubled and violent world. Are there no resilient, strong gay teens who cope, survive, and thrive? (179)

Savin-Williams does not suggest that statistics on the prevalence of anti-LGBT harassment and violence are incorrect; however, he asserts that focusing on gay youth as maladjusted or "at-risk" makes invisible the lives of the many LGBT young people who are happy, healthy, and socially content and further solidifies the dichotomy between youth who are considered "normal" and those who are not. The current model of responsive intervention supports a paradigm in which LGBT youth are powerless to overcome their own oppression. Thus, even through well-intentioned support, school officials often perpetuate the harmful environment from which they seek to protect LGBT youth.

The Theatre for Social Justice Institute is built upon a theoretical framework that seeks to promote agency in youth; it reimagines schooling and curriculum as sites to disrupt cultural reproduction and to enact a radical pedagogy. Rather than respond to LGBT youth as victims, the Institute turns to them as experts on their experience, strong enough to recognize and challenge the inequities they face. We empower our students to imagine equality. Through theatre, we seek to reframe a response directed at challenging the discriminatory environment rather than problematizing the individual. By acknowledging and teaching about injustice, we empower students to critically examine their own experiences of oppression and to act upon the root injustice. In other words, by facilitating an opportunity for students to develop an original theatrical production, we can help them to change their world and to envision themselves as agents of this change.

This effort to radicalize education by engaging students in critical reflection requires a transformation of how we view the roles of educators and the schooling system. Henry Giroux echoes other critical theorists when he posits that "transformative intellectuals," as he calls progressive educators, must make their pedagogy a form of radical praxis. He defines this concept of radical praxis as "combin[ing] reflection and action in the interest of empowering students with the skills and knowledge needed to address injustices and to be critical actors committed to developing a world free of oppression and exploitation" (333).

If we start with reflection, we examine histories of oppression as lived by students. During the Institute, we did this through a storytelling session designed to create a safe space for students to share their experiences with homophobic behavior, experiences that would then serve as the foundation for their play. Giroux asserts that the purpose of reliving such interactions is twofold: "Uncovering the horror of past suffering and the dignity and solidarity of resistance alerts us to the historical conditions that construct such experiences. This notion of liberating memory does more than recover dangerous instances of the past, it also focuses on the subject of suffering and the reality of those treated as 'the other.' Then we can begin to understand the reality of human existence and the need for all members of a democratic society to transform existing social conditions so as to eliminate such suffering in the present" (333). Liberating memory serves to remind students of lived experiences of inequality. However, rather than reinforcing a victim mentality, the process of exposing and challenging injustice reminds students that there is also a history of struggle and resistance that has prompted social transformation. In this sense, starting from the recognition of victimization is not the same as building a reactionary response to troubled youth. Rather, it liberates students from their fears by allowing them to imagine a better world. Indeed, as Paulo Freire has suggested, "It is only the oppressed who, by freeing themselves, can free their oppressors" (*Pedagogy of the Oppressed* 42).

Freire makes explicit the link between the fear students encounter as they liberate memory and the generative power of such remembering. Confronting fear, Freire (as cited in Darder) suggests, channels energy into agency to effect change: "The more you recognize your fear as a consequence of your attempt to practice your dream, the more you learn how to put into practice your dream!" (26). As students shared their stories during the Institute, at first timidly and later with pride and courage, they realized that their own lives could inspire social change. This became apparent early in our storytelling session when one student, Jessica, shared a shocking experience about a former boyfriend. After they had been dating for five months, he told her he was gay. Jessica was devastated and turned to her close friends for support. Just a few days later, Jessica's now ex-boyfriend knocked on her door, bloody and disoriented. He had been beaten up by friends who had heard the rumor that he was gay.

Jessica told this story almost as an afterthought. We had already completed our storytelling circle, during which she had chosen to pass rather than to share. However, once she told us her story, she said she felt a weight had been lifted from her shoulders. Her story later became the keystone for our theatrical production, *We Are Who We Are*. In this instance, the residency structure provided a forum in which Jessica felt safe to confront her own guilt and fear and to discover that by so doing she could actually effect change in herself, in her peers, and in her school.

Following a ten-week storytelling, scriptwriting, and rehearsing residency, we presented four performances of the student-generated play *We Are Who We Are* on December 8 and 9, 2005. Each of the performances ran approximately twenty-five minutes, followed by a ninety-minute facilitated discussion between the audience and cast members. The post-show discussions began with student participants' stories of how they got involved in the production and how the experience affected them, followed by an open forum for the audience to ask questions and make comments.

Perhaps because the audience was aware that the story enacted onstage was a composite of true events, or perhaps because student participants were forthcoming about their own struggles creating the play, audience members were equally unguarded in their responses. Although there were both supportive and hostile comments from audience members, most were delivered with a degree of respect that engendered meaningful dialogue. Many audience members shared stories about friends, family members, and classmates who had been subjected to name calling and harassment and, as a result, had taken their own lives. When these stories were shared, a hush came over the packed auditorium. I was stunned by the number of people who knew a lesbian, gay, bisexual, or transgender individual who had committed suicide. As one student shared a story about her cousin's death, I noticed that one of our cast members began to cry. Instead of shrinking into the background, he approached the microphone onstage and through tears said, "He shouldn't have to die for us to realize that words do hurt." He received a standing ovation.

Participant surveys completed after the performance revealed the writer-performers' perceptions of themselves as activists and reflections about the success of the play.[4] Overall, participants reported that they felt they had accomplished something major and were proud of their role in the project. Prior to the performance, many students voiced concerns about being targeted for harassment after appearing onstage. Some worried that being in the play at all would lead people to assume they were gay. Afterward, one student took pride in the fact that a classmate mistook her identity: "There was this one guy that asked me [if] I came out in the play . . . because I was lesbian. I told him that I was [a lesbian] even though I'm not and he just stood quiet." Whereas before the performance, students seemed to think they needed to shield themselves from possible attacks, they left the residency experience feeling strong enough to weather criticism.

I suspect that the students' increased self-esteem was the result of several contributing factors. These students worked together for nearly two months on a project that was close to their hearts. They encouraged one another as they performed their own and other students' life experiences in improvisation exercises and ultimately onstage for the school. This close-knit work environment helped them to develop a community of support. Likewise, student-ownership in the play led to a greater sense of accomplishment when it was well received. There was far more at stake in this performance than in the standard school musical—students made their own lives transparent onstage and determined the lens through which their stories should be told. When they received accolades, not only from administrators and faculty but also from their peers, the students discovered that taking on challenging topics and inspiring people to think can be "cool."

Based on audience survey responses, it seems the play did inspire a positive change in students' attitudes and behavior regarding LGBT issues. One teacher wrote: "Many of my students were surprised to find out that the play was based on real experiences of the student performers. At the end of the play many students were shocked to realize that hate crimes and discrimination do exist toward LGBT students."[5] Another teacher shared: "When we discussed the play after viewing it there were positive outcomes: One student was able to tell another student that he hates being teased. The other students joined in and gave advice and encouragement to both students. One of my students now catches himself and apologizes to the class whenever he says something disrespectful or insulting." Perhaps the greatest indicator of whether social change was achieved was the feedback from audience members regarding what they felt they could do to stop discrimination on campus. In response to this open-ended question, 98 percent of the respondents provided positive, though sometimes vague, feedback. The most common comments included "Respect others for who they are," "Stop name calling," and "Speak up." One student wrote: "Create more plays like this one to show that we are all human. Having more of this kind of opportunity will change people's views slowly."

Even if the play didn't succeed in transforming Woodrow Wilson High School overnight into a safe and supportive environment for all students, it has demonstrated one thing: theatre can be used as a means of engaging dialogue on social justice issues. It is a forum that requires collaboration and thus the creation of a community committed to working productively toward a common goal in spite of participants' diverse backgrounds. Theatre provides a safe space for people to explore issues of social justice and to posit alternatives to violence and harassment. For the school community at large, the play provided a lens through which students were able to examine their own prejudices and assumptions. The residency offered a first step toward empowering students to create a better world.

Too often, classroom teachers view students, especially youth from disadvantaged, underserved communities, through a deficit lens. They see only those academic skills that our students have not mastered and standardized test scores that label them "far below basic." The effect of the deficit lens is compounded by a tendency to label LGBT youth as "troubled" and in need of intervention in dealing with the "problem" of their identity. Through the residency, students were able to demonstrate that they are resilient and proud, and have highly developed critical thinking skills that simply need relevant application to become apparent.

The experience of conducting this inquiry into community-based theatre and education offered me an opportunity to develop and mature my philosophy of social justice education. I realize now that a pedagogy that seeks to critique social injustices in a relevant and meaningful way must include an element of action. Through theatre, I was able to learn about the lives of twenty-five remarkable students and witness their ability to develop this sense of praxis as they infused their reflections with action. I was also able to see that a pedagogy that lacks an emphasis on subverting inequities lacks meaning. Students desire opportunities to make their education meaningful. They need schools to become centers for critical thought and social action.

Like the students with whom I participated in the residency, I am very proud of the critical action we took to imagine and begin to create a better world. Reflecting upon her role in the residency, one student declared, "It has been amazing. This has been a very powerful, emotional journey." Certainly for me, the experience of bringing this residency to Wilson High School exceeded my expectations. I am amazed, too, at the ability of young people to reflect upon their lives and to inspire others. The experience has transformed the way I look at students and teaching. I realize now that it is not possible to teach social justice to students. I must mediate opportunities for young people to discover within themselves the ability to shape a more just world.

Notes

1. Throughout this essay, I use the terms LGBT and lesbian, gay, bisexual, and/or transgender to refer to individuals who identify as members of, and with issues pertaining to, the lesbian, gay, bisexual, and/or transgender communities.

2. Students' names have been changed to respect confidentiality.

3. For more information on the act, please access the following website: http://cta-glbtc.org/docs/California%20Student%20Safety%20and%20Violence%20Prevention%20Act%20of%202000.pdf.

4. This assertion and those that follow are based on responses to the participant post-project surveys administered between December 9 and December 16, 2005 (unpublished).

5. Quotations from audience members have been extracted from responses to post-show surveys administered to Wilson High School students and faculty between December 9 and December 16, 2005 (unpublished).

Bibliography

Bourdieu, Pierre. "Cultural Reproduction and Social Reproduction." In *Knowledge, Education, and Cultural Change*, edited by Richard Brown. London: Tavistock, 1973. 71–112.

Darder, Antonia. "Teaching as an Act of Love." Reclaiming Our Voices: Emancipatory Narratives on Critical Literacy, Praxis, and Pedagogy: An Occasional Paper Series for Entering the 21st Century, edited by Jean Frederickson. One of a series of complete stand-alone papers. Covina: California Association for Bilingual Education, 1998.

Diaz, Esteban, and Barbara Flores. *The Best for Our Children: Critical Perspectives*. New York: Columbia University Press, 2001.

Freire, Paulo. *Pedagogy of Freedom: Ethics, Democracy, and Civic Courage*. Lanham, MD: Rowman and Littlefield, 1998.

———. *Pedagogy of the Oppressed*. New York: Continuum, 1970.

Gilstrap, Samuel. "Understanding the Social Environment Survey: Report on Hollywood Senior High Pilot." One of a series of complete stand-alone papers. Los Angeles: Los Angeles Unified School District Program Evaluation and Research Branch, 2001 (unpublished).

Giroux, Henry. *Teachers as Intellectuals: Toward a Critical Pedagogy of Learning*. Granby, MA: Bergin and Garvey, 1988.

National Mental Health Association. "'What Does Gay Mean?' Teen Survey Executive Summary." Media: International Communications Research, 2002. www.nmha.org/whatdoesgaymean.

Oakes, Jeannie, and Martin Lipton. *Teaching to Change the World*. New York: McGraw Hill, 2003.

Savin-Williams, Ritch. *The New Gay Teenager*. Cambridge, MA: Harvard University Press, 2005.

4

Creating a Safe Space and a Great Show

There is a raging debate about "Safe Space" in the field of Theatre and Social Change. Fringe Benefits' position is somewhere in the middle: while our primary focus is on creating effective activist performances, we have taken care to develop a process and a working environment in which everyone feels included, respected, and clear about the "rules of engagement." Over the years, we have experienced a wide range of responses to our workshop guidelines,[1] packed agendas, and facilitation style. Some have found our approach insufficiently safe and too demanding; others have found it to be overly cautious; and still others have found the process fun and invigorating. This chapter comprises essays detailing and critiquing some of the procedures and guidelines Fringe Benefits has developed in an attempt to balance the need to create Safe Space with the need to create great activist theatre. The final essay in the chapter details some of the accommodations and considerations that must be addressed to enable people with and without disabilities to collaborate successfully.

"It's Safe to Say," coauthored by internationally recognized playwright and community-based theatre practitioner Bernardo Solano and solo performer and teaching artist Paula Weston Solano, provides a look at various ways Safe Space can be achieved and what happens once participants trust it to the point of sharing personal stories for the first time. Central to the essay is a comparison of the different Safe Space guidelines developed by Fringe Benefits, Michael Rohd, and John O'Neal, especially as implemented by the authors in three different community-based collaborations. The Solanos describe how "the personal becomes political" when participants work together to transform the intimate and often painful details of their lives into theatre that compels social action.

Xanthia Angel Walker, a community-based theatre scholar and practitioner and winner of the American Alliance for Theatre and

Education's 2009 Winifred Ward Scholarship, contributes the second essay in this chapter. In her thought-provoking "Pronouns, Play Building, and the Principal: Negotiating Multiple Sites of Activism in a Youth-Focused Theatre for Social Justice Project," Walker tracks defining moments of empowerment and disenfranchisement during a project she led as a college senior. She examines the ways in which Fringe Benefits' primary preoccupation with concerns about "product" clashed with the process-centered approach to which many of the youth participants were accustomed, paying close attention to the impact of the resulting ruptures on the youth and on the show.

The next essay offers a contrasting perspective. In "Creativity or Carnage: An International Theatre for Social Justice Project," Selina Busby and Catherine McNamara, both faculty members at the Royal Central School of Speech and Drama (University of London), tell a cautionary tale about the danger of fostering overly protective stewardship of Safe Space. In their essay, they interrogate the interplay between such factors as the education and training of MA Applied Theatre students, the participation of individuals with widely diverse backgrounds and expectations, and the use of Fringe Benefits' play-devising methodologies. They also call attention to the danger of setting up a false binary by expecting theatre practitioners to bear primary responsibility for shaping the dramatic material and by expecting community members largely—or worse, exclusively—to play the role of simply providing the stories or raw material for the script.

We close the chapter with Kathleen Juhl and Lindsey Smith's "Adapt the Space! Working with People of Diverse Abilities," in which the writers share a number of thought-provoking reflections and ideas regarding respectful collaboration among artists with various abilities. Feminist theatre scholar, coeditor of *Radical Acts: Theatre and Feminist Pedagogies of Change*, and Southwestern University Theatre professor Juhl brings to this important issue more than twenty years' experience working with diversely abled students and with the Texas theatre company Actual Lives Austin. The Institute for which she served as project coordinator engaged a dynamic blend of writers and performers, a number of whom were people with physical, intellectual, and/or emotional disabilities. One of those writer-performers, cowriter Lindsey Smith, was inspired by the Institute to start a student-run Theatre for Social Justice organization. As a result of that group's first show, which addressed disability issues at Southwestern University, numerous structural changes were made throughout the campus to increase accessibility. Juhl and Smith expand the Safe Space discussion with their revealing and candid account of some of the lessons they learned about communication, accommodation, and inclusion while working on these plays.

Note

1. Fringe Benefits' workshop guidelines are included in "It's Safe to Say" by Bernardo Solano and Paula Weston Solano, found in this chapter. Additional guidelines can be found in appendix C.

It's Safe to Say

BERNARDO SOLANO AND PAULA WESTON SOLANO

Exactly what is a "Safe Space" when it comes to working on a collaborative theatre piece? In our experience, it is essential to establish guidelines for Safe Space early in the process, but if you front-load too many safety guidelines, it can actually instill fear or trepidation among the participants, leading them to wonder, "What exactly are we going to *do* in here?" The process of sharing, taking risks, and exiting one's comfort zone is a gradual and cumulative exercise; too much preparation or information can send neophytes into a state of anxiety and/or freeze them up. The key is to find the right balance for the particular group and project. A combination of guidelines in conjunction with trust-building exercises/activities and the organic process of trust building as a result of sharing stories, improvising, and writing seems to be the best recipe for developing an exhilarating, secure, and creative environment.

This essay draws upon our work with Fringe Benefits, Cornerstone Theater Company, California State Polytechnic University, Pomona's Peer Theatre Program, California State University's Summer Arts Program, and other programs in which we've employed the concept of Safe Space.

Safe Space Guidelines

Because of the very nature of these programs, it is often assumed that most, if not all, of the participants have had little to no exposure to theatre or experience with creating theatre. So we begin at the beginning, at the most elemental level, by acknowledging that all humans are vulnerable creatures, with feelings and thoughts that are som difficult to share because of our fear of being misunderstood, j ridiculed, and/or stigmatized because of our opinions/lifestyles, belief systems, and a dozen other reasons that are ripe for misunderstanding and ridicule. Depending on the age of the participants and the particular circumstances of the project, we need to find the best possible way to communicate all of that—not necessarily all in one breath or by using those words.

Here are some Fringe Benefits workshop guidelines from which we borrow when leading collaborations:

1. *Raise hand to speak. No side conversations.* This is so that everyone has a fair and equal chance to share his or her thoughts; so that we all can hear each other; so that whoever is speaking doesn't have to worry that others might be talking about him or her (some people may be in a vulnerable state when sharing feelings and don't need the additional angst); and so that the tape recorder can catch the important things!

2. *No putting each other down.* However, in stories and in improvisations, "colorful language" (expletives and put-downs) may be used.

3. *No real names* in stories or improvisations!

4. *Improvisations*:
   a. Put-downs need to be based on the imaginary characters, not the actors!
   b. Physical boundaries: No hitting; no "stage combat."
   c. No touching another person except from the shoulder to the fingertips. (Demonstrate how hard one person may touch another.)

5. *Confidentiality.* No repeating outside of this space what other people said or did. But what you say *may* be used in the play!

6. *No judging* what others say, either verbally or in the form of laughing, groaning, rolling your eyes, and the like.

7. *Speak up!* Say "Ouch!" if you're uncomfortable with something that's happening or being said. Say "Oops!" to acknowledge or apologize for something you wish you had not said or done. This is a brief opportunity to check in. If you need more time to process the issue, please speak with the designated counselor in the hallway and/or speak with any of the facilitators before or after the workshop.

8. *You have a right to "pass"* on any/all invitations to share your ideas,

opinions, and stories and/or invitations to participate in theatre exercises. You may also call "UNCLE!" mid-sentence (and not continue speaking) or mid-exercise (and step out of the exercise). Take care of yourself.

9. Give each other the *benefit of the doubt*.

10. Please be *brief and to the point*.

11. *Mandatory Reporting Law*. In the United States, teachers are required to report any information they see or hear regarding youth involvement in physical or sexual abuse, as well as suicide attempts (past, present, and/or future).[1]

12. *Step up/step back*. If you haven't been participating a lot, "step up." If others need "air time," "step back."[2]

Another set of guidelines is the "ground rules for a safe space" that Michael Rohd sets out in his indispensable book, *Theatre for Community, Conflict, and Dialogue: The Hope Is Vital Training Manual*. Rohd's approach has time and again proven itself in his work with Sojourn Theater and in communities across the country. His guidelines that duplicate those of Fringe Benefits, with minor differences in language, are confidentiality, non-judgment, and the right to pass. On to others:

1. *Respect*: We show respect in the way we talk, listen, and take care of each other.

2. *Openness*: "Share what you can." We get out of this as much as we're willing and able to put in, "not in terms of secrets and private stories, but of who you are and the degree to which you bring what is special in you to the group process."

3. *Honesty*: "When you choose to share, do so truthfully. Don't create stories to make an impression."

4. *Anonymity*: At times there will be chances for everyone "to write down a question or an issue that they would like the group to address." You don't have to put your name on it; all of the papers go to the center of the room, so no one need know where specific questions or issues came from. (This is especially helpful when dealing with delicate subject matter.)[3]

We should also consider John O'Neal's guidelines for Story Circles. O'Neal is a seminal figure in community-based theatre, from his groundbreaking civil rights–era days with the Free Southern Theater to the present-day vitality of Junebug Productions. Two points from Junebug Productions' Story Circle guidelines, not explicitly covered in Fringe Benefits' nor in Michael Rohd's guidelines, are relevant to this discussion:

1. Don't make too many *rules*. Less is more.
2. *Listening* is more important than talking. You mustn't be thinking about what you will say while someone else is talking. Trust the circle to bring your story to you. You don't have to like other people's stories, but you must respect their right to tell them.[4]

Case Studies: Safe Spaces in Action

How can we draw from each of these sets of guidelines to create the most effective and efficient set possible? In order to determine this, perhaps it would be helpful to examine how these diverse guidelines functioned in the following case studies.

Case Study 1. *Theatre on the Edge: Unheard Voices*

A collaboration between California State University's Summer Arts Program, Fringe Benefits, and Fresno CORAL (Communities Organizing Resources to Advance Learning), summer 2004.

CSU Summer Arts is a yearly summer program that offers university students two-week intensive workshops in all the arts; professional artists are invited to lead and teach the workshops, culminating in public presentations. In 2004, Fringe Benefits (FB) co-facilitators Norma Bowles and Paula Weston Solano were the invited artists. CSU faculty Bernardo Solano and Shannon Edwards coordinated the course. The community partner was CORAL, a Fresno nonprofit organization created to support and promote student success by developing and providing quality out-of-school programs for children and youth. Eighteen university students were invited to participate in the course, in which they would learn the methodologies of Los Angeles–based theatre companies FB and Unusual Suspects. The first half of the course focused on a collaboration between FB, the university students taking the class, and a group of middle and high school students enrolled in the CORAL program. The participants as a whole represented a wide range of ethnic and socioeconomic backgrounds.

After an orientation with the university students, FB co-facilitators Norma and Paula facilitated afternoon sessions with the combined

CSU/CORAL group and morning sessions with the CSU students to debrief the previous afternoon's work and plan the next CORAL session. The basic idea was that the CSU students would be "learning by doing" and, in theory, would be able to leave Summer Arts with enough knowledge and experience to run such a program on their own—a tall order given the short amount of time, but that's the nature of these things: dream big and achieve the most possible.

One of the first challenges we faced was the fact that there were eighteen CSU students and, at best, ten or twelve CORAL students. Add the FB and other guest artists to the eighteen, plus the faculty coordinators of the course, and the result was a large group of people "testing" their theories on a small group of unsuspecting guinea pigs—or so we worried it would appear. These lopsided numbers seemed to be something over which we had little control; clearly we'd have to make the best of the situation. One solution came rather naturally: because the ages of the CSU students and the CORAL students were at least in the same ballpark, the CSU students might be considered by the CORAL students as peers and would therefore achieve a more immediate level of trust. This proved to be mostly true. We also decided that the CSU students and the faculty should all spread themselves throughout the circle, thus intermingling participants of all ages. We also encouraged everyone—FB facilitators, CSU faculty and students, as well as CORAL students—to share their stories about discrimination.

Another challenge came with the fact that the course was going to be documented via video recording. This decision may or may not have been ill-advised, as no one was really sure if the camera (operated by a CSU student documentarian) would be construed as an invader and thus inhibit participants and lead to self-censorship. The fact that there would be a video camera was introduced gently and with an understanding that it would be turned off if any individual so requested. Also, it was made clear that permission had to be granted before anything could be put into a documentary and that it would be possible to edit out anything objectionable. In the end, no one ever complained about the camera; if anything, it seemed to have a positive effect on the participants, almost as if the camera added to the validity and importance of what was happening in the room. But did a participant ever self-censor because of the camera's presence, or not share a story out of fear that the "no real names" or confidentiality guidelines could be violated? Perhaps. We'll never know for sure.

Another unusual circumstance was that the focus of the piece would be conceived with the CORAL kids during the first session. Usually, FB Institute project leaders determine the focus of the piece months in advance in concert with their partnering school, community, and/or theatre organization. Would we be able collectively to conceive and execute the entire project in just one week without the customary advance work? Then again, as Cornerstone Theater and other community-based theatre companies often find when they engage a given community, the element of surprise, of discovering the need of the community, is a truly exciting element of the process. And so, in this case, all participants would have a voice in determining the "what" as well as the "how" it would be achieved.

It probably goes without saying that if Safe Space had not been present during this discovery phase, it's likely the participants' statements might have been forced and/or downright untruthful because they might have been expressed out of a need to impress, or conversely to say only "safe" things that would neither offend nor dig deeper than the first layer of skin. Thanks in large part to the improvisations and the confidentiality guidelines (camera notwithstanding), the "cry" of the project was discovered almost immediately: the discrimination high school students are subjected to based on their weight.

A turning point in the process came when one of our high school students improvised a scene wherein she asked one student to play her father while she acted as herself. During that improvisation, she brought out the frustration and anger she felt about her father criticizing her and telling her she needed to lose weight. That scene spoke to the general feeling of the students: they often felt misunderstood, labeled, criticized, and generally not heard. If not for the feeling of safety in the group, that raw and honest sharing would not have been possible.

An additional technique that provides "safety" is the FB practice of assigning roles/lines in performance to students who had not shared those specific words or stories during the script development process. This both preserves confidentiality and creates a "pact" in which members of the ensemble trust each other to invest importance and integrity in the portrayals of their experiences.

The final play, titled *Weight?! Wait, Don't Tell Me!* was honest and penetrating due to the atmosphere of trust and non-judgment that was nurtured throughout the process.

Case Study 2. Peer Theatre

A yearly collaboration between California State Polytechnic University, Pomona (CPP) and Pomona Unified School District (PUSD).

This program brings university students together with PUSD high school students to create an issue-based play that is written, designed, and performed by the PUSD students. The CPP students mentor, dramaturg, direct, and coach the PUSD students throughout the year-long process, guided by Bernardo Solano, who has run the program since 2002 and who will therefore narrate the following.

The program relies heavily on maintaining Safe Space throughout the play development process but particularly in the beginning as the ideas, concepts, and initial script are being developed. As the program brings together students from five different high schools, at the beginning most of the youth know only the few students who also attend their own school. There is a natural unease about working with strangers: Am I going to like them? Are they going to like me? Can I trust them? The process must move quickly because the combined CPP/PUSD group meets only once a week in two-hour sessions, and a first draft needs to be ready by the eighth or ninth session. Hence, building trust is the number-one priority. The first session is all about games to break the ice and to begin building trust among the participants. By the second session, a definition of Safe Space, mostly utilizing Michael Rohd's guidelines, is presented to the students in the form of a contract they and their parents must sign.

Every year brings new individuals with their heartaches, their victories, their dreams and hopes just barely hidden under the surface of protective armor. The Safe Space we work hard to construct offers enough protection to encourage everyone to let others have a glimpse of who they really are. By the third meeting, we have a brainstorming session during which the students shout out all the topics, issues, and problems that are currently in their lives. This is relatively easy for them because it's still not personal and they don't have to own the issues they name. Now that there are topics "on the table," we begin to narrow down the focus. Students are asked to provide examples of what they mean when they cite "people who disrespect other people," for instance, as a potential topic for a play. By design, the topic is still at a safe distance. By the fourth session, we have a giant Story Circle, and this is where Safe Space is really tested. Now there's a tape recorder in the middle of the circle. But we have all agreed on the basic principles of respect, listening, being able to pass, and so on, as described in John O'Neal's Story Circle guidelines, in addition to the guidelines they've already committed to in their contract. I have also learned to add, "If you don't have a personal story to tell, maybe you know of someone who has experienced the topic of discussion, maybe a friend or a relative." This provides one more safety valve of "it didn't necessarily happen to me" that helps some individuals get over the hump of sharing the scary stuff.

Every year, the CPP students who take this journey are amazed and touched by how, in only six hours (the total time of the previous sessions), these high school students make the decision to share some of the most intimate moments of their lives. Once one person takes the plunge, others follow suit. If anything, the person who shared is suddenly familiar, a stranger no longer. The whole room is right there, silently taking it in, bearing witness to the pain, the suffering, and the courage of that individual. One year, once it was decided that the play was going to be about abuse, three girls admitted to having been sexually abused. The dam had burst and the healing had begun.

Case Study 3. Cornerstone Theater Company / El Nido Family Center

A twenty-one-week project in Compton, California, teaming Cornerstone professional theatre artists Paula Weston Solano and Sigrid Gilmer with Compton youth, fall 2008–spring 2009.

This program was populated overwhelmingly by male youth in Compton, ages fourteen to twenty, who were on probation and for whom this program fulfilled an anger management mandate. The armor for survival in their community/surroundings was a face void of emotion and a general distrust of anyone and everyone. The goal was to create a play that would speak to the issue of "justice." (Cornerstone was in the midst of "The Justice Cycle," which examined the issue in collaboration with several communities over the course of four years.) The question posed—What do we need to create a safe space?—was met with stoic faces and crossed arms, hiding a probable lack of understanding in general of what the hell was being introduced. The only suggestion offered by the group was that no one should touch anyone or get in another person's space. We then offered the group Safe Space suggestions such as confidentiality, respect, the right to pass, no putting each other down, saying yes to opportunities, and taking risks—all of which were met with suspicion and cursory agreement. What turned out to be the most effective device for building trust (clearly, "trust falls" were out of the question!) was the sharing of writing. It was easier for the youth to write from the point of view of someone they picked from a pile of photos than to speak from their own experiences. As they shared their funny and tragic monologues in sometimes surprising enactments, the walls began to melt. Just showing up for these youth every week—on time, no matter what—was also a powerful binder. Eventually, they were casting, directing, and acting out improvisations of "The Dinner Table" and ultimately what justice or the lack thereof looked like in their lives. By the end, the large twenty-year-old who was trying to complete his anger management mandate for the third time and who had divulged to us that he didn't speak as a way to control his anger was hugging and joking with his peers as well as with the visiting artists. As one participant shared with an invited audience at the group's first reading of the play, "I learned it's okay to get to know somebody else."

Where Does This Leave Us?

So, where does this leave us? Is Safe Space an essential component of a successful collaborative theatre project? Does Safe Space look the same from project to project? As evinced in the above-described case studies, circumstances (population, parameters of the project, time limitations, external pressures) will influence the approach. And perhaps this is for the best. If we are too inflexible and rigid with the "rules," we open the door to an inflexible and rigid atmosphere and run the risk of making art that doesn't affect participants and audiences alike.

Do the previous three case studies demonstrate appropriate and effective implementations of Safe Space guidelines? In each case, project leaders came in with specific guidelines but were also flexible enough to adapt them to the particular circumstances. Had all the guidelines to the El Nido group been forced on them without discussion and consensus, the project might not have moved forward at all. Had anonymity been strictly enforced with the CORAL youth in the Theatre on the Edge project, the usefulness of a documentary filmmaker's presence would not have been discovered. And the Peer Theatre program could not even exist if it weren't for the daily evaluation of "Did we go too far?" and "Was it safe enough?" As to whether or not these projects represent the best possible implementations of Safe Space, it may be most accurate to say that every project "could have been safer" for its participants, and every project could have yielded more stories, more insights, and more healing.

What we can say for sure is that project leaders need to remain open as they determine which "rules" will help the group create a working environment that will encourage participants to dig deep, take the risks, and share the stories that will both empower them and affect the intended audiences the most. But when this process is rushed or if critical steps are missed or implemented without appropriate sensitivity, Safe Space is put in peril, as is the integrity of the entire project. It is not a perfect science, but with balance, specificity, and humility, Safe Space can be achieved and can build the foundation for real creativity.

Notes

1. See the federal policy at http://www.rainn.org/public-policy/sexual-assault-issues/mandatory-reporting-child-abuse.

2. Slightly paraphrased from Fringe Benefits' "Theatre for Social Justice Institute Curriculum" (unpublished).

3. Except where we have included direct quotes, we have slightly paraphrased these items excerpted from Rohd's "Ground Rules" (130–31). The parenthetical sentence in the fourth entry is our editorial comment.

4. See John O'Neal, "Story Circle Process Discussion Paper," http://www.racematters.org/storycircleprocess.htm. Accessed December 10, 2012.

Bibliography

Rohd, Michael. *Theatre for Community, Conflict, and Dialogue: The Hope Is Vital Training Manual.* Portsmouth, NH: Heinemann Drama, 1998.

Pronouns, Play Building, and the Principal: Negotiating Multiple Sites of Activism in a Youth-Focused Theatre for Social Justice Project

XANTHIA ANGEL WALKER

It is Day Four of the Minnesota Theatre for Social Justice Institute. The principal of Sunnyside High School, who is attending the workshop for the first time and can stay for only a few hours, just referred to one of his transgender students by the wrong pronoun—again. The workshop session is focused on feverishly editing the play we've written. The group is stuck on the locker room scene, in which a transgender student is being bullied. The principal is objecting to the scene, arguing that this would not happen at his high school and that it is not appropriate for performance in a school. "It's really what happens—it's based on reality," counters one of the youth participants. The principal's transgender student is out in the hallway with a trained counselor processing his feeling of not being safe in this space. I wish he was in the room so he could say to his principal that this has happened to him at their school. We are between a rock and a hard place.

The Institute project planning began in April 2006 and culminated in a high school tour in April 2007. Fringe Benefits collaborated with the University of Minnesota Department of Theatre Arts and Dance, a local suburban high school (referred to here as "Sunnyside High School"),[1] and a local drop-in center for lesbian, gay, bisexual, transgender, and queer/questioning (LGBTQ) youth.

Fringe Benefits explicitly identifies its Theatre for Social Justice (TSJ) Institute projects as activist (Norma Bowles, personal communication). I posit that our project in Minnesota was definitely an example of activist theatre. I believe that activism and community cultural development work go hand-in-hand. Arlene Goldbard's fifth unifying principle of community cultural development work states that "cultural expression is a means of emancipation, not the primary end in itself: the process is as important as the product" (43). In this essay, I will explore the multiple sites of activism that emerged in the creation, rehearsal, and performance of this piece, framed by the project's partnership with Sunnyside High School. I will identify the specific spaces where activism lived in this project, as well as the moments where we missed opportunities for activism in process, product, and performance. Moments of "emancipation"—of embodied, transformative activist theatre—occurred in all phases of this project.

The project began with a six-month series of workshops at the drop-in center with its already-established theatre group. The core group of youth participants, all in high school or recently graduated, passionately articulated their frustration with the lack of Safe Space for LGBTQ youth in their high schools. This became the crux of our project: creating a piece of theatre to address bullying and the lack of Safe Space in suburban high schools. Unfortunately, very few high schools in the area were willing to take on a dialogue about LGBTQ themes, and hosting the play project was considered by the schools to be too big of a risk in the face of potential backlash.

At this phase of the project, the youth participants stated both verbally and nonverbally, through their commitment to showing up and participating, that they felt agency over the project. They were actively engaged in the process of creating and participating in workshops; they decided how they participated in the space, stepping in and out as they pleased; and they drove the decision-making process for determining the theme of our play project. One of the youth, known to us as "Mark,"[2] attended Sunnyside High School. At Sunnyside, he was not out as transgender. He identified as Mark in most of the social parts of his life but at school was still known by his birth name, Mary. Mark was adamant about getting our play into his school, and he convinced his school counselor to have a meeting with us about building a partnership. Mark's push to get Sunnyside to partner with our project was a site of activism. Before the theatre-making even began, Mark was already engaged in an emancipatory experience in his efforts to get the administration to meet with us and ultimately to become a partner on the project. Mark, the other project coordinators, and I had a series of fantastic meetings with the school counselor and a series of challenging but productive meetings with the school principal. The principal agreed that Sunnyside could participate in the development of the play and would host a performance of the play.

Fast-forward to the Institute: five days of long, fast-paced workshops and deep dialogues focused on getting people from all parts of this project and the community into one room to participate in the creation of our play. Facilitated by Norma Bowles and Sara Guerrero of Fringe Benefits, the Institute engaged college students, community organizers, professors, lawyers, community members, and drop-in center youth, staff, and counselors, as well as teachers, students, and counselors from our partner school. All were highly invested in the Institute, but it was an extremely high-stakes experience for the center youth. These young people were talking about issues with which they had direct and, for some, freshly painful experience. Moreover, they were used to a process of creating theatre wherein their voices were the only authorities in the creation of their art, with no "outsiders" involved. Mark's stakes were even higher because our play was going to be performed for his own high school community.

Bowles and Guerrero began each day of the workshop with a check-in, during which each participant was invited to say his or her name and the pronoun by which they preferred to be addressed. Although Mark was not out as transgender to many of his classmates at school or to his principal, in the check-ins during the first three workshops, he specified that he preferred male pronouns. Despite the fact that he had stated this preference several times, fellow students from his school repeatedly referred to Mark as "Mary," and he grew increasingly frustrated.

On Day Four of the workshop, Mark's school principal was scheduled to attend. It was incredibly important to have the principal there, as he had to approve of the play's content in order for us to be allowed to perform at Sunnyside. About forty-five minutes before the start of that day's workshop, Bowles, Guerrero, Mark, the counselors from the drop-in center and the school, and I discussed the arrival of the principal, as well as Mark's desire to specify a male pronoun for himself in the workshop. With full awareness that the principal would be in the room, Mark decided to continue to specify in the check-in that he preferred male pronouns and wanted to be called Mark.

As planned, then, during the check-in on Day Four, Mark identified as male. As the day progressed, I noticed that he was spending more and more time out in the hall with the counselor, talking about how he did not feel safe in the workshop. And as Mark began to grapple with the reality of having his own school participate in this high-stakes conversation, his drop-in center crew rallied around him to support him. As a result, the center youth spent a larger portion of time engaged in the process of supporting Mark and less time participating directly in the *playwriting*.

Reflecting back on that day, I see missed opportunities for activism. There were two parallel tensions at work: tension surrounding Mark's feeling of not being safe, and tension surrounding the facilitators focusing disproportionately on feedback from the school principal, a "gatekeeper" with the power to determine whether or not the show could be presented at his school. Thus, the principal, who already held a position as an agent of the space, accrued exponentially more power. He became the primary editor, the censor. The center youth became angry with the principal's editing and also with the facilitators for catering to his edits and opinions. They felt unheard in relationship to the principal. Our focus for those five days was to write a play that we could bring to Sunnyside, but the center youth became unable to participate actively in writing the play when they felt the balance of power in the room tip toward the person who, from their perspective, was the oppressor.

An important opportunity for activism was lost at this stage in the process in the interest of serving the product. I wonder, however, if stopping the workshop would have served our activist goal. Was it the "right" decision to push forward with the play creation and not take the time to have a whole-community dialogue about Mark feeling unsafe in the workshop and about the principal being a primary agent in the space? I am unsettled by the fact that the youth participants, who were meant to be central agents in the creation of this play, were largely absent from this phase of the process.

At the end of the five-day Institute, we had a script called *The Punch . . . Or How I Became an Ally*. In the world of the play, students face the challenge of dealing with LGBTQ issues in an environment where there are no safe spaces for LGBTQ youth and allies. As the play unfolds, they confront discrimination in classrooms, hallways, and locker rooms, and it all escalates to the point of violence. At the turning point, the protagonist, a popular kid who has never thought much about LGBTQ issues before, learns what it means to be a straight ally when he steps into a fight that started as a result of hate speech. The script, based on true stories and experiences of bullying and hate speech in high schools, was approved by Sunnyside's principal.

When the cast and crew met together for our first rehearsal, over a month had passed since the Institute. There had been some attrition in the core group of youth participants from the drop-in center: some of the youth had left due to life circumstances, and some had left because they felt the play was not enough of a direct reflection of their own realities and experiences as a result of the lack of agency they had felt in the playwriting workshops. The already-existing drop-in center youth theatre troupe's methodology for creating work was focused on youth writing, editing, and performing theatrical pieces based on their own real-life stories for audiences of LGBTQ and allied youth and adults. Feeling that Fringe Benefits' devising methodology had been too big of a departure from the approach they were accustomed to, and troubled by the events involving the principal, some youth opted out of the project after the Institute. Mark stayed on as a participant in the project and became a driving force in gluing the ensemble back together. As we began to rehearse and made a few small adjustments to the script, many of the youth came to feel that it did in fact reflect their experiences and the message they wanted to send.

Our cast comprised the drop-in center youth, University of Minnesota students, and youth from local high schools. The attrition of some of the center youth after the Institute phase of the project created space for actors in the play who were not affiliated with the drop-in center. This became a surprise gift to the process. The rehearsal space became an active site of dialogue about the very issues the play was grappling with and therefore an unexpected site of activism. The inclusion of college student actors alongside drop-in center youth actors provided opportunities for meaningful mentorship within the cast. The rehearsal room became a space wherein we not only rehearsed the play but also invented and rehearsed strategies for dialoging with administrations about creating gay-straight alliances, for speaking out against hate speech when we witness it, and for using our play as a jumping-off point for both dialogue and the initiation of policy changes in schools.

A few weeks prior to our scheduled performance at Sunnyside, the principal decided to change the performance from an all-school event to an after-school event. He said he didn't feel equipped to deal with the aftereffects of such a "risky" performance at the all-school level. This was deeply disappointing. We knew that the after-school audience would be students and faculty who already supported the activist aims of our play. So our performance at Mark's high school, our most anticipated performance, was for a half-full auditorium of students and teachers. The principal did not attend. We could only preach to the choir. At the same time, however, the act of coming full-circle, of performing at Sunnyside, despite all of the challenges that were a part of getting there, was a deeply important experience. Even though it was an after-school event, we had shared a play that opened a door for dialogue about Safe Space. We left the school that day feeling conflicted yet proud of our work.

How artist-activists build stronger partnerships that both complement and work within necessary social systems (such as public schools) while simultaneously challenging the oppression that those systems inherently work to sustain is a large question that I am left with years after the culmination of this project. The missing link may have been to center the project at the school itself instead of positioning it as a touring piece that entered the school community from the outside. I wonder what could have happened. As it was, however, it's noteworthy that Sunnyside High School students, counselors, and the principal participated in the creation process, and the project had a significant impact both within and outside that school community.

It is vital to recognize the sites of activism that occur *within* youth-focused activist theatre projects as well as those that occur as a result of sharing work with a larger community. An equally important goal in youth activist theatre work is for the youth participants both to be activated and to activate—to have personal emancipatory experiences throughout the process *and* to reach and touch a target audience with the product. This balancing act is ever-evolving and unique to each project.

In respect to this balancing act, it is possible to see this collaboration as a failure. The high school with which we had invested the most time and energy, with which we had collaborated to create the play, backed out on its commitment. Our project did not change a single policy at any of the schools we toured. Still, I know this project did not fail. There is a truth about this work: it is often messy and fraught with complication, and sometimes projects do not end as they begin, because the work is about real people and their real lives. In tracking our journey, I see messy and challenging sites of activism throughout all phases of development and production. In tracking the youths' journeys, I see that they, Mark especially, clearly were both activated and activators. We had worked together in a meaningful, challenging, and transformative process, and the product of this process was a transformative, well-crafted, quality piece of theatre.

As I continue to develop activist plays with youth, I hold this collaboration with the University of Minnesota Department of Theatre and Dance, the local LGBT drop-in center, Sunnyside High School, and Fringe Benefits close to my heart as an invaluable experience that I still draw from.

Notes

1. The name "Sunnyside High School" is fictional.
2. The names of the participants are also fictional.

Bibliography

Boal, Augusto. *Theatre of the Oppressed.* New York: Theatre Communications Group, 1993.

Freire, Paulo. *Pedagogy of the Oppressed.* New York: Continuum, 2000.

Goldbard, Arlene. *New Creative Community: The Art of Cultural Development.* Oakland: New Village Press, 2006.

Creativity or Carnage: An International Theatre for Social Justice Project

SELINA BUSBY AND CATHERINE MCNAMARA

This essay explores a collaborative Theatre for Social Justice project that took place in London, United Kingdom, in 2008 and involved fifty participants. The key question we ask is, What are the key challenges when bringing student and community participants together to create theatre? We will start by outlining the nature of the international collaboration and then will unpack some of the tensions that emerged during the process of making a play and in relation to the play as product of the process. We will conclude by considering to what extent we were successful in creating quality art and effective theatre, playfully questioning whether this project was a creative success or a site of carnage.

The Context

From the outset, as project coordinators, we felt that we were taking more risks than usual in bringing so many different stakeholders together. Members of Fringe Benefits (FB) were visiting London as part of their first overseas project. Their part in this collaboration was to facilitate the writing of a play for performance in secondary schools. Gendered Intelligence is a UK-based organization that delivers arts projects with young transgender and queer-identified people. Its lead practitioner, approximately thirty LGBTQ young people and their allies, and other community participants joined the project. The Royal Central School of Speech and Drama is a small, specialist, higher education institution and a college of the University of London. Eight of its MA Applied Theatre students and their program leader engaged with this project, as did a number of students from five other programs and several members of the faculty and staff. Everyone identified as LGBT, as queer, or as a straight ally. The MA students had a significant dual reason for attending, though, in that they were all at Central to study applied theatre or theatre that has a social imperative. They were participating in the creative process but also rigorously analyzing it and reflecting deeply on the method of practice. The complexity of intra-cultural dialogue across, between, and among these sets of people was great in several ways.

Over a period of eleven days, a forty-minute script was created. The group was together for twenty hours, over five four-hour workshops. Between sessions, improvisations were transcribed to form drafts of dialogue (the typical FB model), and out of it, *Brief Encounters* was created. Fringe Benefits left us after the final writing workshop, and the script was put into production and rehearsal. An accompanying workshop exploring issues of gender diversity and sexual orientation was planned, and the package was initially delivered to seven secondary schools across the United Kingdom, as well as in a variety of other settings. The play and workshop have been toured twice in subsequent years, thus reaching a total of twenty-two schools and approximately 2,000 young people.[1]

Norma Bowles, artistic director and lead practitioner of FB, is clear about her desire for project partners to have activism-related goals similar to FB's, as opposed to empowerment-centered goals. FB's process is product-driven, and the structure of the process is tightly geared toward writing a play that can be performed for the specified target audience. Our goals in collaborating with FB were creative (bringing together a group of LGBTQA people to write a play), educational (having MA students learn about this model of practice), and political (using a piece of theatre to enter into discussion and debate about gender within statutory school settings). In this sense, our "fit" appeared to be a good one, though the process wasn't without its challenges.

Points of Tension

Points of tension that emerged in the course of this collaboration included concerns about the process and about the product. Both FB and our applied theatre master's program have a strong emphasis on creating and maintaining emotional safety for participants in creative processes where personal experience is elicited. However, the methodologies and approaches taken generally within Theatre for Social

Justice, or applied theatre more broadly, may still be perceived to be putting participants' emotional wellbeing at risk and potentially can create obstacles to uninhibited and creative collaboration for a variety of reasons.

A Point of Tension about the Process of Collaborative Writing

One key strategy or technique of FB's model of practice is story sharing. Storytelling is a tried, tested, and contested applied theatre practice. Richard Kearney in *On Stories* outlines the way in which we tell stories to make sense of the incongruent parts of lives. He says that telling tales makes our experiences comprehensible, and "in this way, storytelling may be said to humanize time by transforming it from an impersonal passing of fragmented moments into a pattern, a plot" (4). We are warned to be mindful of the ethical implications of asking people to disclose personal stories. James Thompson cautions that "without extreme care theater projects that dig up narratives, experiences, and remembrances can blame, enact revenge, and foster animosity as much as they can develop dialogue, respect, or comfort" (151).

In this project, we would assert that appropriate care was taken for the most part, though the idea of what that care involved was a significant part of the negotiation between Central and FB. We engaged in a lengthy process of creating a Memorandum of Understanding that specified all parties' responsibilities; we talked at length via email and telephone about the fact that the MA student participants needed to demonstrate evidence of having met learning outcomes and to submit work for assessment for their master's qualification after their involvement in the project; Bowles and McNamara met in person three days before the first session of the Institute and discussed possible cultural collisions between the working practices that the community participants were familiar with and those of Fringe Benefits.

The FB model of practice dictated that stories were gathered in the first session, so within an hour of meeting, people were divulging personal experiences or things they had seen or heard happen, both to strangers and to people they knew. The construct used here was to request that people offer a story or anecdote to the (very large) circle of thirty-seven people with a view to these stories being used in a play— the play that we were all there to write together. We did this by literally going around the circle and speaking a story aloud to the group, and into the tape recorder for later transcription. This construct worked to make people aware that they could and should self-select stories and share what they were happy to share and what they felt might be appropriate in a play about gender variance and sexual orientation for school audiences. Further, we were asked to consider whether we would be happy to see our stories developed by the group or would prefer them to be dropped. The dynamic in the room was brisk—not one that invited slow, emotionally laden storytelling.

Bowles acknowledges in an interview with Ann Elizabeth Armstrong, published in *Radical Acts: Theatre and Feminist Pedagogies of Change*, the potential risk that this exercise holds for participants: "We're not trying to lead therapy sessions, so we've got to make sure that we're not inviting people to think of us as therapists . . . the moment when someone is sharing can be very, very delicate—not the time to pass judgment, but not the time to be completely detached either" (Armstrong and Juhl 294). Bowles also asserts that the structures and strategies she builds into the process make the environment a productive and functional one. Through brisk discussions, pragmatic decision making about structure, and a fast series of improvisation exercises, the group adapts and dramatizes the stories in a variety of ways. The stories are then retold or performed in the touring performance by different people, rarely the original teller, sometimes whole, but sometimes very much changed. FB and Central agree that drawing on personal stories as a way of generating a script is neither dangerous nor safe per se but is something to be utilized in conscious and structured ways.

Approximately thirty stories were told in the first session, and of those that survived and made it into the script, some were adapted quite extensively and others were used almost verbatim. Claire's story of coming out to her mother as transgender was adapted and became the main narrative thread, for example.[2] Another story—Jane's, where Jane was the subject of a nasty practical joke because of her gender identity—was used as told in the workshop. Listening to Jane tell her story was a poignant moment in that first workshop. The response from the group was tangible. Some participants were shocked at the way she had been treated by other young people. In translating that story into performance, it was made more theatrical in that the character of Emma (an LGBTQA youth group leader) tells the story to her youth group as something that had happened to her in her own youth. Thus the story is embedded within a scene that serves to make a point about the existence of support groups for young queer-identified people. Our secondary school student audiences were keen to know if this story and the other events portrayed in the play were "real." The poignancy and realness was what engaged the young audiences, and this story created one of the key moments where learning took place in that the telling of this "real" story evoked empathy and stimulated deep-level discussion and reflection.

By writing this play, people were making themselves the subject of their own stories rather than the object of another's. Deirdre Heddon says, "Through their stories, then, the storytellers not only claim identities for themselves, but they may also attempt to rewrite what those identities mean. . . . The act of writing enacts the writer, bringing [him or] her in to existence, as matter" (221). The project participants' own understandings of the complexity of gender challenged popular conceptions, such as those found in television documentaries and in what J. Gamson calls "freak show" presentations in the talk show genre. The group, and ultimately the play, aimed to portray the consequences of living with the stigma that young transgender and queer-identified people encounter due to those misconceptions. By entering into mainstream settings and using personal stories to challenge these views, there was an insistence on demonstrating the right to be as a gendered person.

There was a range of perspectives about the extent to which we navigated the potential minefield of dangers that Thompson warns about. Some student participants did voice concerns about their perceptions of the lack of emotional safety of the story-sharing exercises, though none of the community participants raised concerns about their own emotional safety with members of the team. Erasmo Tacconelli talks about his role as clinical psychologist within the process of this particular project later in this anthology. A small number of community participants attended one or two of the writing sessions but did not stay with us. We asked those who left the project to tell us about their experience; their reasons for not returning to the project were primarily about the lack of opportunity to interact with other young queer-identified people on a personal and social level rather than because they felt emotionally unsupported. One participant said:

> I did go there to do the project but I had also been hoping it'd be
> pretty social as well, and it wasn't, because there was only one

ten-minute break in 4 hours. At sci:dentity [a previous project run by Gendered Intelligence for young trans people] at least people could chat while they were doing the work and we had breaks to get to know each other in. I know this was different because we only had 20 hours to write a whole play, but I wasn't comfortable with the way it was go-go-go all the time and I found it hard to keep up with the pace. (email to the authors, June 2008)

A Point of Tension about the "Product"

Within the project, there was also a tension between the desire to create good art and the desire to educate. The tension existed primarily for the students of applied theatre, who on the one hand had anxieties about this being a weak play that would preach an overly moralistic message and cause audiences to switch off and disengage and on the other hand felt (along with the community participants) that it was important to use theatre to develop understanding and awareness about gender diversity in school settings. The point of the tension was about how to accomplish the latter without somehow accidentally doing the former. This clash is not a peculiar one. There is a general consensus that experiencing good theatre will always be educational—that one will gain new knowledge about something, whether it is about a particular subject or about the human condition more broadly. However, when theatre is produced by a company working together as a community group, and that group is made up primarily of people under twenty-five years of age, there is a tendency for some to conclude that aesthetic values and "quality" will be reduced.

Lowell Swortzell argues that "art, of course, cannot be created by committee" (in Jackson 241). Educational theatre is sometimes not considered good art because it is presumed to be moralizing or so primarily concerned with the transmission of knowledge that the complexity of the narrative and characters are lost. Good educational theatre balances the art with the educational aspects of the work such that these two elements are mutually dependent. Overwhelmingly, the community participants seemed to have strong faith in the project and repeatedly asserted the sentiment that "this will be a brilliant play." The MA students were, however, acutely aware of the ways educative theatre can be perceived. Several of them brought the weight of anti–Theatre in Education feeling with them and lacked faith that this model of practice could produce a "good" play script. When reflecting on the quality of the play, one student, Amy, said: "I was very negative and worried about the situation. . . . When we were reading the play, I really didn't see how it could possibly turn into what it did. I didn't have faith in it at all and I thought it was a bit crap. I thought it was . . . quite cheesy and I was really worried about working with non-actors and well, most of us are non-actors. And I just didn't think it was going to be very good, to be honest" (verbal communication, June 2008).

We suggest that in this case, the students' critical position could have adversely affected their experience of participating in specific aspects of the project, in particular the writing of a play with a message. Central's MA Applied Theatre students are encouraged to develop a critically reflective attitude as part of their journey through the program. We have come to wonder, though, whether the critical position can become overly dominant and therefore potentially impede both the learning and the creative experiences. We are asking whether the applied theatre students can get so caught up in what is ethically right or wrong that on occasion they cannot see the woods for the trees. When applied theatre practitioners bring their questioning, problematizing minds to the room, can this stifle rather than stimulate creativity?

One of the assumptions underlying FB's devising methodology might also have contributed to the difference of perspectives between the applied theatre students and the community participants. Bowles says this about bringing students and community members together: "Community group participation in the institutes is crucial, because their stories provide the primary material from which the plays are made and their knowledge about the issues and their activism experience guide the decision-making process regarding the target audience and how best to reach them. The participation of theatre department students and faculty in the institutes helps ensure that improvisations—which are the source of all the dialogue in the plays—and the dramatic structure of the play are as theatrical, powerful, and lively as possible" (in Armstrong and Juhl 297). This binary between the "real people" being the ones with stories and the students being the ones with expertise in playwriting seems problematic. That binary did not seem to hold true for this group, and it was not always possible even to make a distinction between these different categories of participants. Two of the student participants' experiences as a lesbian and as a trans-woman, for example, were as integral to the play as the community participants' stories. Many of the community participants had theatre experience and improvised high-quality dialogue that was as powerful as the Central students' improvisations. In terms of the skills and experience required to participate and contribute, there wasn't a discernible difference between the community and student participants.

Prior to the project starting, Bowles requested a meeting with the MA students in order for her to begin to get to know them. She asked if they would arrive early for each session and help to set up the space, meet and greet the community participants at the beginning of the first session, and take on other organizational responsibilities. There was desire on both sides (FB and Central) for these students to have some responsibility and agency and to be more actively involved with the facilitation since they were required to meet learning outcomes relating to their Writing with Communities course. These learning outcomes specifically involved making decisions independently, addressing firsthand the development of a particular group through an engagement with drama and theatre.

We were concerned, though, that this prior briefing ahead of the first session of the Institute could establish a hierarchy of sorts and contribute to a potentially problematic dynamic by setting the students up as experts before the community participants arrived on the scene. Even when the community participants' expertise (their stories) became the focus, a culture of ownership and insider knowledge had already been produced, to a degree. We suggest that this contributed to a disjuncture of perspectives during the writing phase in that the subtle hierarchy and the positioning of the applied theatre students as insiders or project assistants was in conflict with their role as participants in the creative process and positioned them outside that community. This conflicted position may have influenced the critical analysis of the process they were part of, leading them to form some negative judgments about the process and the quality of the product that was emerging. What happened in the end was that all participants were invited to support the process (arriving early to set up the space before sessions, tidy the space after sessions, transcribe and edit between sessions, and the like), and a number of participants were happy to do so, community participants included, but the expectation that the applied theatre students would assist the facilitators did remain.

That said, the extent to which the students' opinions and feelings changed between the end of the writing workshops and the end of the tour was surprising. Amy, who had expressed negative feelings about the play, said this five weeks later: "I think that I did a complete shift really. I loved the process. I loved the rehearsal process and the touring process. . . . It's really clear and it's really down to earth and it's just saying what it's saying. There's no ambiguity there . . . which I think can really mess with people's heads, which can make them a little more silent in the workshop. . . . It's just a basic play . . . but I think that it set up exactly what we needed for the workshop. . . . [I]t was very educative, which I didn't think it was going to be" (verbal communication, July 2008). We understand that this shift in attitude and perception came from the student seeing the play lifted off the page in production and viewing the positive and engaged responses to it from young people in school settings.

We would suggest that not fully engaging in an experience until it is over diminishes the potency and full potential of the experience and therefore the learning. With an overly dominant critical position in place, students of applied theatre may miss things. Another individual started to lose her trust in the process when we structured the play in the third writing session and did not regain her trust until she started reading the feedback forms after each school performance. Then she saw that, despite her anxieties, nobody felt preached to or confused. While she was in a state of mistrust, with a critical position that led her to see disaster looming on the horizon, she lost hope. bell hooks tells us, "When we only name the problem, when we state complaint without a constructive focus on resolution, we take away hope. In this way critique can become merely an expression of profound cynicism, which then works to sustain dominator culture" (xiv).

Did We Create "Good Art"?

Finally, we come back to the question of whether the project achieved its aims and, in doing so, created good art. Alan Read asserts that "from the pedagogy of theater to the performer's obituary, via the critic and the arts mandarin, there is continual negotiation of what constitutes an 'acceptable standard'" (3). He suggests that we question the traditional foundation of the conditions of recognition of what that standard can be "and the way such conditions determine public opinion outside their own limited domain." He is talking in *Theater and Everyday Life* about innovative, experimental theatre that happens in the "shadows" of theatre buildings—"a theater resistant to official views of reality" that cannot be described with the language of that officialdom (4). Success for this project could, then, center on the ability of the final performance piece to effect the desired change in the target audience, or on its educative potential.

There were several indicators that audiences thought more deeply about the subject, learned new vocabulary around gendered identity, and reconsidered behaviors and attitudes toward LGBT people: "When we asked students if they had ever in the past helped to stop or challenge anti-LGBT behavior, 31% said YES and 44% said NO.... When we asked 'Having seen the play and participated in the workshop, do you feel that in the future you might intervene in anti-LGBT behavior?,' 47% said YES and 17% said NO. That's an increase [in the number of people who would intervene] of 16%" (Gendered Intelligence 10). Some 35 percent of school students thought that anti-LGBT behavior was a problem in their school, and more than half the students we worked with commented that more should be done in schools to raise awareness and to have debates about LGBTQ lives and experiences (9–10).

The school audience's positive feedback and learning experiences centered around the real stories, the genuine and the authentic, and this comes from the fact that the script was created "by committee," from a lacework of stories from within that committee. One could argue that the play would have been better had one skilled playwright transformed the stories from the committee or community of storytellers, but we would argue that the play would have been different, not better, and that there is a place for both models of making theatre. The young people in schools engaged with the play and its characters, which led to their shift of perspective on gender, identity, and sexual orientation (Gendered Intelligence 9–10). The dramatization of the personal stories provided new information for some audience members, but the strength of the work was found in the dramatization's ability to augment knowledge with evocative and tangible examples that were transformative because of the artistic experiences the spectators had. John Dewey suggests that "knowledge is transformed in an aesthetic experience . . . because it is merged with non-intellectual elements to form an experience worthwhile as an experience" (290). The target audience experienced moments and stories from the lives of the writing community, and the learning resulted from the unexpected direct disclosure of often concealed and unspoken experiences.

Swortzell's assertion that art cannot be created by committee does not stand up here. The fact that this piece of theatre was devised collaboratively by fifty people was its strength. The project met its and its participants' aims in that the school audiences responded with respect and empathy and engaged in dialogue. There was not an extreme change in understanding for every single one of the 2,000 school students who saw the play, but there is a clear indication that they learned something new about gender, from the meaning of words such as "trans" and "genderqueer" to the ways that some people live and express their gender in complex ways.

Kathleen Gallagher posits that "the distinctive educative force of theater—its dialectic—invites us to take up points of intersection and confrontation, so that our dramatic explorations do not simply calcify cultural and ethnic boundaries and limit . . . our students' abilities to affiliate with multiple cultural identities . . . and develop capacities for functioning in diverse situations" (11–12). Were we affiliating with multiple cultural identities here? Identities such as student and community participants were multiple and often overlapping; queer and straight people from a range of backgrounds and nationalities worked together to create Theatre for Social Justice; participants identified variously as artists, activists, theatre practitioners, and theatre novices.

The structure of the whole project enabled new creative encounters across multiple cultures because of the matrix of subjectivities present. As a result, the end product and the process were facilitated via a border pedagogy, to draw on Henry Giroux's words, that was "attentive to developing a democratic public philosophy that respects the notion of difference as part of a common struggle to extend the quality of public life" during which our students became "border crossers in order to understand otherness in its own terms" (51) and, in turn, along with the other participants, enabled the school audiences also to start to cross borders. What was evident was that all the participants eventually felt an emotional connection to the project and to each other and that this bond enabled a complex network of exchange that was supported and supportive, educational, political, creative, and thought-provoking, perhaps somewhere on the spectrum of "creative carnage" rather than at either end of a binary.

Notes

1. Please visit the Gendered Intelligence website at http://www.genderedin-telligence.co.uk.

2. All names have been changed as a way to honor the participants' requests for confidentiality and anonymity.

Bibliography

Armstrong, Ann Elizabeth, and Kathleen Juhl. *Radical Acts: Theatre and Feminist Pedagogies of Change*. San Francisco: Aunt Lute Books, 2007.

Dewey, John. *Art as Experience*. New York: Perigree Penguin, 2005.

Gallagher, Kathleen. "(Post)Critical Ethnography in Drama Research" In *Research Methodologies for Drama Education*, edited by Judith Ackroyd. Stoke On Trent, UK: Trentham, 2005. 63–80.

Gamson, J. *Freaks Talk Back: Tabloid Talk Shows and Sexual Nonconformity*. Chicago: University of Chicago Press, 1998.

Gendered Intelligence. "Brief Encounters Information Pack." http://www.gende-redintelligence.co.uk/downloads/Brief_Encounters_Information_Pack. pdf.

Giroux, Henry. *Border Crossings: Cultural Workers and the Politics of Education*. 2nd ed. New York: Routledge, 2005.

Heddon, Deirdre. *Autobiography and Performance*. Basingstoke, UK: Palgrave Macmillan, 2008.

hooks, bell. *Teaching Community: A Pedagogy of Hope*. New York: Routledge, 2003.

Jackson, Tony, ed. *Learning through Theater: New Perspectives on Theater in Education*. 2nd ed. London: Routledge, 1993.

Kearney, Richard. *On Stories*. Abingdon, UK: Routledge, 2002.

Read, Alan. *Theater and Everyday Life: An Ethics of Performance*. Abingdon, UK: Routledge, 1995.

Thompson, James. "Digging Up Stories: Archaeology of Theater in War." *The Drama Review* 48, no. 3 (2004): 150–59.

Adapt the Space! Working with People of Diverse Abilities

KATHLEEN JUHL AND LINDSEY SMITH

Through descriptions of our experiences with the shows *As Seen on TV* and *A Mystical Quest to Slay Normalcy*, this essay will detail some of the accommodations and considerations that must be addressed when devising, rehearsing, and performing a show that includes people with disabilities. We will, for the most part, focus very specifically on our experiences in the context of these two projects, and so our descriptions will not be comprehensive, especially in terms of shows that might be produced outside an educational setting. We will reveal a journey and some of the lessons learned along the way.

The journey began in the fall semester of 2006 when Fringe Benefits came to Southwestern University to lead a Theatre for Social Justice Institute for which we had identified our topic as racism and our target audience as high school students in the Round Rock and Austin, Texas, areas. Southwestern University alumnus Aaron Johnson, a drama teacher at McNeil High School in Round Rock, and Kathleen worked together to gather a group of fifty students, teachers, counselors, and administrators from both McNeil and Southwestern. Through the Institute, this team collaboratively developed *As Seen on TV*, a play featuring parodies of popular TV shows such as *Law and Order, South Park, The Colbert Report*, and others, along with racist commercials. Our goal was to portray racism in a way with which we thought our target high school audiences could identify. Specifically, we wanted to spark constructive dialogue about racist stereotypes and humor. Responses to post-show surveys indicate that the student audiences found the theme and tone of the play engaging and that it motivated them to challenge racist assumptions and behaviors.[1] As an added benefit, many of the university students involved in the Institute were inspired to form their own student-led Theatre for Social Justice (TSJ) organization so they could continue the work. The new student organization began by supporting the rehearsal process and tour of *As Seen on TV.*

Pam and the Not-So-Level Playing Field

One of the Institute participants, who was later cast in *As Seen on TV*, was Pam, a young woman who has cerebral palsy and who uses a motorized wheelchair.[2] The Institute sessions were held in McNeil's drama room, which was equipped with a small elevator for accessibility. Often, the elevator did not work or the teacher who kept its key was not present. The classroom space was designed with seating risers that did not accommodate Pam's wheelchair, though she could enter the space from the back of the room above the risers. We accommodated Pam during the Institute by widening and opening up our work-group circle and positioning chairs for other participants on the risers alongside Pam. This was workable but not ideal because participants were not able to see or hear each other as well as would have been possible in a smaller circle on a level floor. During rehearsals, which were held in the same room, issues of accessibility for Pam became a more serious problem. When the elevator wouldn't work or the key was not available, we could not fully rehearse the play because Pam could not get to the stage.

Once we began touring the show, we discovered that some schools did not have accessible stages. We very quickly learned to go to the schools ahead of show dates to check whether or not stages were accessible. At times, Pam's wheelchair could not be accommodated, and she could not perform. As each role was double-cast, with one actor from McNeil and one from Southwestern, getting another actor to replace Pam was usually possible but, of course, not ideal.

Observing how difficult it was for Pam to participate in rehearsals and performances, many of the students in the newly formed student TSJ organization who were involved in the cast and production crew of *As Seen on TV* decided that their next project should be a show about disability issues on our university campus. During the summer of 2007, we (Lindsey and Kathleen) wrote a grant to the Associated Colleges of the South organization to create the show. We received a large grant and began planning our "disability show" to be devised, rehearsed, and performed in the fall semester of 2007.

We decided to focus our show on issues ranging from access to buildings and classrooms to academic and social issues for students with visible and/or invisible disabilities.[3] The result was *A Mystical Quest to Slay Normalcy*, a show that dealt with a plethora of these issues. The cast for the show was made up almost entirely of students with visible and/or invisible disabilities. In fact, because of Lindsey and Pam's involvement with Advocates, a campus organization for students with disabilities, the TSJ group attracted many Advocates members who subsequently became members of the *Mystical Quest* cast. Gradually, through the theatre activist efforts of a coalition of students, faculty, and administrators along the dis/ability spectrum, awareness began to grow that accommodations would have to be made if the university was to continue to recruit and admit students with disabilities and hire faculty with disabilities.

In conjunction with the *Mystical Quest* production, the cast and production staff of the show met with senior Southwestern administrators in a conversation focused on disability access. This conversation was required by the grant from the Associated Colleges of the South that funded the production. According to Bob Mathis, who attended the meeting with the cast and production staff and is associate vice president for facilities and campus services, an audit focusing on accessibility was conducted on campus in the summer of 2008 as a direct and indirect result of the show and the conversation with senior administrators. Moreover, as a result of this audit, automatic doors, ramps, and curb cuts (more than are required by the Americans with Disabilities Act) were installed, and some restrooms were remodeled for accessibility.[4] While the work is not complete, improvements continue to be made.

An "Ethic of Accommodation"

In her article "The Actual Lives Performance Project," Chris Strickling provides a comprehensive discussion of some of the complex issues of accommodation that she and her collaborator Terry Galloway encounter as they work on their Actual Lives production projects. The great majority of Actual Lives actors are people with disabilities, and their shows are performed for broader community audiences. Galloway's notion of an "ethic of accommodation" is useful for our purposes here, as well. As described by Strickling, "the ethic of accommodation recognizes a fundamental disjuncture, between disabled bodies and 'mainstream' environments, and provides a model for moving through obstacles in both the physical and social environments to ensure the fullest inclusion possible" (289). For both *As Seen on TV* and *A Mystical Quest*, it was important for us to negotiate both "physical and social environments" for which accommodation was necessary if our actors with disabilities were to fully participate. But *A Mystical Quest* was an activist production that very specifically promoted Galloway's "ethic of accommodation."

Below, we will describe some of the lessons we learned about negotiating physical and social environments in rehearsals and performances for *As Seen on TV* and *A Mystical Quest to Slay Normalcy*. In addition, we will describe some of the issues we presented in *A Mystical Quest* that had to do with accommodating disability in a university setting.

Early, Open, and Ongoing Communication

It is crucial to begin the devising and subsequent rehearsal processes with an open discussion—including the whole cast and production staff—about the challenges participants with disabilities negotiate in their lives and what accommodations will be necessary to ensure full participation by everyone in rehearsals and performances. This conversation must be handled diplomatically without singling out actors and production staff with disabilities. Ideally, this conversation can be part of larger discussions around Safe Space and/or intercultural communication, in which a variety of issues might also be considered, including individual desires and needs regarding preferred gender pronouns, physical contact parameters, and scheduling around religious holidays. This initial group discussion should be followed by more detailed private conversations between the director and stage manager and the actors and/or production staff members with disabilities. It is important to create multiple, diverse opportunities for sharing this crucial information early on—full group, small group, private, written, anonymous, and so on—in order to ensure that each individual can discuss his or her situation in a manner that feels best to him or her.

We ran into several communication issues during *As Seen on TV* and *A Mystical Quest to Slay Normalcy* that could have been proactively addressed through such discussions. During the writing process for *A Mystical Quest*, we began by discussing our disabilities. We did not, however, discuss the participants' accommodation needs for the writing, rehearsing, and performance processes. Here are some of the lessons we learned as we embarked on the journey that led to *A Mystical Quest*:

1. The batteries for the cochlear implants one hearing-impaired actor used often ran out unexpectedly. If we had created an opportunity to discuss such issues at the beginning of our work, this issue might have come up and the stage manager could have added extra batteries to her kit.

2. One actor who used a wheelchair needed her attendant to help her use the restroom. This took coordination with the attendant and extra time that should have been built into rehearsals.

3. Another actor had cataplexy, a disorder that causes temporary body paralysis that cannot be relieved by intervention and must simply be allowed to run its course. When such an episode occurred during a rehearsal, cast members and production staff members tried to help. If we had known simply to wait until the episode had ended, the actors and production staff would not have acted out of futile fear and misplaced sympathy, and the actor would have been spared embarrassment.

4. One hearing-impaired cast member could read lips. The leaders within the production collective often reminded others to make sure Joanna could see their lips to read them, but Joanna was never given the opportunity to explain how often she wanted her colleagues to be reminded. Because she was singled out so frequently, Joanna felt embarrassed. We should have negotiated a way for Joanna to take agency in this situation and to ask people herself to turn toward her when they spoke.

5. Pam and John, who have cerebral palsy, could not negotiate handwritten correspondence (schedules, rehearsal notes, and the like). They needed all communication to be electronic because they could not write by hand but could navigate computer keyboards. On the other hand, Rachel, who is blind, could not access certain forms of electronic communication, such as PDF email attachments and Google Groups, with her Braille computer device. We later discovered that Facebook communication could better accommodate everyone.

6. Several members of our production team who had learning and/ or physical disabilities would have benefited from the availability of transcribing and/or note-taking assistance during the devising process. Either production team members or students trained in transcription through Southwestern's Center for Academic Success could have provided such assistance.

When communication channels are opened early and remain free and clear, there are myriad ways that diversely gifted and diversely abled individuals can work together to ensure that everyone can participate fully. As Strickling has said, "All of these accommodations produced a sense of give-and-take between cast members and a respect for each other's needs and abilities" (290), and "Accommodation is a way to guarantee an individual's ability to participate, while collaboration asks that enabled individual to bring their creative energy into a partnership with others in order to produce the best theatre possible" (292).

Spaces and Accessibility

It's imperative to check out any and all work and performance spaces thoroughly! Actors, production staff, and audience members with disabilities must be accommodated for both rehearsals and production. For example, as we discovered during our first devising sessions, elevators must be calibrated for four hundred pounds in order to accommodate motorized wheelchairs. If a key is required to access the elevator, the stage manager must have a copy of the key. These are fire safety issues as well as accessibility issues.

We set out to raise awareness about these issues in *A Mystical Quest to Slay Normalcy.*[5] The staging of the show required performers and audience members to move from space to space around campus. We did this so that we could point out problems with physical accommodation at Southwestern. We performed humorous and serious scenes in a variety of venues, from steeply raked lecture halls to the pathways that are often blocked by bicycles carelessly dropped by students in a hurry to get to class.

One particularly powerful scenario took place in a problematic theatre on campus. Ironically, the theatre we chose is an arena space that easily accommodates actors with mobility issues, while the audience seating situation is a nightmare. There are only two places where audience members who use wheelchairs can be accommodated: onstage, where they are lit by stage lighting and risk being in the way of the action of a play, or in the back of the sharply inclined seating area. The second alternative involves traveling up an elevator and through three heavy doors and a black box theatre space where classes, rehearsals, or even performances might be taking place. Our scenario pointed out these kinds of problematic audience seating issues by having an actor who had maneuvered her way to the back of the theatre complain bitterly about the fact that she couldn't see the action onstage clearly and that she couldn't sit with her friends. Another group of actors, some of whom were people with disabilities and some of whom were their able-bodied friends, came into the theatre from the onstage entrances where they were intercepted by the usher, who suggested they all go to the back of the theatre. After deliberating loudly about where to sit, they decided to sit onstage to make a point about the problem with the space by being visibly in the way of the action onstage.

The audience seating issues represented in this scenario are typical of most theatres and lecture hall classrooms. People with disabilities must sit in either the front or back of the space and often have to navigate a difficult and confusing path to get to their seating area. Usually this is exacerbated by stages that are impossible for disabled actors and production staff to access and by equally inaccessible restrooms for actors, production staff, and audience members with disabilities.

Space accessibility issues are so important that we would like to mention a few that we did not run into but that might be encountered when doing a production out in the community. Often painful choices must be faced: the rehearsal space that is accessible is too expensive, or the affordable and accessible space is not near any public transportation and/or is located in a dangerous neighborhood. Further, a space may have accessible restrooms but not gender-neutral restrooms to accommodate transgender members of a production team. Finally, perhaps the performance space is accessible and safe but is not a place where audience members feel inclined to go. It is crucial to take time to consider the pros and cons of your rehearsal and performance space options very carefully. Often it will not be possible to find a space that meets all of the important criteria, but with some forethought, negotiation, creativity, and elbow grease, spaces can be adapted to be as comfortable and accessible as possible for the production team and audience members. Make a checklist of the issues you need to consider and leave no stone unturned![6]

A Final Thought

Do not assume that people with disabilities are unhappy with their situation and want special treatment. In general, they do not. "Slay normalcy" by recognizing that members of your production team with disabilities simply need to be treated with respect because they are human beings and not because they have "special" needs. Communicate, accommodate, and imaginatively create accessibility solutions proactively, subtly, and respectfully. Be sure that actors and production staff with disabilities have agency. "Slay normalcy" by challenging your own assumptions about disability and "normalcy." Ask questions and provide ways for production team members with disabilities to participate as creative, talented theatre artists who have stories to tell.

Notes

1. This information was gleaned from audience members' responses to post-show surveys, filled out after each performance (unpublished).

2. To protect their privacy, all the names of student participants mentioned in this essay are pseudonyms.

3. Visible disabilities include physical impairments that lead to visible accommodations such as wheelchairs, hearing aids, and canes. Invisible disabilities are impairments that are not manifested visibly and include physical impairments such as chronic pain as well as learning impairments such as dyslexia, emotional impairments such as depression, and neurological impairments such as epilepsy.

4. Bob Mathis, telephone conversation with Kathleen Juhl, August 4, 2011.

5. Additionally, by including scenes highlighting the stereotypical ways that people with disabilities are thought of and treated, we were able to inspire thought-provoking post-show discussions about social accommodation issues. One of the most discussed scenes, "Superheroes," included the characters Always-Help-All-the-Time-Woman, Christian Healing Man, and Pedestal Man. These "heroes" portrayed the many ways that individuals approach people with visible disabilities and how unwelcome such attitudes often are.

6. Again, this article focuses primarily on lessons learned about accommodation in the course of devising, rehearsing, and producing two plays. For more ideas, you might wish to consult the texts included in our bibliography, the "Guidelines for Project Facilitators" in this volume (appendix C), and the DisAbility Project, at www.disabilityproject.com, which provides a helpful glossary and a compendium of web resources, plays, and study guides about disability issues.

Bibliography

Fox, Ann M., and Joan Lipkin. "Res(Crip)ting Feminist Theater through Disability Theater: Selections from the DisAbility Project." *NWSA Journal* 14, no. 3 (Fall 2002): 77–99.

Kuppers, Petra. *Disability and Contemporary Performance: Bodies on Edge.* New York: Routledge, 2003.

Lewis, Victoria Ann. *Beyond Victims and Villains: Contemporary Plays by Disabled Playwrights.* New York: Theatre Communications Group, 2006.

Sandahl, Carrie. *Bodies in Commotion: Disability and Performance (Corporealities: Discourses of Disability).* Ann Arbor: University of Michigan Press, 2005.

Strickling, Chris. "The Actual Lives Performance Project." In *Radical Acts: Theatre and Feminist Pedagogies of Change,* edited by Ann Elizabeth Armstrong and Kathleen Juhl. San Francisco: Aunt Lute, 2007. 281–302.

5

The Many Players: Perspectives on Diverse
Project Roles and Responsibilities

In this chapter, collaborators share their "nuts-and-bolts" and critical perspectives about the responsibilities they took on for various Theatre for Social Justice Institutes and productions: project coordinator, show director, counselor, participant, vocal coach, marketing director, and Forum Theatre actor, among others.

We open with an essay by two cultural workers and theatre artists from "Down Under": playwright, producer, and director Rod Ainsworth and producer Jude Pippen, named Cultural Development Worker of the Year in 2006 by the Queensland Community Arts Network for her work with Indigenous and culturally diverse communities in the Bundaberg Region. In their lively narrative, Pippen, the Institute project director, and Ainsworth, the show director, take on one of the most pernicious, recurring issues host communities face: cleaning up the mess after the "carpetbagging" visiting artists leave town! "Ripples over the Great Barrier" is a moving, hilarious, and at times harrowing account of the transition from the cozy sharing of ideas and democratic, collaborative decision making with visiting theatre activists to the disciplined rehearsing of a play with local theatre artists. Ainsworth and Pippen bring their expertise in both theatre and community development to bear in their thoughtful analysis of this complex issue.

The next two essays address the diverse roles each of the two writers played in our UK Institute. First, internationally recognized voice teacher Rebecca M. Root contributes "Voicing Your Gender, Gendering Your Voice," an examination of how the Institute provided an opportunity for transgender and genderqueer youth to give their genders voice and how, as a vocal coach, the author worked with these youth (non-actors) to "voice" their genders in their roles. Next, in "Psychological Reflections on an LGBTQI Theatre for Social Justice

Project," London clinical psychologist Erasmo Tacconelli discusses the rationale for including a counselor in projects involving the collaborative development of theatre from personal stories and considers some of the factors that contributed to obviating the need for his professional interventions during our London Institute.

The two theatre practitioners whose commentaries conclude this section take on some of the sometimes vexing, sometimes rewarding challenges theatre activists face when presenting their work. In her essay "Forum Theatre and the Power of 'Yes, and . . . ,'" University of Winnipeg theatre major Jessy Ardern gives us a spirited description of how she adapted classic improv techniques to rehearse for and perform the role of the antagonist in improvised responses to spect-actors' Forum Theatre interventions. "By Hook or by Crook! Luring the Oppressor into the Lair," Daniel-Raymond Nadon's second essay in this anthology, shares the ingenious marketing plan he and the Kent State Institute team constructed to ensure maximum attendance of their target audience—conservative male freshmen—at performances of their pro–LGBT acceptance play.

These are but a few examples of the myriad perspectives participants have shared about the various "roles" they took on during the Institutes, productions, and post-show engagements. The perspectives of diverse co-facilitators, project coordinators, diversity experts, students, community members, and others (including one legal representative) are integrated into articles in other chapters throughout the anthology.

Ripples over the Great Barrier

ROD AINSWORTH AND JUDE PIPPEN

The Bundaberg Region in central Queensland, Australia (population circa 98,000), has a varied landscape ranging from bush to river and sea, from bird-thronged wetlands and turtle nesting beaches to rich-earthed farming country rippling with sugarcane, and sits at the southernmost tip of the Great Barrier Reef. Bundaberg is a regional city bounded by the Wide Bay and the World Heritage–listed Fraser Island in the south and by the Burnett River in the north. The original Aboriginal inhabitants and the waves of immigrants that have come into the region share a love of this country and delight in the outdoor living possible in the temperate climate. Most of the amenities needed for a healthy and productive life are here. The rhythm of life is slower than that of the rush hour just four hours away in the state's capital, Brisbane.

The play that is the focus of this essay started in Bundaberg and toured Maryborough, a smaller rural city an hour's drive to the south; Nambour in the Sunshine Coast hinterland, a three-hour drive south; Kingaroy, a small rural center three hours' drive to the west; and Murgon, a very small rural community twenty minutes' drive east of Kingaroy. Bundaberg, Maryborough, Kingaroy and Murgon are part of what is called the Wide Bay Burnett Region. Bundaberg still feels like a safe place to be, where children can grow up happily with plenty of room for recreation and access to quality schooling. Yet there can be a sense of disillusionment and frustration in young people. It is proven that the Wide Bay Burnett Region has one of the poorest socioeconomic indicators in the state (Anglicare). The region is also an aging one. Young people often opt out, heading for the cities in the hope of finding a more diverse and exciting life. In comparison to the youth in our capital cities, the young people of this region, in particular, are not taking up places in higher education or available traineeships. They are not seeing themselves as having an ongoing role in a regional success story (National Institute of Economic and Industry Research). Moreover, this is traditionally a conservative place. Those working out their sexual identity do not have ready access to support structures to help them through. According to social services workers engaged through the development of the play, the region has one of the highest suicide rates among young people in the state, a significant percentage of which seem to be lesbian, gay, bisexual, and transgender (LGBT) youth.

One might hope that the rich cultural history of the region would generate a climate of tolerance. This project showed that the opposite is true: that there is intense pressure to conform to the dominant white, straight culture. This place, where the Great Barrier Reef begins, harbors a strong undercurrent of prejudice against LGBT people.

The First Wave: Setting the Scene

Jude Pippen, one of the directors of the newly formed, nonprofit regional production company Creative Regions, receives a blast from the past through her email inbox. Norma Bowles, a fellow student with her in Paris twenty-five years prior, has found her. She has a theatre company, project funding, a small team of writers, and a mission—to combat prejudice against LGBT youth in communities across the globe. The transpacific partnership between Fringe Benefits and Creative Regions begins.

Rod Ainsworth is another one of the founding directors of Creative Regions. Like Jude, Rod is theatre-trained and theatre-wired. Both are excited by the prospect of this new partnership, but, as two straight people, they have some insecurity about leading a show about LGBT issues into production with any sense of authority. They talk through it and realize that their involvement has nothing to do with authority but is to be about listening, learning, and being true to the devising process. They agree to, as Australians would say, have a go.

In the beginning, one issue seems insurmountable—finding the LGBT community in Bundaberg and the surrounding region. It becomes obvious that LGBT people in this region find networks in private, in order to avoid public displays of prejudice. The team realizes that this is a strong indicator of intolerance and lack of acceptance.

After much research through phone calls, emails, and visits to LGBT people, a strong queer network is found in Maryborough, led by Sally Cripps, a woman who becomes a vital link with LGBT communities.

Through Sally's determination and support, articles make it into a quarterly publication called *Bay Pride* and online through various networks spanning a radius of two hundred kilometers. Creative Regions joins an organization called the Queensland Association of Healthy Communities (QAHC), which provides funding for public education projects around LGBT issues; the organization becomes a friend and a financial supporter of the project. With the funding pledged by Fringe Benefits providing leverage, additional financial support is granted from the Australian government's Regional Arts Fund.

Months go by, and there is some response from the LGBT communities. A small number of people have agreed to participate in the project. Partners have been found: the local university provides assistance with design, printing, and performance space; an amateur theatre company provides workshop space; a government public health unit agrees to spread the word through the LGBT community; and the local community development office pledges secretarial support and rehearsal space for the production. A local masseur, who has struggled through her own coming-out process, provides a donation to the project that funds the printing of T-shirts; these become the costume for the actors and a treasured souvenir for the participants. The project finally seems possible. And, with the US team on its way to Australia, that is just as well.

Local schools are approached to garner their support as potential production sites, but phone calls and emails to principals are not returned. The team gets frustrated. The regional executive director of education is called to discuss the issue. However, while she gives her blessing to the project, she says that negotiations must occur with individual schools. Perseverance is the key. Schools are called again. The guidance officers are not responsive. Finally, allies are found in the drama teachers, who understand what the project is about and provide access to the principals, who then agree to support the production. The engagement of schools is another time-consuming exercise, but eventually there are five high schools committed and contracted to receive the production: three in the city and two in rural communities.

Three public venues are also identified to provide wider community access to the production: the Criterion Hotel in Maryborough (a

Rod Ainsworth and Jude Pippen

supporter of Youth Diversity, an LGBT youth program run by Sally), the CQUniversity Australia campus in Bundaberg, and a small art space in Nambour known as ArtSync, which will take the production into the territory of one of the sponsors, the QAHC. The tour is set.

One week prior to the project starting, only a very small number of LGBT people have agreed to come to the workshops; most are straight allies. The team is concerned. More calls are made, some additional community announcements are placed in local newspapers, a radio interview goes to air, and people start to get in touch—anonymously at first, until they realize the company is trustworthy.

By this point, hundreds of hours of voluntary service have been committed to the project, far exceeding initial expectations. All the preparatory work seems worth it, however, when thirty-five to forty people come to the first workshop; most stay for the entire devising process. This is an incredibly diverse group, and stories begin to flow about being LGBT and/or allied in the Wide Bay Burnett Region.

The Second Wave: The Social Justice Institute

The Fringe Benefits team runs a very intensive and strict devising process. Chosen stories from the group are brought to life through improvisation and tape-recorded. Audiotapes are transcribed, drafted, and redrafted into the night to be ready for the next session. All decisions are voted on by the group: the identification of the target audience, the choice of stories with the most impact, the genre and style that would be most appealing to the target audience, and any changes to the drafts of the script as they emerge. It is an intense, passionate, and robust experience where people jostle about characters, lines, words—even punctuation—to make the script the best it can be. The last workshop involves casting the play and ensuring that the actors understand the time commitment in the following weeks to get the show on the road.

In order to reach its target audience of fourteen-to-seventeen-year-old males, the group decides to structure the play, *Game On!*, as a sporting event—specifically, Rugby League and the much-coveted State of Origin competition between Queensland and New South Wales, which is a hot topic at the time of the Institute. The plot revolves around a true story shared by a participant about his experience coming out to his best friend, who then betrayed him by putting posters all around their high school announcing he was a "fag." This story and the humorous observations and thought-provoking reflections of three fictional rugby commentators link the events of the play in which the school campus becomes a rugby field with the students and faculty as the players of the game.

> CANDY: Well, that's the siren for Half Time. Looks like Lily took the ball in that intense scrum!
>
> DAISY: Bit 'a blood and sweat, but where are the tears? I'm giving my 4 points to Steve! He is a riot! Runs the ball hard for a try every time.
>
> CANDY: No way! That was an atrocious play. I'm disappointed in the player Steve's becoming.
>
> DAISY: C'mon! He's just being a kid, playing the game. That's what high school is about.
>
> CANDY: Well, I'm giving 4 points to Addie. She's holding strong, playing right down the line and sticking to her guns. And Lily really backed Addie up—got the teacher right round the middle and went for the tackle. I'd say she gets 2 points for that kick. What great sportsmanship! In all my years of commentating, I don't think I've seen such passionate players![1]

After the script is developed, the Fringe Benefits team travels home, and the production is taken up by Creative Regions. Those on the creative team, including a composer and a cast of eleven actors, seven of whom are school age, have ten days to get a tour on the road.

The Ripples Begin: The Rehearsal Process

The transition from devising to producing a show in such a short time becomes the most challenging aspect of the process, one that needs some unpacking in order to inform future work. With the rehearsal schedule beginning the day after the Institute finishes, the compressed time frame, the high-pressure concerns of people putting their sexual orientations into a highly public arena, and numerous family, employment, and other personal frustrations, a pressure cooker of emotion is created that needs to be negotiated.

Another factor complicating the situation is that the producer and director have been intricately involved in the devising process, in the same capacity as any other participant. So far, it has been a highly democratic process where everyone has had the opportunity to edit the text. Everyone has had a say about everything. Many of the Institute participants, now members of the cast and crew, have also been involved with the writing process in the days between the workshop sessions, transcribing and reworking the scenes. The first hurdle in the production process is for the director and producer to move from their positions as fellow participants to leaders in getting the show on the road.

Given the very short time to get production-ready, this transition and renegotiation of roles becomes problematic. The director is concerned about short time frames and wants to get down to business. Those in the cast, all working voluntarily and most without any prior theatrical experience, want to continue the negotiation process. But in a rehearsal schedule as compressed as this, there is no time for the actors to exercise the same sense of democracy over the rehearsal process that they have had in the devising process. There is a sense of torn loyalty, a period of emotional withdrawal and realignment of energy and focus. A new set of relationships has to be built. The youth feel dispossessed and disempowered. They own the project so deeply that they find it hard to trust someone taking charge. There has to be an end to the continual editing, and the director needs to be given permission to create something that sits well with the company's production standards and those afforded (or not) within the project budget.

The director finds that one actor wants to resist all of his suggestions, another struggles intensely with learning lines, and others express frustration with the the power differential by arriving late, disrupting the ensemble, and falling in and out of focus. The rehearsals have immediately followed the intense ten-day Institute, and the group is flagging emotionally. The script and the performance concept require a tight, emotionally connected ensemble, and the first week of rehearsal is anything but. Valuable rehearsal time is wasted as these power struggles are negotiated.

The producer and director discuss the management of this situation. Why is this happening? Group members are committed and really want to get the show on the road. Why the blocks? There is an air of "Norma said" in the group. Due to their attachment to Norma and her well-managed democracy, the culture of negotiation is strong. It is concluded that there has not been an adequate handover in terms of expectations. Certainly, roles have been discussed, but the necessity for the script to be interpreted by a director and the nature of the rehearsal phase and extremely tight time frames have not been clearly articulated to an amateur cast by the Fringe Benefits team. Norma and her group are viewed as the experts, and nothing the production team says seems to be taken in. There is much discussion—and navel-gazing!—between the producer and director. Should this have been something that everyone discussed in the first hour of rehearsal? Should the producer and director have been distinguished more during the devising process and/or engaged separately or differently from the other participants? Should they have made sure that they were acknowledged and had their roles clarified more at the close of the devising process? The answers are not obvious at the time. In a phone call with Norma during the rehearsal process, she suggests that Fringe Benefits has never toured a show in the same semester in which it was devised.[2] This is a critical piece of information. In hindsight, some distance between the devising and rehearsal process should have been programmed. Time and space are required, and this group has had neither.

The director wonders if his stylistic choices should have been more conservative, given the time allowed for rehearsal. Much of the script is naturalistic, reflecting the schoolyard language and everyday experiences of young people.

> TYLER: Hey Mackenzie, wait up!
> MACK: What's up?
> TYLER: Ah . . . not much. . . .
> MACK: Sorry about calling you a loser, I was just jokin'.
> TYLER: It's okay.
> MACK: Got a hot date for the formal yet?
> TYLER: No. You?
> MACK: Well, I really want Steve to ask me.
> TYLER: Steve? Ahh come on, Mackenzie. You can do better than
>   that.

It is felt that this naturalistic dialogue could be heightened theatrically to transform the piece into a high-energy style reflecting the feel of a Rugby League game. The director is asking a group that has spent ten days finding the naturalism and the truth in dialogue to somehow move stylistically into a metaphorical world of theatre. How could the two extremes meet?

There is virtually no production budget, and the demands of performing in schools (where the space is not known prior to arrival), a pub, a university "drama barn," and the foyer of an arts space dictate that simplicity is a must. During the Institute, Norma had seeded the idea of using milk crates as seats, and this idea is taken up. The group needs Norma's voice to be present, and the crates are a symbol of trust and inclusion of the project leader. The devising team has discussed design, and these ideas need to be incorporated wherever possible to respect decisions made during the devising process and to maintain trust between director and ensemble. An emphasis is placed on building a soundscape through grunting, chanting, cheering, and screaming. This creates a lighthearted approach to finding the soundtrack to the piece. Peter Rankine, the composer working with the group, has developed additional ideas and facilitates some musical devising sessions—including recording a rap song he has written—with the entire production team. Unity is found in collective beat-boxing. The ice is broken.

This work translates into the key metaphor of the performance. The actors, backs to audience, create the soundscape throughout the drama, creating the chants, hoots, whistles, and cheers—the highs and lows of a Rugby League game. The action emerges out of this wall of sound. It is a simple but very effective solution where rhythm, timing, and musicality become critical to the storytelling. It is a style that allows no one time to rest. Every moment of the script, every actor (and the stage manager) is engaged in every scene—if not physically, vocally. High levels of concentration, energy, and precision are required, and the ensemble rises to the challenge. The rhythm and music, the T-shirts, the milk crates, and a simple screen painted in a graffiti style by one of the devising team become the symbols of togetherness. There is ownership at last.

On the Saturday of the opening performance, press coverage in Bundaberg is extensive. The front page of the local newspaper reads "Bashed Just Because They're Gay" with a full-page article highlighting the stories of two of the ensemble members. Morale is high. The energy of the game can be felt in waves.

Measuring the Waves: Reflections

The aim of the project was to create a play that promoted respect for and understanding of the complexity of sexual orientation and gender and to combat prejudice, bullying, and cruelty toward LGBT youth. Over four hundred people saw the production; three hundred of them were high school youth. Schools were a logical entry point to the fourteen- to seventeen-year-old males whom the production targeted. Questionnaires were handed out after each performance; in the case of school performances, information kits for youth at risk were also distributed. The response was overwhelmingly positive, regarding both the vibrant theatricality and the compelling activist message of the production.

The responses to the audience questionnaires demonstrated that LGBT put-downs were rife and that LGBT students did not feel safe in the school environment. Comments were often made by audience members about the play being an "eye-opener." There was a feeling that audiences were now ready to "stick up for their friends," as one of the characters had. Audiences identified what they could do to assist LGBT friends, and most responses were very positive: "Stop my own bad habits: saying things like 'that's gay,'" "Attend to my own language and behaviour." The responses were very rewarding for the production team, but there were also some reality checks evinced by a few comments such as "Keep hitting them between the eyes." The crew watched the audiences carefully and saw, in the school shows in particular, the discomfort experienced by some. A few mid-adolescent males reacted negatively to the play by laughing and/or causing a disturbance throughout. The actors felt this, too. However, debriefings with the team confirmed that this level of discomfort was a positive thing—that we had made a difference by putting this in front of schools.

Despite the small number of people who reacted negatively to the show, the dynamic between actors and audiences was electric. For the most part, the age of the cast closely matched the age of the target audience in schools, creating an immediate bond both during and after the performances. Audience members, tears in their eyes, hugged the cast, and, particularly in Murgon, the place where the team expected the most resistance, audience members talked for over half an hour about their experiences, family life, issues in the schoolyard, and prejudice from teachers. A true connection was felt, a connection that could not have happened with a professional cast that had little or no association with the stories discovered during the Institute.

One of the most memorable moments in the entire tour involved one of the actors bursting into tears during the final scene at the Bundaberg performance as she recounted, as part of the script, the true story she had heard in the Institute:

SHELLEY: My name is Shelley, and I'm a straight ally. There was this really nice girl named Teagan who participated in the playwriting workshops. . . . Her dad used to beat her just 'cuz he was mad about her coming out as lesbian. He even told her "When I get a gun, you'll be the first to go!"

The audience was captivated. The emotion, the bond between actors and audience, was astounding.

Another highlight of the tour was the response of one audience member at the final performance in Nambour. A man who was a notable gay activist in the 1970s made his way over to the ensemble at the end of the show, wiping tears from his eyes. "This made the struggles of the '70s worth it," he said. After the last performance of the tour, these few words created not just ripples but a tidal wave through the cast and crew, a torrent created in a mere twenty days.

Postscript: Two years after the Game On! *project, the* Bundaberg News-Mail *published another article about prejudice against LGBT people. One of the participants in* Game On! *was interviewed; she said that she is seeing a change in the community and knows of at least two young women at one of the schools where the play was toured who now feel comfortable to be out while at school (Emery).*

Notes

1. This and all script quotations are derived from the final draft of *Game On!* (unpublished).

2. Editors' note: While it was rare, some TSJI and other FB plays have been performed during the semester in which they were developed. The turnaround time for this collaboration in Bundaberg, however, was the quickest on record. A longer turnaround time is recommended, especially for controversial topics and for complicated productions and/or tours.

Bibliography

Anglicare. *A Scan of Disadvantage in Queensland 2010: From Analysis to Innovation in Place-Based Practice.* Brisbane: Anglicare, 2010. http://www.ucareqld.com.au/SocialJustice/index.php?option=com_content&tas=view&id=133&Itemid=20.

Emery, Leigh. "Gay Play Helped Destroy Barriers." *Bundaberg News-Mail,* November 19, 2010. http://www.news-mail.com.au/story/2010/11/19/gay-play-helped-destroy-barriers/.

National Institute of Economic and Industry Research. *The Wide Bay–Burnett Region: Demographic and Economic Change—A Perspective and Prospective Analysis.* Maryborough: Wide Bay Burnett Regional Organization of Councils, 2006. http://www.wbbroc.org.au/uploads/summary_report.pdf.

Voicing Your Gender, Gendering Your Voice

REBECCA M. ROOT

The human voice tells many stories. It is not only the words we use but the way we say them that can reveal a good deal about our age, upbringing, socioeconomic profile, and education; how confident or awkward we are as we conduct ourselves in relationships; our mood and tastes; and our gender.

That gender is a social construct has long been acknowledged. Simone de Beauvoir stated, "One is not born, but rather becomes a woman" (295). She might as easily have written "man," since the pressure to conform to either of the principal genders can be intense and lifelong. People brought up as a "boy" or a "girl" tend to believe they should sound "male" or "female." Aural perception that matches the visual leaves no room for ambiguity in a binary world of black or white, good or bad, male or female.

It can be distressing and disorientating to question or doubt the gender identity with which one has been raised. Some people seek to redress the perceived imbalance by assuming the role (and, often, social status) of a different gender. This state is known as transsexuality. A transsexual (TS) person may be defined as someone who has undergone surgical/hormonal intervention to attain his or her desired gender, whereas transgender (TG) may denote a person who emotionally and psychologically identifies with a different gender from his or her own but who has not as yet undergone the permanent transition to that gender.[1]

Assuming a person does undergo surgery to attain his or her felt gender, the accomplishment of that physical transition does not necessarily predicate anonymity as TS. To go undetected as someone who has lived in a previous gender role—to "pass"—is a highly desired goal for many transsexuals. Beyond the spectrum of the visible identifiers of breasts, facial hair, and exterior sexual organs, the spoken voice may stand as one of the most challenging to adapt to a new gender presentation.

Research has shown that the factors most commonly associated with the speech differences between the male and female genders are pitch, resonance, intonation, articulation, and vocabulary.[2] These are chiefly the consequence of differing anatomies: for example, males are typically larger than females and may have longer and thicker vocal folds.[3] The denser folds vibrate more slowly than thinner, tauter female folds, and a deeper voice results.

In the case of the female-to-male TS person, gender-specific modification of the voice is normally achieved by hormonal therapy. Increased levels of testosterone in the biologically female body simulate male puberty: the vocal folds increase in bulk and the voice "breaks." The story is somewhat different for the male-to-female TS. Estrogen treatment does not affect the pitch of the voice: speech therapy and vocal resonance placement training is often necessary to acquire a voice that is deemed acceptably "female"—to the subject, at least.

Theatre for Social Justice Institute, May 2008

I participated in the Theatre for Social Justice (TSJ) Institute at the Central School of Speech & Drama, University of London, in May 2008. The Institute began with a series of play-making workshops and culminated at schools and festivals with performances of the devised play *Brief Encounters*.[4]

My involvement in the project combined my experience as a professional actor with my burgeoning specialism in voice training for the TS population. Both have been, to a degree, influenced by my own TS identity, and I considered this as possibly my most significant contribution to the TSJ project. During the development of the play, I related episodes from the period of my gender transition from male to female some five years earlier. Although I had previously preferred to bury the details of those often difficult times, I now welcomed the opportunity to share stories which I'd not hitherto articulated. The nature of the Institute, egalitarian yet deliberately controlled, allowed me to assess and reevaluate such experiences in the light of my subsequent successful transition and my newly discovered confidence in myself and my gender identity. Among so many others' tales, whether

TS-related or not, my own history became simply part of the wallpaper of the project: visible and invisible, present and absent, happy and sad. This made it a remarkably safe place for candor, embracing all generations, genders, and sexual orientations.

The improvisational components of the Institute appealed enormously to me as an actor. My earlier acting career took something of a downturn when I transitioned to the female role, and I have described this experience in greater depth elsewhere.[5] Any opportunity to perform nowadays is seized upon with relish; the *Brief Encounters* project provided some intense moments to dramatize. One scene concerned an instance of transphobic bullying. In an ironic twist of casting, I took the role of a male bigoted thug on the brink of committing a brutal hate crime upon a young transman. Perversely, despite the savagery of the episode, the transphobic character was funny, pathetically so. The insanity of his behavior was seen through the prism of gallows humor. As actors and audience we laughed at him, not with him; as transpeople we despised him; ultimately, as humans I believe we pitied him. I later reflected on the incongruity of my birthing such a monster. It had been unnerving yet peculiarly cathartic to reenact a moment that had once happened to me (albeit obliquely) in reverse.

The second but no less significant role for me within the project was as voice coach for the cast. This was a teaching practice placement module toward my MA in Voice Studies, also at Central.[6] My responsibilities were to help the actors, many of whom were young and inexperienced, with their overall vocal technique and to lead pre-rehearsal voice warm-ups. Once the play was in fuller shape, I gave voice notes following rehearsals.[7]

One performance was especially challenging to coach. With so much of the play's focus being trans-centric and so many participants themselves TS/TG, when it came to the matter of a biologically female performer playing male-to-female TS, I almost became dizzy by the very circularity of the situation. This performer needed to produce a voice that sounded as if it had once belonged in a male body but was now quite at home in a female one. Near-Shakespearean in its scope, the undertaking has been tackled before, by actors including Olympia Dukakis (in the television series *Tales of the City*, 1993), Vanessa Redgrave (in the television feature *Second Serve*, 1986), and, more recently, Felicity Huffman (in the acclaimed motion picture *TransAmerica*,

2005). It was the first time I had had the chance to coach this kind of gendered performance myself.

Working backward, we used the actor's existing female voice as our "template." Exploring her lower resonances, she constructed a "male" sounding voice, experimenting with lower pitch and flatter intonation, accompanied by more direct vocabulary and stronger physicality. The actor buried these foundations deep inside her character's emotional core and layered "female" qualities back on to it—more inflected tone, lighter pitch, slightly more breathiness—while "remembering" the male sound she had previously obtained. The result was a voice that sounded "female" with "male" undertones: occasional roughness, intermittent monotony, and a hint of directness that seemed unusual in a female speaker. More than anything, the actor was able to connect the voice *emotionally* to the character she was portraying: the gendered voice was "real" to her, and so it would be to her audience.

This character work was essential for all the trans-identified roles, whether performed by actual trans-people or not. Aware that the exercises used in my voice rehearsals—varying pitch and resonance, changing intonation and volume patterns, and so on—would bear some relevancy to the everyday lives of the cast, I took care to illuminate parallels between performance and life. Conviction, clarity, and emotional integrity are as necessary on the stage as on Main Street.

Of course, in theatre as in life, there is no such thing as a *definitive* "female" or "male" voice. Certain traits may be accepted as pertaining to one gender or another, but there are no hard-and-fast rules. For many TS/TG people, one of the top priorities of passing is to use a voice that they feel is appropriate to their felt gender. I can speak from experience. During my transition, I underwent extensive speech therapy and subsequently surgery to help my voice maintain its higher pitch.[8]

Years later, I now attest that, in fact, what is most important to maintain is the personal creed that the voice you are using is yours and yours alone. As playwright David Mamet says, "What comes from the heart, goes to the heart" (63). A voice might be noticed as belonging to a TS or TG person for maybe the first two minutes of conversation, perhaps less; after that, it is normally accepted that the interlocutor is the gender that he or she presents. And the truth of this is even more evident within the context of theatrical presentation, for between audience and cast there exists an unwritten contract that states, "This is the world of make-believe; let's play."

The project with Fringe Benefits provided me with much raw material, which fed directly into my thesis for my master's degree; this now forms the basis of my professional practice as I turn my attention to the broader discussions of voice and gender. Developing my range, I have taken my knowledge to San Francisco, where the city's main LGBT Community Center hosted my workshop in late 2008. In 2009, I presented my thesis at Harvard University, where I expanded on the theme of male/female vocal presentation and adaptation. The paper was published as "There and Back Again? Adventures in Genderland" (see Cook).

Reflecting subjectively, I believe the most significant outcome of my participation in the project was the realization that I'm not alone. I may be the only male-to-female TS voice teacher in the United Kingdom, but I'm not the only TS person. The TSJ Institutes certainly foster collaboration and creativity and break down the barriers of social intolerance; but more important, to my mind, they instill connectivity between humans. In the process of making theatre, we are given permission to speak to one another with voices we are proud to use and unafraid to call our own.

Notes

1. These terms are fluid and the identities of TS/TG often overlap; TG is often regarded as the umbrella term for all gender identity issues.

2. The interested reader is directed toward Adler, Hirsch, and Mordaunt, whose bibliography and references lead to extensive further background reading. Rees contains several peer-reviewed essays and articles on the nature and manifestation of voice and gender identity.

3. Average fold lengths are 9–13mm (adult female) and 15–20mm (adult male). Borrowing an analogy from stringed instruments, the tighter the vocal fold (or string) the higher the note, and vice versa. For an amplification of the physiology of pitch and the human vocal folds, see Shewell, 184–94.

4. The production was reprised in 2009 and again in 2010. On each of these occasions, I was voice and speech coach for the cast.

5. See my chapter "There and Back Again? Adventures in Genderland" in Cook.

6. The degree provides training for teachers of speech and voice production for actors and other public speakers.

7. The role of the vocal coach within the theatrical environment is discussed in depth by Feindel and Withers-Wilson.

8. The procedure known as "crycothyroid approximation" involves the repositioning of two of the cartilages within the larynx (the "voice box") so that the vocal folds are held in a tighter position than before. While this does not in itself increase the pitch of the voice, it does remove the lower notes from the speaker's range,

thus reducing the chances of sounding "male" at inopportune moments. Success is not guaranteed, however; I am still occasionally addressed on the phone as "sir."

Bibliography

Adler, Richard, S. Hirsch, and M. Mordaunt, eds. *Voice and Communication Therapy for the Transsexual/Transgender Client—A Comprehensive Clinical Guide.* Abingdon, UK: Plural Publishing, 2006.

Cook, Rena, ed. *Voice and Speech Review: The Moving Voice.* Cincinnati: Voice and Speech Trainers Association, 2009.

de Beauvoir, Simone. *The Second Sex.* Translated by H. M. Parshley. London: Vintage, 1997.

Feindel, Janet. *The Thought Propels the Sound.* Abingdon, UK: Plural Publishing, 2009.

Mamet, David. *True and False.* London: Faber and Faber, 1998.

Rees, Mandy, ed. *Voice and Speech Review: Voice and Gender.* Cincinnati: Voice and Speech Trainers Association, 2007.

Shewell, Christina. *Voice Work: Art and Science in Changing Voices.* Chichester, UK: Wiley-Blackwell, 2009.

Withers-Wilson, Nan. *Vocal Direction for the Theatre: From Script Analysis to Opening Night.* New York: Drama Book Publishers, 1993.

Psychological Reflections on an LGBTQI Theatre for Social Justice Project

ERASMO TACCONELLI

Supporting LGBTQI People

I am a clinical psychologist and psychotherapist experienced in supporting clients regarding a range of mental health, physical health, and sexual health needs. Over the past thirteen years, I have helped many clients presenting with issues relating to their sex, gender, sexual identity, and sexuality, including those expressing non-heteronormative sexualities, such as lesbian, gay, or bisexual; those who are transsexual or transgendered, including transmale and transfemale people who have changed or are changing sex; those who are gender-queer or gender-diverse; and those who are intersex with genital and sex identity issues. I have supported clients who have struggled with their identities, and I have also supported clients who are confident about who they are.

My Psychological Roles with the Institute

I was asked to participate in the Theatre for Social Justice workshops at the Central School of Speech & Drama. I was told that the workshops aimed to create a play with LGBTQI (lesbian, gay, bisexual, transgender, queer, and intersex) content that would be performed in secondary schools and that my role was as a counselor for the workshop participants. Sharing personal stories and discussing and creating a play about LGBTQI identity and anti-LGBTQI discrimination experiences could certainly trigger rather difficult memories and emotions for some participants. I was asked to be present during the workshops to help participants should they become distressed due to the material disclosed and discussed. Much needed to be accomplished, and quickly: from nothing, a script had to be created in five workshop sessions.

I was very excited about the chance to help with this initiative because I realized what an amazing opportunity it would be to help the LGBTQI youth. I have always been motivated to help people with sex, gender, and sexuality issues, and I enjoy helping people feel good about being LGBTQI. I know that there are multiple problems around the understanding and acceptance of LGBTQI people in society, so to use my training alongside the creation of a drama production with the youth participants was a novel and exciting prospect. While discussing my role, I was mindful about the potential emotional impact that creating a play based on personal experiences might have on participants. My contribution was therefore agreed to be based on the following three main roles:

Supportive role. I was asked to let participants know at the beginning of each workshop that I was available to offer support if and when the need arose. Participants knew that if difficult thoughts or feelings were triggered by what was discussed or happening in the workshop, they could indicate to me that they wished to talk privately, and we could sit outside of the room and explore their feelings and concerns, one-to-one. I was there to help when needed. It was made clear to participants at the start that I would not be providing formal therapy but facilitating a supportive space to process immediate feelings and to help think of a way forward.

Consultative role. I was asked to offer my psychological ideas about LGBTQI identity, development, problems, relationships, acceptance, and so on. The script needed to reach as many people as possible, simultaneously highlighting sensitive and taboo ideas but not putting people off nor reinforcing unhelpful narratives. The play needed to include an acknowledgment of participants' struggles and difficulties but also recognition of empowerment and normality. Additionally, while the one-to-one discussions I might have with participants would be confidential, I was asked to raise any concerns, questions, or issues participants may have shared with me generally to help with the overall process and to share my own thoughts about the process with the workshop leaders throughout the program. I was also asked to be available whenever possible following the workshops to help out with planned productions in schools and to help facilitate post-show interactions with the audience.

Participative role. I was asked to be a participant in the process as a whole and in the play development. This included taking part in the exercises, group discussions, and improvisations. My engagement in the process helped foster an open environment, encouraging the participants to do so too. I was mindful about how this particular role could influence my overall position as a counselor. I agreed with the facilitators, however, that my engagement in the process as a co-deviser could be additionally beneficial.

The Workshops

I was amazed by the large turnout and diversity of both youth and adult participants. The gender and sexual orientation spectrum of society was well represented. Additionally, participants were of various ethnicities and from different backgrounds, cultures, and nations, which diversified the range of experiences aired and shared.

The facilitators started the workshops with an overview of the guidelines for participants and leaders, discussing respect, confidentiality, a nonjudgmental approach, how to participate, and so on. The scene was set and a safe space was created for all participants to explore sensitive issues so that the work could develop productively. The workshop agenda and goals also were made plain. It was clear what to expect from facilitators and what was expected of the participants. It felt safe, and I could sense the emerging energy and creativity in participants. The passion, fun, and dynamism throughout the process made it apparent to me that we would all create something special together.

The workshops were facilitated at a fast yet appropriate pace as the facilitators' energy and creativity helped focus our work. I was impressed with how many powerful psychological themes were elicited and documented as the beginnings of the script were emerging. All of the participants were encouraged to have a voice and an opportunity to be heard as they disclosed their stories and experiences of growing up LGBTQI. It appeared that many participants enjoyed having their voices heard, sharing their experiences, and being publicly recognized for who they are. Each participant in turn had the opportunity to verbalize both positive and negative societal responses to his or her sex, gender, and/or sexuality. Sad stories, traumatic stories, anger-provoking stories, and triumphant stories of transfemale, transmale, gender-diverse, gay, lesbian, and bisexual people and their straight allies were shared. I witnessed familiar stories of bullying, rejection, and isolation being disclosed by participants. Participants communicated experiences of their identity awareness and how their resulting self-development was negotiated within families, with peers, and in schools. Feelings, relationships, hopes, wishes, desires for acceptance, and the struggles that could occur were communicated. It was clear that the experience was cathartic for all. I was amazed by the way everyone participated in the workshops. I could sense the community spirit and togetherness that developed. It was great that people could share their experiences openly, freely, and nonjudgmentally.

As the workshops progressed, a few poignant and representative stories were chosen by participants, which were then developed through improvisation into a play script. The stories came to life and, with them, the rich array of experiences and related feelings, from traumatizing experiences of homophobia and transphobia to joyous experiences of successful identity expression and acceptance. At each stage, emotions were monitored by the facilitators and me. Throughout the creation of the script, I was acutely aware that, in order to educate and not alienate members of the audience, blame was never assigned to the perpetrators. Education was our primary goal. I was witnessing stories that I so frequently hear in my clinical work being transformed into theatre. I knew that what was being represented in the play reflected what is happening to LGBTQI people today.

My Experience of My Psychological Roles

My primary responsibility was to help create and maintain a contained and safe space. Throughout the workshops, I made sure that I was open and available to all the participants, and I used every opportunity to engage and interact with them so that, should they need to talk to me more, they would have already established a relationship of trust with me and could say what they needed to, no matter how difficult. Although, in the end, I was not formally asked to help anyone in overt distress, I had many discussions with the participants about their identities, experiences, and realities.

I also tried to remain vigilant regarding the range of ways that participants' behavior, both verbal and nonverbal, might signal a cause for concern. Even if distress was not obvious, I was aware that participants might keep their difficult and/or internalized shame-related feelings quiet. I observed how participants were connecting with personal stories of hurt, confusion, and rejection and how the process of verbalizing and sharing these stories affected them. Sometimes, when participants shared particularly emotionally triggering experiences, I would later approach them and validate what they had shared and acknowledge that their contribution was welcomed, heard, and understood. Still, again, throughout the process, I observed that participants seemed to experience the workshop environment as safe and contained as they appeared able to share difficult memories and experiences without feeling overwhelmed by the emotions that were triggered.

If there had been a situation in which a participant expressed extreme distress due to a past or present concern, I had a clear idea of the processes I would have followed. I would have initially attempted to address this with the participant confidentially by letting him or her talk and then by listening, empathizing, and, where appropriate, helping problem-solve. Should there have been a concern regarding severe depression or self-harm, I would have informed the participant that I would have to respond to his or her needs in a more formal way. I would have communicated my concerns *with* the participant's knowledge to workshop facilitators and have helped to liaise both with appropriate London-based voluntary LGBTQI organizations and/or with the participant's local health services to ensure that his or her mental health needs were being addressed. I knew that within my role, I could pave the way forward if help was needed.

But, again, the participants seemed to feel safe to be themselves and were not afraid to show it. I believe this was due to the fact that the workshops were so well facilitated. For example, if a participant openly shared a distressing past experience of being bullied, the workshop pace was adjusted to ensure that what was being communicated was recognized and validated. Perhaps, too, my presence created a containing influence in that the participants were aware support was there for them should they need it. But one thing was for certain: everyone experienced and expressed their feelings of solidarity, which created an amazingly supportive structure.

I gradually realized that the whole experience was important for me, too. I was asked to help, but *I* was actually helped. I was part of a community, a gathering of like-minded people working together and sharing common stories. I personally understand the issues sex, gender, and sexuality pose for people. I am gay, and I too had had some similar experiences with bullying at school. I had a difficult adolescence due to this, and I remember being scared about being gay. As I grew up, I gradually came out and felt better, but my journey was not that easy as I lost some significant relationships as a result of coming out. Although older, I was in many regards no different from the youth who were attending the workshops: I am part of the community and dealing with many of the same issues. My experience of high school would have been amazing if I had heard the words "gay" or "trans" mentioned positively. Instead, my experience was that they were mentioned only derogatorily. In the Institute, however, I really felt part of a community and embraced by those who attended. The fact that I was part of an intervention that created an LGBTQI play for schools was also important for me.

Psychological Reflections on the Process

It seems essential for a counselor to participate in Theatre for Social Justice Institutes (as well as in similar endeavors) and that his or her role is viewed as supportive, consultative, and participative. It was recognized by all that what was talked about during the workshops was very personal. It was clear that some participants were stronger as a result of the adversity they had experienced in their lives but that some were not and were still dealing with past and/or current events. Everyone was on a personal journey. The process was exciting and innovative throughout; nevertheless, the telling and hearing of stories, the acting in or observing of an improvisation, and the speedy group process and decision-making process triggered many emotional responses that needed to be attended to in some way. Participants talked to me about their personal experiences from the past and the present, and I sensed that my input and presence were valued.

The project as a whole, including the performances in schools, was unique and multidimensional; moreover, I believe it successfully achieved its objectives. I was very impressed that, through drama, real, *lived* LGBTQI experiences were captured so well. Through facilitated group work, a large gathering of diverse individuals was able to take part enjoyably in the creation of a serious play about human nature, form friendships through the process, become stronger within the LGBTQI community, and ultimately disseminate the created play within secondary schools to empower and educate many other people. It seemed to me as if all participants were empowered and strengthened through communal catharsis. And, as it led to a successful and useful product, I believe that the process and product helped everyone, from the participants to the audience it was intended for.

A few months after the Institute, I attended a transgender conference where the play was performed with audience questions at the end. As I took part in the discussion that ensued, it seemed clear that the audience valued the play. It was also clear that the participants who acted in the play had gained a lot from presenting it in diverse secondary schools. I so wish I had seen a play like that presented at school when I was young. Still, to have been part of such an initiative with such confident LGBTQI youth has made it clear to me that the future is better for LGBTQI youth in schools.

I reflect on the whole process with fondness, both professionally and personally. Being a participant in my counseling role, I helped demonstrate and acknowledge to the participants that they were important, their experiences were recognized, and their accomplishments in overcoming barriers were respected and praised. While I have extensive experience supporting people with sex, gender, and sexuality concerns, I believe that the psychological role within projects such as this simply requires a counselor who has at least some familiarity with and understanding of supporting clients living with LGBTQI experiences (or whichever experiences are to be the focus of the project) and, if not, is open to and validating of these very personal identity issues. What I witnessed inspired me. Addressing personal identity-related psychological issues through the medium of theatre is a wonderful way of accessing and helping many people.

Forum Theatre and the Power of "Yes, and . . ."

JESSY ARDERN

Just about every improv class ever taught has started with a game called "Yes, and . . ." (Seham xxiv). It's an extremely simple game. Character #1 makes a statement; Character #2 accepts the premise and builds on it. *The cat ran away*. Yes, and I'm afraid it will get lost. *I need to find a job*. Yes, and you need to do so before we are evicted.

When I first began to learn improv, this game made me want to chew my own face off, and I was as vocal as anyone else with my complaints: *Do we have to play this? We get it. It's boring. Can we do something else? Can we do something REAL?* The answer was always, *Later. After we've learned this. After you know how to say "yes."*

The fact is that as an actor, as an improviser, and as a human being, learning to say "yes" can sometimes be very difficult. When I was approached about working on a Forum Theatre play about racism in my hometown of Winnipeg, my kneejerk reaction was not "yes." It was something more akin to "Thanks, but I think I'd rather drink Drano." I had done message-driven theatre before, with unhappy results. No one likes to be preached to. Especially teenagers. (Especially teenagers bearing fruit, I once had the misfortune to learn.) No, I thought. No, no, no. And then, somehow, the voice of my high school improv coach came floating up through the recesses of my brain. *Nothing interesting ever happens with "no." Nothing is ever created with "no."*

And so I signed on. And I stayed on, from the first day of work-shops through the last day of performance. I came, I sat, I did my best to shut up and listen. I heard, I was touched, I was humbled. And in spite of my still-rampant pessimism, when asked to act in the show's workshop production, I said "yes." When asked to play Crystal, the show's thoroughly hateful oppressor, I said "yes."

At that point, you see, I had learned my lesson. Saying "yes" is not only an essential tool in performance; it is a catalyst for personal growth in real life. When we began rehearsing the collaboratively created Forum Theatre play *No Offense . . .*, it provided a tool that I could never have lived without. In a situation wherein every audience intervention is different, the worst thing that you can possibly do is shut yourself off. "Yes" is always the answer. "Yes, and . . ."

In an improv, everything that your scene partner says or does is an "offer" (Seham xxiv). To get anywhere, you must say "yes" to every offer that comes your way, no matter how different it is from where you think the scene should go. Blocking someone else's ideas may get a laugh, but it also usually stops the scene cold, as in the following scenario:

> BILL: I've brought you to the museum, the site of our first date, to ask . . . *(kneeling down)* Will you marry me?
> KATE: What? We've never been on a date. I don't know you. And we're not in a museum, we're in a rocket ship.

Not only is the scene over before even getting started, but the trust of the actor playing Bill is shot to hell. Why should he offer anything new when his partner is just going to reject all of his ideas and build her own scene? In our Forum Theatre performances, if an audience member was going to be bold enough to come up onstage and try something out, then we had a duty not to betray that trust and run roughshod over him or her. Otherwise, new volunteers would be low in supply.

I tried to take this idea to heart as much as possible while preparing to work with audience members. As we drilled interventions over and over in rehearsal, with cast members filling in as our rehearsal audience, I kept a constant refrain in my head: "What are they offering me? What are they telling me? How can I accept that information and allow it to change the scene?" These questions were sometimes tough to answer, but eventually the practice of analysis and response became easier, almost automatic, and I made increasingly stronger, character-driven choices in our improvised dialogue:

> CRYSTAL: Guess who's back? Raven da drunken Indian! I can smell her from here!
> AUDIENCE MEMBER: *(taking over the role of Crystal's friend)* Whoa. Crystal, that's completely inappropriate.

CRYSTAL: "Inappropriate"? What are you, a teacher?

AUDIENCE MEMBER: I'd rather be a teacher than your friend when you talk like that.

CRYSTAL: Are you saying that you'd quit being my friend just because I made a little joke?!

AUDIENCE MEMBER: It's not a little joke. And yeah, that's exactly what I'm saying.[1]

For the most part, audience participation looked a lot like this. Plenty being offered, and therefore plenty to react to.

There were, of course, times when a volunteer made me want to bang my head against a brick wall. When you're trying to illustrate a character's attitude change, what the heck are you supposed to do with this?

CRYSTAL: You guys are a bunch of drunken half-breeds! *(Laughs)* No offense.

AUDIENCE MEMBER: *(as the friend)* Uh, you should, uh . . . I don't know.

CRYSTAL: What are you talking about?

AUDIENCE MEMBER: That's uh, y'know . . . like . . . not nice. I guess. I don't know . . .

After spending weeks getting into Crystal's mind, my instinct was to tear into that unfortunate audience member. A weakling! ATTACK!! It was very challenging to find ways to "lose" in situations like that, because I had been doing my best to embrace Crystal's win-at-any-cost attitude. Finding reasons to accommodate people who did little more than mumble halfhearted protestations went painfully against the grain. In the end, a piece of advice from the director provided me an "aha!" moment: *You must value your friends as much as you value your power.* Shockingly simple, shockingly effective advice. It's just another way of saying "yes"—in this case, to accepting and preserving a friendship.

You must value your friends as much as you value your power became a mantra that helped to ground our interventions and to raise the stakes realistically. It forced me to remember that everyone is searching for more than one thing in life. I began to examine in every intervention not only what my character was trying to win but also what my character *risked losing.* When I looked at it that way, I began to understand how she might be genuinely affected by every new of-fer. Even a mumbled protestation, a raised eyebrow, or a groan might unnerve or set Crystal off.

Of course, allowing these less dynamic interventions to affect my character sometimes involved helping audience members communi-cate their intentions more clearly. Although I tried to avoid putting words into people's mouths, sometimes I engaged in a bit of creative extrapolation:

> CRYSTAL: You guys are a bunch of drunken half-breeds!
> AUDIENCE MEMBER: *(as the friend)* That's uh . . . y'know . . . like . . . I don't know . . .
> CRYSTAL: You're acting weird all of a sudden. You know I'm just kidding, right?
> AUDIENCE MEMBER: Um . . .
> CRYSTAL: Jeez, can't you take a joke?
> AUDIENCE MEMBER: Uhmmm . . .
> CRYSTAL: God, stop looking at me like that. I hate it when you get all judgmental.
> AUDIENCE MEMBER: Well, it's . . . y'know . . . like . . . y'know . . .
> CRYSTAL: Look, if you're going to go all weird on me, just forget it. God, you're so sensitive!

Taa-dahh! When the audience member doesn't give you strong or clear offers to say "yes" to, you make it up. This was not the most realistic or fascinating of exchanges, true. But now the audience has seen a situa-tion wherein even a tentative intervention has changed the dynamic of the situation—not a profound or long-term transformation, perhaps, but at least a small shift, a small step forward.

A potential problem with modeling a positive change in an antago-nist in the absence of a truly effective intervention is that it could lead audience members to have unrealistic, perhaps even dangerously high expectations about what similar interventions might achieve in the "real world." Optimistically, however, one might have reason to expect that witnessing a positive outcome like this might inspire people *in real life* to stand up for what's right, even when they feel nervous and shy. At the very least, the audience has seen that there is nothing to be afraid of *onstage* and will most likely become bolder.

And the bolder the better, I say! I have never felt so much glee on-stage as when I was confronted by a young man who came up, took over the role of a classroom instructor, and called me out less than two lines into a scene.

> CRYSTAL: Nice to see you back, Raven! Nice to see you sober, eh!?
> AUDIENCE MEMBER: *(as teacher)* Get out.
> CRYSTAL: Huh . . . What?

As an actor, I was genuinely stunned by the force of his response.

> AUDIENCE MEMBER: Get out of my classroom right now. Report to the principal's office!
> CRYSTAL: But I—
> AUDIENCE MEMBER: *(interrupting)* I have a zero tolerance policy when it comes to insulting other students. Come back tomorrow.
> CRYSTAL: You can't just—
> AUDIENCE MEMBER: *(interrupting)* Now, please.
> CRYSTAL: I have the right to express my opinion!
> AUDIENCE MEMBER: Not by being insulting.
> CRYSTAL: But—
> AUDIENCE MEMBER: You can leave now or I can have you suspended.
> CRYSTAL: *(exiting in high dudgeon)* I'm getting my dad to call the principal. He's going to get you fired.
> AUDIENCE MEMBER: I'd like to see him try. Good-bye.

In general, I found that the more confident the volunteer was, the more confident my character could be. Incidentally, "I have the right to express my opinion!" was my favorite line to throw at the confident volunteers, because the statement is used by bullies the world over. It is recognized as such, and when I offered the line to smart and secure volunteers, it often resulted in very strong and realistic responses.

I often had the most fun onstage when I found myself outmatched. An audience member would occasionally offer a serious challenge, which I always loved to accept. Such challenges afforded me the opportunity to struggle vigorously, exposing in the process more of my character's true colors and providing the interveners glorious opportunities to take me down a peg. The audience also seemed to have the most fun when watching moments like this unfold:

> CRYSTAL: Look, I'm just saying that we already know this stupid Aboriginal history!

AUDIENCE MEMBER: *(as teacher)* Well, obviously not, young lady,
as you've already failed this class twice.

Luckily, on that occasion, the whoops and applause of the audience were loud enough that I didn't need to come up with an immediate rejoinder. Neither I nor the character could think of one. We just sat there looking shocked and furious, peripherally aware of the audience's glee and cognizant that all of the reactions—from the volunteer, from the audience, and from my fellow actors—were authentic responses to a class bully being called out. In any sort of art, truth is what we strive for, and when you hit it, everyone knows.

Looking back on the show, I am always a little surprised by the number of volunteers who joined us onstage, braving the scrutiny of their fellow audience members. Without these volunteers, we would not have accomplished very much with our show. But up they came, tentatively at first, and then with more confidence and strength of will. Thinking back on it, I realize that by walking onstage they were answering a crucial question. *Will you help? Will you speak up?* Yes. Yes.

All of my worries and fears regarding this project are long over. Looking back, I am tremendously relieved that I made the decision to participate. The skills that I gained, the friends that I made, and the respect that I have come to have for this marvelously audience-trusting form of theatre are all things that I will carry with me for a long time. I have no doubt that the next time I am asked to do something that scares me a little, I will remember this experience and just say "yes."

It makes me laugh now to think back on those frustrated protestations in improv classes: *Can we do something else? Can we do something REAL?* It has taken me several years since my first improv lesson to learn that the "Yes, and . . ." game is very real. I have questioned the principle every step of the way—as did, I'm sure, everyone else in our cast. The answer was always yes. It's the only way to accomplish anything. And in the end, it is what we want to empower our audience to say. *Are there issues that need facing?* Yes, and they can be pretty formidable. *Is it scary to tackle them?* Yes, and sometimes it's tempting to look the other way. *Can we change our views? Can we change our attitudes? Can we change the world?* Yes. Yes. Yes.

And . . .

Note

1. Dialogue from interventions in *No Offense...* has been reproduced to the best of my recollection.

Bibliography

Seham, Amy E. *Whose Improv Is It Anyway? Beyond Second City.* Jackson: University Press of Mississippi, 2001.

By Hook or by Crook! Luring the Oppressor into the Lair

As the project coordinator for the Theatre for Social Justice Institute at Kent State in 2007, my jobs were primarily administrative. Guidelines were agreed upon and set for the planning and implementation of the Institute process. Our Kent team, along with Fringe Benefits' administration, mapped out a detailed schedule and set of expectations that would begin at the time we signed our contract and continue through Fringe Benefits' arrival at Kent State and until the time when the completed pre- and post-show surveys were submitted to Fringe Benefits—from the time we conceived of the idea until the results were tabulated and the numbers were crunched. My team and I worked tirelessly to be sure that the schedule and expectations were met, a diverse representation of participants arrived, copies were made, attendance was taken, food and beverages were served, technology was available, phone calls were made, letters were sent out, and so on. The scaffolded structure of the Institute is precise, consistent, and tested. It is designed to offer groups the best chance to achieve the final objective of reaching and inspiring change among their target audiences through their devised play.

The Kent State Institute participants wanted to respond to recent anti-LGBT hate crimes on campus through our play, *True Lives: I'm a Kent State Freshman*, and to aid in the development of Safe Space for incoming LGBT freshman. To do this, we hoped to reach a target audience of freshmen, primarily straight male freshmen. It was determined, by the collaborating team, that this group would, most likely, be resistant to attending events with LGBT subject matter and would perhaps be hostile toward LGBT students. Immediately following the

Institute, we began strategizing how to locate and entice this target audience into viewing our play.

Among the many jobs of the project coordinator is that of marketing director, both for the Institute and for the final play. It soon became clear to me that my usual marketing methodology would prove to be ineffective in marketing this play. My instinct as a theatre producer and marketing director is to discover and target the audience *most* likely to be interested in the show, then to strategize how to reach and entice that particular audience (rifle-shot marketing), while simultaneously working to reach the general community (scatter-shot marketing) through posters, press releases, and direct mail.[1]

The project needs turned my usual process on its head. First, we were charged with the assignment to reach—to rifle-shoot— the audience *least* likely to come willingly to our show. So, in initial marketing conversations that took place during Day Five of the Institute, we decided that the best practices with regard to this were to (1) make it mandatory (thereby removing the option to self-select *out* of attending) and/or (2) try to avoid signaling the LGBT content of the show (thereby tricking audiences into attending willingly and surprising them with the focus of the show upon their arrival). We needed to get them by hook or by crook, by enticement, force, or deceit—by any means necessary. In spite of the moral implications of baiting our hook with trickery and deceit, we forged ahead bravely.

We agreed that the best time to reach our target audience of freshmen was early in the semester. At this time, members of our target audience were most likely still carrying their prejudices from home and from high school; this might be the time when they would learn to act on their prejudices, thereby increasing the unsafe environment of the campus. However, as they were newly adjusting to campus life, they might also be open to accepting new ideas and information as part of their new culture. Most important, perhaps, before the semester began, these freshmen would be treated to a week of scheduled programming, which could offer us opportunities to lure them in (although we wondered how successful we would be in mandating their attendance at our play). Logistically, we also discovered that, given our performance-space restrictions, we would need to have two separate performances to achieve our goal of reaching five hundred freshmen. Given these circumstances, we decided we would need to bring in our audiences both by hook *and* by crook to get the job done.

The first strategy would be implemented the week before classes started. Part of the university's programming to help freshmen adapt to this "new culture" is a series of events called "Week of Welcome." Freshmen are called to campus before the rest of the students and required to attend a selection of events. A schedule is printed, and freshmen must attend roughly half of the events from the master list. Most of the daytime events are educational (addressing such issues as the differences between high school and college curriculums), while most of the evening events are social (parties and other gatherings) or cultural (art, music, theatre). A select number of events involve diversity (increasing students' awareness and understanding of racial, gender, and sexual difference).

We approached the Week of Welcome committee to ask if our play could be listed as a "Mandatory Event." Despite much painstaking negotiation, we were not able to get the show on that coveted list. Still, the administration was excited to use our play as a "Featured Cultural Event" and thrilled that it would also serve as a "Diversity Event." Two birds . . . We selected a late date and time (Friday evening) directly before the big "night out on the town" when the freshmen were likely to attend parties and break loose. This timing would work in two ways to encourage our target audience to attend: first, as it was near the end of the week, students might be running out of events to fulfill their obligations, and second, they might see it as a perfect launching pad for their Friday night festivities.

To further increase the likelihood that this target audience would attend our event, we informed the Week of Welcome staff about the Institute process and goals and the LGBT content in the show (they were surprisingly eager to support our efforts), but we kept the marketing materials vague regarding the play's content and themes. The flyers and posters featured a variety of students—young, hip, attractive, socializing—with only the title, time, and location mentioned. We were successful at attracting the maximum theatre capacity of 250 freshmen (and others), and the ratio of males to females was surprisingly high. The atmosphere entering the theatre was festive and charged. It was Friday night. The show was well received, and the talkback session and post-show surveys yielded insightful and encouraging commentary. Round One was complete.

The second strategy for reaching our target audience was also embedded in the university's welcoming process for freshmen. As part of their first semester course load, freshmen must take an orientation class titled "First Year Experience" in which they discuss a variety of topics to help them make their transition into the university. Among these topics is diversity. A willing set of instructors who had been informed, in general, about the LGBT script content agreed to include a second performance of our play on the list of cultural activities that they encouraged their students to attend. Once again, the performance was not mandatory, but, as it was positioned early in the semester, with only the aforementioned marketing materials, we were able to fill the house.

This time, too, we suggested to instructors that, for our marketing purposes, they not discuss the event beforehand with their classes. We hoped that our request would be honored, but we could not be certain. Additionally, we were not sure to what extent members of our first audience might "taint" our marketing efforts by warning the target group about the LGBT content, thereby possibly steering them away from attending the second performance. We have reason to think that our "by crook" marketing efforts were not thwarted, however, as, according to the audience survey results, chronicled in detail in Susan Iverson's essay in this volume, the demographics of the second audience were similar to those of the first. Iverson's pre-show surveys also registered a similar profile with regard to LGBT acceptance and support.

All in all, the exercise of purposely recruiting and gathering audience members likely to be least interested in and perhaps most hostile to our show proved to be a positive and rewarding growth experience. We were able to entice our target audience to attend the show by using my usual rifle-shot strategy along with a carefully orchestrated "by hook *and* by crook" marketing campaign. As a result, we were able to dialogue directly with student audience members who were either resistant to or uncertain about our message, as well as to give students in our audience who were allies to the LGBT community a contained and constructive context in which to hear and engage strong voices of dissent. The pathway to promoting social change, however uncomfortable, requires dialogue among people of different minds. While our strategy was somewhat deceitful (by crook) and a bit manipulative (by hook), we feel that we achieved this kind of meeting. We succeeded in bringing people with diverse points of view into the room and created a context in which they could engage each other respectfully and productively. The rest is up to them.

Note

1. These are general marketing concepts often described by a number of different titles. My use of the terms "rifle-shot" and "scatter-shot" extends from John Baldwin's theatre management class at Michigan State University in 1983. For an example of this concept, see the following website: http://xpandmarketing.co.uk/blog/2011/01/10/sniper-rifle-approach-market-segmentation-vs-shot-gun-approach-hit-hope/.

6

A Transformative? and Empowering? Experience

The essays in this chapter consist of reflections about the personal impact of facilitating or participating in a Theatre for Social Justice Institute. Community-based arts projects can move people to examine, reexamine, and rededicate their lives. Some people discover strengths and talents they didn't know they had; others gain tools and inspiration that transform their work and/or their lives. These collaborative efforts can also open or reopen personal, intra-community and inter-community wounds, especially when gaps in the safety net allow conflicting agendas to collide or when promises and/or expectations are not fulfilled. As chapter 3 focuses on activist impact and chapter 4 focuses on Safe Space issues, we have tried not to retread that same turf here; instead, we include essays that problematize the notion of empowerment and/or celebrate the transformative impact on individuals and communities in the context of the Institute.

We open with "The *Wiz*dom of Us: Reconsidering Identities and Affinities through Theatre for Social Justice," which explores how participants' understandings of themselves and others were deconstructed and rebuilt within a group of university students and faculty and well-to-do, working-class, and homeless community members as they worked to devise an anti-classism script. The author, Brooke Kiener, teaches acting, educational theatre, and community-based theatre at Whitworth University in Spokane, Washington, where she served as the project coordinator for the Institute. Kiener paints an exquisitely detailed picture of encounters between individuals with radically different perspectives, some of the ruptures that ensued, and some of the almost shamanic transformations that evolved.

Personal and pedagogical transformations of two thoughtful teaching artists are teased out in the next two essays. Educator and grief/trauma counselor Laura Reed Goodson's "Wade in the Water" is both an elegy and a paean to a North Carolina Institute with homeless

LGBTQ youth, a life-changing event that transformed the writer's perception of the power of social advocacy and change. In "True to the Course: The Learning Curve of a New Teaching Artist," Natalya Brusilovsky vividly and humorously describes her growth as a teaching artist/activist in five journalistic snapshots of challenging moments in the project: when a student threw a projectile at her, when another student took jabs at fellow participants, when a co-facilitator called her out, when the lead actor stormed out of dress rehearsal, and when the audience started jeering. Arrestingly honest, Brusilovsky lays bare her ongoing internal battles to stave off her internal "drill sergeant," remain true to her core values, and create powerful, transformative theatre. A Fringe Benefits company member since 2004, Brusilovsky has co-led Institutes, residencies, and workshops in New Hampshire, Pennsylvania, and California.

The collection ends on a powerful and haunting note with Crystal Grills's "Bricks and Stones: Bashing Back with a Fistful of Words" (written with Flint). On the first day of an Institute, in the presence of thirty-five strangers, Grills, a young, out lesbian from rural Australia, shared her story of being the target of a brutal hate crime. She then worked with the group to dramatize her story in the play *Game On!* As one reads Grills's account, it's difficult to resist wondering what might have happened if Matthew Shepard had lived to contribute his voice to *The Laramie Project*.

The *Wiz*dom of Us: Reconsidering Identities and Affinities through Theatre for Social Justice

BROOKE KIENER

In the winter of 2004, my Whitworth University colleagues and I decided to host a Theatre for Social Justice Institute focusing on issues of socioeconomic discrimination.[1] Our intention was twofold: to create a piece of theatre that would unveil socioeconomic realities in Spokane, and to build bridges between Whitworth and the larger Spokane community.[2]

One of the things Whitworth students experience quite distinctly during their college years is a strong sense of campus community and connection to each other, but they also experience a disconnect from anything beyond the campus. Students joke fondly about living "behind the pinecone curtain" (our campus is covered with pine trees), where they are tightly linked to each other but virtually cut off from the rest of the city. We hoped that the Institute would introduce our students to theatre as a form of activism and also provide an opportunity for them to move beyond this physical and psychological barrier and interact with residents of Spokane.

Without giving away the ending, we did in fact accomplish both goals—our script detailed many of the socioeconomic disparities in Spokane, and the Institute brought together over fifty participants from vastly different backgrounds and neighborhoods and created a space where we could respectfully learn more about each other. Reflecting on the Institute, however, I discovered another thread that I think is an equally important result of the work—students and community members alike were challenged to consider how identities are constructed and negotiated and how they are complex and interconnected rather than singular and isolated. The purpose of this essay is to discuss our Institute, highlighting moments in which identities and affinities were deconstructed and rebuilt within the group. By doing so, I hope to make the case that the act of creating theatre together can be a uniquely powerful activist tool for social justice initiatives.

Story Circle

On the first night of the Institute, fifty students and community members convened in our black box theatre space and were invited to talk about instances of socioeconomic discrimination they had witnessed or experienced. The stories were all incredible—eclectic, personal, and rich in detail. Looking around the circle, it was not uncommon to find mouths gaping, eyes opened wide, heads nodding in agreement or shaking in disbelief. It was a moving experience just to be present in the room and to witness the honesty and vulnerability of total strangers from disparate walks of life. Here are a few of the stories that were shared:

> My family owns a farm, and I've talked to people from more urban settings who seem to expect that my dad is a big, bad employer who is mistreating migrant workers. But my family has worked hard to get where we are, and we all still work really hard. People think we're just this privileged class and that we haven't done anything to deserve it.

> I work for a sexual assault victims' hotline, and I get calls from hospitals to go in and sit with the victims and listen to them and give them information. And I've gotten to the point where, on the phone, right away, I can tell what class the victim comes from, because if it's someone from a lower class, the person at the hospital will call and say, "This person claims they were sexually assaulted," or, "This person says they have been assaulted." But if it is a higher-class person, then they will call and they'll say, "We have a young woman here who is just devastated; she's been sexually assaulted." They are a whole lot nicer about it, and they are like that with the victim too. Somehow they think that the lower-class people deserved it.

> We did a presentation at this hoity-toity affair, and we were talking about welfare reform and telling our personal stories

and how we've been affected. And afterwards, people made comments like, "Oh, we just wish more welfare people were so well spoken. You're so special!" And I know this lady is trying to compliment me, but why doesn't it feel good? It was like she wanted to keep her own stereotypes in her head, not reexamine or confront those stereotypes, but just look at me as a special exception so she can keep thinking about welfare recipients the way she always has.[3]

I was impressed right away by the level of engagement in the group; it seemed obvious that people needed to tell these stories, to hear and be heard. But as the night went on, I also became peripherally aware of a widening gap. As the community members became more activated, empowered by the act of speaking their truth, a resistance started to surface among some of the students who, as you might expect, tended to come from more privileged backgrounds. Similarly, community members sometimes responded to student stories dismissively, arguing that their points of view were uninformed or naive. I want to be clear that this was not a clean divide—there were many students and community members who did not display resistance or dismissiveness. My intention isn't to criticize or "villainize" one side or the other; rather, I hope to point out that from the very start, the play-building process was both creating ruptures *and* sewing sutures in our individual and group identities.

Charting Identities

On the first night of the Institute, in addition to inviting story sharing, we asked participants to create a bubble diagram detailing their key identities.[4] At the center of the diagram was the participant's name, and then extending from that center were words or symbols that represented the roles, characteristics, or other descriptors that made up his or her identities. One of the participants, "Martha," displaying her diagram, introduced herself by telling us the story of her people and her family: "In the center of my molecule, I put 'Tsuts Poo'; that's my grandmother's name from my mother's side of the family. I am a strong Nimi'ipuu *ayat*[5] [pronounced *nee-mee-poo eye-it*], which means I am a strong woman. I am a descendant of Chief Joseph. Those are in my center. In my bubbles around it, I put I am traditional, energetic, love-in-motion, forgiven, educated, mother of six adult children, and grandmother of twelve." Later in the evening, she further explained her background:

> I've been in this community for several years. I've had to argue with caseworkers about my treaty rights. I became a social worker. And to me as a traditional Indian woman, those credentials behind my name, it's like, so what? Now what's next? Because for me and my people, our status is about where we are at in that sacred Medicine Wheel. Where are we mentally, emotionally, spiritually, and physically? And I'm entering into the fourth cycle—elder. I appreciate my education and everything, but what's most important to me is education and culture. And to keep active in the community. I go to these community meetings, and I feel like the cinnamon dot in a bowl of milk. Where are my brothers and sisters; where are the people of color in these different communities? Sometimes I feel like the Lone Ranger. I look like Tonto, but I feel like the Lone Ranger.

I have to admit that I didn't understand all of this at first. Her narrative structure was unlike mine, and I didn't always see the connection between her thoughts. And I observed others in the room who were uncomfortable with Martha's point of view. At the conclusion of our first session, the participants were each given an opportunity to make one final remark regarding their hopes and concerns for the project. One of the first students to speak challenged Martha's perspective:

> Okay, I hope this won't be offensive, but I think it's important that we make sure that we focus on what we want to learn. And not that we disregard what we've learned from our past, but we can't control what happened to us, or what our ancestors did to other people or what they experienced. So I hope that we can focus on what we want our children to have and the legacy we want to leave for them.

A few minutes later, when the tape recorder passed into her hands, Martha responded, unfazed:

> I personally am a reminder from the Northern-Western European's past. And I'm going to stay on that path, as long as I live. And I hope that by me speaking out about all this Indian-versus-Northern-European people/dominant society, about being

an invisible nation within a nation, I hope people hear that. Because whose land are we walking on? We're walking on the bones of others. And I love pushing people's buttons and getting them heated up because they get defensive, y'know? That's good! Because it's time for change. Conflict means change. You have to look at your past before you can go forward. I'm not here to hurt your feelings or your historical background, but that's what people need to look at, their history! I'm recovering from historical, generational greed, oppression, everything we're talking about. Me and my people are recovering from that.

The exchange was respectful, but there was tension in the air. On the drive home that night, I thought about the visual image of the bubble diagram, all of those lines extending from the center, creating a web of identity that is interconnected and overlapping. I began to realize that it would be impossible to isolate our discussion of socioeconomics apart from the other histories, beliefs, and assumptions held by individuals in the group. Racial identities and spiritual beliefs had already come to the surface and were complicating (in a positive way!) our activity of writing a play together.

Blurring the Lines

On the second night of the Institute (and for the rest of the week), the group shrank, as expected, from fifty to between fifteen and twenty participants.[6] This smaller number created a more intimate setting, and we intentionally provided more opportunities for exploring identity and building affinity. We began this second night with a cultural mapping game called "Come to My Island" in which participants took turns inviting others to "Come to my island if you . . ." and then offering an identifier. We started with a simple, noncontroversial invitation: "Come to my island if you like chocolate ice cream!" The participants rushed to join the speaker, enjoying this lighthearted common ground. As expected, the invitations moved toward deeper convictions and more emotionally charged material. At one point, a Whitworth student invited people to "Come to my island if you have accepted Jesus Christ to be your Lord and Savior." All of the participants except for Martha and the two Fringe Benefits Institute co-facilitators joined her. We suddenly had a very clear image of another divide that was present in the group. I can only speculate about what participants on either side may have been thinking during this moment, but I can imagine that both sides worried about being judged by the other. In any case, this theatrical activity revealed, or established, majority/minority distinctions and alliances among the participants, thus creating and disrupting power and status structures in the group while also drawing our attention directly to those structures.

Later that evening, the participants engaged in an Image Theatre[7] activity, through which they physically depicted current tensions among and rifts between local socioeconomic groups and explored literal and symbolic first steps toward bridging those divisions. After each step, each participant articulated one thing his or her character might be thinking in terms of a motivation to take that first step. When it was Martha's turn, she murmured, "Creator, bless them." The facilitators urged her on—"Keep going." Martha then pulled a feather out of her pocket and waved it over the various participants who were frozen in the sculptural image: "Creator, bless this young lady's feet. Bless her heart that lifts the heaviness. Bless her female organs so that she has healthy babies. Same with this young man, soften his mind and his heart, help him to help people, give back some of what he has to share. Creator, bless this young lady that she learns what she's learning and she goes out and teaches what she learns. And bless all these young women and men here, that what they learn here today they will take and continue to teach others." The air in the room was thick with emotion. I was so overwhelmed I could hardly breathe. At the beginning of the blessing, I could feel that some of the students were uncomfortable—*Is she praying to the same god I pray to, and if not, what does this all mean?* They shifted in their frozen positions and waited to see what would happen next. But as she continued, I sensed a shift in the group, overcome and humbled by her heartfelt prayer. We had expressed frustration and disbelief toward her, and she had pushed back, insisting on her territory. But now she was taking a different tactic; any skepticism or resistance that she had perceived from the group did not stop her from revealing her true intentions—*Creator, bless them.*

Wizdom at Last?

Early in the process, a student remark during a debriefing session gave us an idea for a structural concept for the play. In essence, she said that her image of Spokane was being shattered and her eyes were opening up to a new city that she didn't know existed. "You're not in Kansas anymore!" another participant joked. And from this simple reference to *The Wizard of Oz*, our script was born. We titled it *The Wizdom of SpokOZ* and loosely structured our plot around a college student who gets lost in a strange new city and tries to find her way home with the help of some new friends. Participants worked on individual scenes in groups of four or five, which were intentionally diversified so that each group had a mixture of community and university members as well as diverse ethnicities and genders.

In our script, "Dorothea" is a Whitworth student who comes from a less privileged family than her new dorm-mates. One evening, she falls asleep on an on-campus bench and wakes up in downtown Spokane, where "Tsuts Poo," a Native American woman, helps her find a path that will lead her to "*Wizdom*." The Scarecrow is a multi-degreed homeless man in a soup kitchen line; his character is based primarily on the experiences of an African American man who came to most of the workshops and talked about being black, unemployed, and invisible. The Lion is a working-class citizen on a picket line outside of a Walmart-type organization, again based on a regular attendee, a white woman who talked about her experiences with government-subsidized healthcare organizations. The Tin Man is a corporate CEO who cuts checks for a never-ending line of open hands but feels he is cut off from his family and the people he is trying to help. This character is based on the stories of a white Whitworth student who talked about her dad and how much he worked when she was growing up so that she and her siblings could go to college.

On the final night of the Institute, we handed out scripts and read through the latest draft of our collaborative work. Then, as was our habit, we passed the tape recorder around and shared our thoughts. At first, the mood was celebratory: everyone seemed pleased with the work and impressed that we had actually created a complete play. And then a student, reaching for the tape recorder and clearing her throat, referenced a line from the Scarecrow scene:

> DESIREE: *(transgender, male-to-female, wearing tasteful feminine attire)* Heck, I can't get a job! And this is practically the only charity that doesn't turn me away. I was at Good News Mission and I blew this guy a kiss, and they kicked me out—blacklisted me! At Urban Ministries, they make

you pray to Jesus before they'll let you have a meal—and I was raised Jewish! And they won't even let me in the door at Auburn Hall, 'cuz they don't see me as a woman! I just wish people would accept me for who I am![8]

This piece of the script (as is true of roughly 90 percent of the script) was taken directly from a personal story, shared by one of the many participants. But the student with the recorder was incensed:

I have a real concern over the character Desiree and the part where we name the Good News Mission and we say that at Urban Ministries they make you pray to Jesus before they let you have a meal. Urban Ministries is a church and so it's part of their mission and part of what they do. And I totally support them and what they do. And I think to name them in the script and to put them down in that way can only harm them, and I don't think it can do them any good. And I think if that's what they're about, that's great, and I don't think that we should be putting them down. And I don't think that's in line with Whitworth's mission, either.

The mood in the room instantly changed, and the next thirty minutes were dedicated to the discussion of this one passage. Some thought the passage should be dropped because it misrepresented the church-based charities in our community; others thought the passage was necessary because it showed an unfair gap in services. Some participants suggested that fictionalizing the names of the charities would solve the issue, but this was still offensive to group members opposing the passage, and they re-entrenched, insisting that if we included this story we should also include a story about all of the good that faith-based organizations do; otherwise, our play was contrary to the college's mission to "honor God, follow Christ, and serve humanity." Again we found ourselves in the midst of a learning moment about the interconnectivity of identity, as some of the participants argued that the socioeconomic issues were eclipsed by naming the religion and sexual orientation of the character—"Our play isn't supposed to be about religion," one student commented, "but this passage makes a strong statement about it. I think we should cut the line." This suggestion of paring down the character's identity to a single identifier made sense to many participants, but others (including myself and the facilitators) advocated for the complexity of the "identity web" that we'd explored on the first night of the Institute. Ultimately, we left the decision to the group.

Mindful of the group's energy and that time was slipping by, we sent the participants back into small groups to work on rewrites for individual scenes and asked them also to submit any suggested rewrites for this particular passage. The majority of their rewrites omitted the names of the charities and changed the transgendered character to a gay character who does not mention his religion. Ultimately, the line came to read:

> MATT: You can't get a job, but half of the time I can't even get a meal. This is practically the only charity that doesn't turn me away because I'm gay. At one religious halfway house, I blew this guy a kiss and one of the directors saw it and they kicked me out—blacklisted me! I'm turned away at most of the religious charities in town now.[9]

For the most part, participants were happy with this compromise, though I did get two remarks on my teaching evaluation that the Institute and the script we created expressed views that were not in line with the mission of the college. The academic dean (who had been very supportive of the Institute and had provided partial funding) emailed me asking for an explanation; I gave her as much information as I could and sent her a copy of the script. We discussed the two student comments, and she reassured me that Whitworth's mission invites both intellectual curiosity and Christian conviction and that the complaints seemed to be attempting to invoke the authority of the college's mission without actually being willing to engage in a discussion of how it might be interpreted and lived out in different ways. I was grateful for *her* wisdom on this matter.

Moving Forward

The questions asked and lessons learned from this Institute about identity and community building are still very much at play in my work. I've facilitated several community-based theatre projects at Whitworth in the last nine years, each full of their own challenges and triumphs.[10] And sometimes I feel as if the mile markers are too few and far between. I often have to remind myself that my own journey toward wisdom has been incremental, sometimes stalled, and still very much incomplete. It's unrealistic for me to expect students or audiences to encounter a perspective radically different from their own and to integrate it fully and immediately into their understanding of the world. I can only ask them to pay careful attention to the new information that they are given, not to ignore it or look away from it. I can only try to create enough safety within the theatrical experience that they will risk stepping inside another character's shoes and attempt to see the world as they do. And I can only hope that the experience will create empathy, understanding, and new perspectives.

I still think about Martha. Quite often, in fact. The memory of this woman, so secure in herself and her beliefs, offering a sincere and heartfelt blessing for people whom she barely knew, inspires me to be generous and compassionate toward everyone whom I encounter, *especially* if their stories challenge or disrupt my own narratives. When I become frustrated—as an educator, as an activist, as a person of faith, or simply as a human being on this slowly spinning planet—I try to remember to pray a prayer similar to the blessing that Tsuts Poo offers Dorothea in our script, when she first meets her on the banks of the Spokane River:

> Have faith, Dorothea; the Creator blesses your journey. *(She begins to slowly circle Dorothea, waving her feather, blessing her.)* The Creator blesses your eyes that you may go forth without the veil that has blinded you; blesses your ears that you may hear truth; blesses your mouth that only truth shall cross your lips; blesses your shoulders that you may continue to stand tall and strong, even when the sharp arrows of self-doubt come at you; blesses your heart that it may remain pure and good; blesses your feet, 'cuz girl, they're gonna get tired. I hope you've got good shoes!

Notes

1. Whitworth is a private, residential liberal arts institution affiliated with the Presbyterian Church (USA) and located in Spokane, Washington. Whitworth's mission is to provide its diverse student body an education of the mind and the heart, equipping its graduates to honor God, follow Christ, and serve humanity. This mission is carried out by a community of Christian scholars committed to rigorous intellectual inquiry and to the integration of faith and learning.

2. We were motivated to focus on socioeconomic discrimination in part because of a recent study that found Spokane County had a higher poverty rate (13.7 percent) than Washington state (11.9 percent) or the United States (12.5 percent). For more information, see the report "Facing Spokane Poverty, 2001–2002." This

report is can be found in WorldCat; copies are available through the Spokane Public Library.

3. Throughout this article, quotes from participants in the workshop are taken verbatim from the tape recordings that were made during the Institute. Names have been changed to preserve the confidentiality that was promised to participants.

4. This activity was based on an Anti-Defamation League diversity-awareness exercise.

5. The Nimi'ipuu were later named the "Nez Perce Indians" by the Lewis and Clark expeditions; *ayat* is the Nez Perce word for "woman."

6. Finding community participants was challenging as most people were too busy to commit to an entire week of evenings, so I decided to aim for critical mass at the first session, an evening devoted primarily to story sharing, even though many individuals couldn't come back during the rest of the week.

7. For more information about Image Theatre, Augusto Boal, and his Theatre of the Oppressed techniques (which Fringe Benefits regularly uses in its work), see Boal's *Games for Actors and Non-Actors.*

8. The names of the charities in this quote have been fictionalized.

9. All script segments quoted in this article are from our January 2004 final draft of *The Wizdom of SpokOZ* (unpublished).

10. In fact, my most recent community-based project was to share "*Wiz*dom" with the Spokane community. In the spring of 2012, over eight years after the Institute, I was able to reconvene two of the original workshop participants (including Martha) to work with a new group of students and community partners to stage the script. The premier performance of the retitled script, Wiz*dom: Making Dollars and Sense,* took place on May 6, 2012, in Spokane and was attended by over 200 people.

Bibliography

Boal, Augusto. *Games for Actors and Non-Actors.* New York: Routledge, 1992.

Wade in the Water

LAURA REED GOODSON

I sat on the edge of my seat, five rows from the stage, as the members of Sweet Honey in the Rock sang about wading into the water. Bernice Johnson Regan, with her African robes flowing down, leaned toward her audience of Oberlin College students. She said: "Go on, wade on in the water, but it's going to really be troubled water. And know this—once you have crossed that water, you will be different." I liked the sound of that. I thought about it a lot, that year when I turned twenty, and a great deal since then, though I only recently began to understand it. I have crossed my own rivers in the interim, some of them filled with profound suffering. However, what has most changed me has been reaching out to others who have suffered, wading into the troubled water of others' stories about coming out and coming of age. Wade on in this water with me, and I will show you what I mean.

My first fall break at Oberlin, I couldn't afford to go home to North Carolina, so I hung around on campus. I had made two friends in the Conservatory of Music who were just "coming out." One was a beautiful tenor named Jimmy.[1] He went home that fall break to see his parents, but halfway through the week, he appeared back at campus, utterly despondent. He said that he'd come out to his parents and that they had kicked him out of the house. So, he had come back to campus because he didn't know where else to go. We talked for a while. I told him, "Jimmy, I don't understand how your parents can treat you like this. But they'll come around; I'm sure they will. You're an extraordinary human being! *Don't you ever forget what you have!*" He seemed to get calmer, and he assured me he'd call if he needed anything. I figured he'd be okay. That Friday, news traveled through the grapevine that he'd committed suicide.

The same day that Jimmy committed suicide, my other new friend, Alex, came back to campus. He'd been kicked out of his home, too! I remember spending hours with him. I wouldn't let him be by himself. Even when he went to sleep, I stayed in his room. I could still hear Jimmy's voice in the conservatory halls for a long time after that. Other singers would be practicing, and I could have sworn it was him.

Twenty years later, a board member contacted me from an advocacy organization called Time Out Youth (TOY) to ask that I direct a theatre project to help raise money for its emergency housing program serving lesbian, gay, bisexual, and transgender (LGBT) youth. She assured me that I didn't need to worry; this would be a collaboration with Fringe Benefits, and experienced facilitators would be coming from California to run the workshops and get this project going. I was completely unconvinced. I thought: "I'm a straight middle-aged white woman—what do I know about youth who identify as lesbian, gay, bisexual, or transgender? Why would they listen to me?" But then I thought of Jimmy and Alex and several other gay friends I had known who had been rejected by their families. And I thought about the heart-opening power of theatre, a transformative power that I'd witnessed and experienced time and time again in my twenty years working as a director, actor, vocal coach, and playwright. Also, no one had bothered to warn me that Norma Bowles can talk anyone into doing anything! I agreed to help.

Norma and her collaborator, Cynthia Ruffin, came to Charlotte to lead five workshops in which youth and adults from our area who identified as LGBT or as allies shared their stories about coming out, getting kicked out of their homes, living on the streets, facing prejudice, finding humor, and seeking love or acceptance. Both women put the participants at ease and drew them out through role-playing and writing and by using prompts or games. We all heard stories that made us pale with rage and sick to our stomachs. So many of the stories centered around individuals growing up gay in the Bible Belt, being judged by religious family members, enduring verbal and physical abuse from family, friends, and strangers, and getting thrown out of their own homes. I spoke about what had happened to my friend Jimmy. One man described being chased and beaten when he was walking down the sidewalk in Chapel Hill. Another young man described the exorcism his family and church had subjected him to when he came out. As we sat together in the basement of a Lutheran church, I realized we had waded into troubled water . . . and there was no turning back. We brainstormed and role-played and cried and laughed together. We sat together, adults and youth, encircled to hold each other steady within the rushing tide of hate, anger, regret, joy, and pain that flowed out as each person recounted his or her tale of growing up, coming out, being rejected, and finding hope. Norma and Cynthia guided us through these waters, sure-footed, kind, and valiant.

My husband, Paul, and I agreed to codirect the play and asked friends who had performed in shows with us before to participate, along with two youth from TOY. I integrated several positive stories from the cast to balance the script and honor their experiences as well. About half of the cast identified as LGBT; the other half identified as allies. The group included a number of experienced actors who embraced the stories in the script. Several of the actors, especially Vito Abate, formerly with the Denver Playhouse, contributed invaluable suggestions about how to improve the script.

We met in the church basement, in TOY's office, in living rooms, at the theatre, and in a sound studio, where we recorded a series of homophobic slurs sounding like whispered threats to help the audience know how it feels to grow up surrounded by hate and prejudice. We also recorded a series of loving words for the end of the play. The artistic director of the Actor's Theatre helped us set up huge speakers behind the risers so that the audience would feel as if they were surrounded by the whispered words.

Our friend who was a lighting designer agreed to help Paul set the lights at no charge. Paul did the blocking, and I worked with the actors and continued editing as needed. The two young actors with little previous theatre experience were apprehensive, so I worked with them in separate sessions until they felt more assured. The experienced actors encouraged them, mentored them, and continued to help us rework and stage the show. Another former TOY youth, Gordon, agreed to sing "Ave Maria" during the story about my college friend, Jimmy. There was a strange, wonderful energy that continued to flow through every rehearsal. As a group, we had decided that this had to work. We had to do justice to these stories. So many people came together to help us honor them. So we waded forward together, holding each other up as we became weary or worried about being ready in time.

And then—oh Mother of God!—it was time . . . all of the workshops, writing, editing, rehearsing, hoping, fretting, and losing sleep came down to this. I sat five rows back, blinking in the dark just as I had when Sweet Honey in the Rock had performed at Oberlin. The stories rolled over us like a mighty stream in whispers, tears, and song. On the first night, the theatre was filled with people who seemed to love the show. Several youth from TOY answered questions during the post-performance talkback session. They were fierce, brave, and honest voices, answering questions directly, no matter how hard they were. And then . . . something wonderful happened. The next night, we sold out, and the audience consisted of many people who had never heard of TOY. People had heard about the show and wanted to know more. Of the people who took the time to fill out our surveys at the end of both shows, *96 percent* said that we had changed their minds about the role of TOY and its emergency housing project.[2] Our cast was so proud of what we had achieved. I realized as we stood on the stage and bowed together that we had waded into the water, reached the other side, and had all been profoundly changed.

One of the most wonderful elements of this process was that everyone who was touched by it seemed to have felt this change, and it continued to have a lasting positive influence. The youth and adults who shared their stories came away feeling heard, validated, and supported. Every cast member said they loved doing the show and wanted to do it again. Two of the actors became long-term mentors for TOY and have continued to do theatre projects for the organization. Both of the TOY youth who acted in the show went on to bigger theatre projects with more confidence and better acting skills. We raised money and support for the emergency housing program, and I, along with many audience members, became a steadfast supporter of Time Out Youth. Our stories, our script, and our production had galvanized all of this love, support, and transformation.

Creating and directing the show was a profoundly transformative experience for me as well. Aside from giving birth to my son, Noah, those two nights of theatre are what I am most proud of in the last three decades of my life. I am proud because Norma was right—it was good work, and it was not about me. It was about the brave honesty of the youth; the creative skill of the writers, cast, and crew; the energy of creation; and, most of all, the stories of suffering, strength, and courage. These young people who had been cast off by family or friends and forced to grow up too soon taught us an amazing lesson about the transformative power of theatre.

For me, it was also about expressing my grief for voices that had been silenced too soon. The stories that we shared, heard, and honored taught me so many lessons in humility, compassion, endurance, and acceptance. I learned that, while I will never completely understand what it is like to grow up gay or to live with prejudice every day of your life, I can go on wading in, reaching out, and lifting up those who have suffered. I can continue to try to understand and to be open to change. I am finishing a master's program in counseling with a focus on helping veterans and gay youth heal their trauma through writing, music, and theatre. I would encourage anyone to embrace opportunities to wade into similar waters. But know this—you *will* be different when you reach the other side.

Notes

1. To protect their privacy, I have fictionalized my college friends' names.

2. Quantitative evaluation about audience feedback and support is based on Debra Wiesenberger, "*Is Somebody Out There?* Audience Post-Show Survey Report," June 27, 2006 (unpublished).

True to the Course: The Learning Curve of a New Teaching Artist

NATALYA BRUSILOVSKY

It hit me squarely in the head. Everything stopped. Everyone held their breath. It was just a paper ball, but I felt embarrassed, intimidated, and at a loss for words.

From the moment I met the students in my project-recruitment presentation at Woodrow Wilson High School in East Los Angeles, my sincerity and strength, along with my commitment to tackling discrimination, were under scrutiny. After the paper ball was thrown at me, I hesitated, unsure of how best to handle the situation. I could ignore the behavior and concentrate on inspiring others in the room to tackle discrimination through our theatre project. But my instincts told me to address the young man and attempt to model the patience and thoughtfulness that I was there to promote. I bent over, picked up the paper ball, shrugged, and winked—making them laugh—and stuffed the ball into my pocket, as if I had just won a prize. Then, as candidly, honestly, and respectfully as possible, I asked the class how often they witnessed this type of bullying behavior or worse. Then I explained that this was precisely why their school wanted to host a Theatre for Social Justice (TSJ) Institute, to address bullying and intimidation and to help create a safer environment. My strategy of directly—but gently—addressing what was happening in the room ended successfully. I even gained the young ball-thrower's respect: he ended up participating in the project and was the only brave freshman to remain through the entire playwriting process and production.

What does it take to stay authentic and true to the course as we work to effect changes in policy or behavior in communities? In this essay, I will explore how authenticity affects the work we do—how remaining true to core values, while strategizing a variety of approaches, will lead to a more compelling, powerful, and meaningful product. I will delve into this topic through an investigation of some challenging moments I encountered while coleading a TSJ Institute in a public high school with a diverse group of staff and students. I hope to paint a picture of how striving for authenticity is the best way to stay true to the course and to propel the work forward.

Once we had a preliminary understanding of the level of violence and fear that LGBTQ students experienced, we worked with the new Gay-Straight Alliance (GSA) faculty advisor to determine the goals of the project. We wanted to help build and strengthen the GSA and, most important, to inspire Wilson's students and staff to be more tolerant toward and respectful of LGBTQ and allied students, thereby creating a safer environment for all.[1] To realize our ambitious goals, we agreed to create a show that would reach the relatively diverse audience of the school's students. We wanted to reflect in our script and on stage the diversity of vernaculars, cultures, interests, and perspectives of the student body and thus needed to recruit a similarly diverse group for the project.

Following our outreach efforts, students showed up for many reasons. Some responded to our flyers because they or their good friends identified as LGBTQ. Drama Club members wanted to check out this new way of creating plays. Emerging artists came to perform. Others were recruited by teachers who saw their dramatic flair or spark for social justice. Thanks to thoughtful planning, effective recruitment, and administrators' support, we had an excited and dynamic group of students, each with his or her particular style, subculture, and interests, ready to tackle anti-LGBTQ discrimination at Wilson through theatre.

The TSJ Institute participants decided that the play should take place at a fictional high school where harassment of students and teachers who are, or who appeared to be, LGBTQ is normalized and generally ignored. At the turning point of the play, a smart, popular quarterback comes out to his equally popular cheerleader girlfriend. Their conversation is overheard by a fellow "jock" who, along with several friends, ambushes and severely beats the young man. (This plot was inspired by a true story, shared by one of the participants.) We titled the piece *We Are Who We Are*.

Goths vs. Jocks vs. Outcasts and Beyond

The focus of one dramaturgical discussion was whether or not our play was vilifying the cheerleaders and "jocks" and glorifying the "goth" characters. The tension began to build between students in the room as we navigated creative ideas from scathing satire to nuanced drama. Vera,[2] a strong-willed, often-harassed Middle Eastern sophomore, asserted, "I don't dress slutty and ridiculously trendy so that everyone can think I'm popular. I'm just me." Upon hearing this indirect insult to the "jock" allies in the room, two young ladies began to visibly disengage— shrunken soldiers, heads down.

The hurtful, demeaning language at Wilson that we hoped to address in our play was rearing its ugly head among us. Had I created this kind of prejudiced environment? Should I just stay silent, allowing the moment to pass, so as not to risk being ostracized as the "everything-must-be-PC" teaching artist? If I don't say anything, would Vera's comment compromise our alliance and undermine our ability to work together? On the other hand, might naming the problem make the situation worse by embarrassing the young ladies or by shaming Vera?

My "gentle warrior" spirit quickly took over, and I recited a personal mantra, "To each their own—everyone has their own style." Vera nodded when she understood that insults would not be allowed the room, and the others smiled and sat up again. I was grateful that the awkward moment did not last long. The impact of this little act of solidarity managed to get the group's creative flow back on track. The students decided to create empathy for all the characters, to depict the beautiful range of complexities present in all human beings.

Lily Called Me Out

The program was well resourced with two main facilitators, several faculty and staff liaisons, and two interns. However, when my co-facilitator's illness forced her to leave the program midway through rehearsals, I became anxious. I took over directing the play and coordinating all production aspects for a few days while training Lily, a former TSJ student-turned-intern, to manage the play's production team. I was doing my best to move forward and stay alert and positive while "leading the troops" through our rehearsal frenzy. We still needed to choreograph a cheer, paint a set, and silkscreen T-shirts . . . and students were busy flirting instead of learning their lines! During one particularly chaotic rehearsal, Lily took me aside and hesitantly explained that my tone was too harsh and my nervousness was becoming contagious—I needed to fix it immediately.

We are not always so lucky as to have a Lily around, someone capable of accessing the maturity it takes to tell a former teacher and current supervisor the truth. When it happens, how do we step back, find grace, and move along, all while contending with the strict time constraints of producing a show? Lily was paying attention to the end goals, and she also understood that the necessary stability to create and perform together and the confidence to facilitate a strong post-show discussion were at stake. Lily stayed true to the course, to the goals, AND to the process and kept her authentic desire to do right by this school as her number-one priority—even if it meant calling me out.

I was confronted by the inconsistency of my own "social justice soldier" persona versus my dedication to being a nurturing ally. My background is such that I sometimes have to fight the inclination to become a zealous dictator, especially in stressful moments. I thanked Lily for her courage and leadership and moved on with a much lighter tone. We had to get to the destination as a team, not as enemies.

Fear Can Paralyze

It was a week before the show, and we were in dress rehearsals. This is a time when, traditionally, actors and crew begin to have doubts, and internal drama ensues. Oscar, the GSA president and one of our lead actors, wanted to quit the show. He abruptly stopped mid-scene, marched off the stage, and sat alone in the back of the auditorium.

Losing the GSA president, the spokesperson for LGBTQ students, would put the primary goals of our project in jeopardy! Moreover, Oscar was our liaison to the administration. If the GSA president left and wasn't going to stand up for his right to a safe education, who was? Perhaps other participants would quit as well. Even if no one else quit, our work might lose legitimacy. Worse still, other GSA members and other marginalized students might not feel strong enough after the show to stand up for themselves. If students didn't feel empowered as a result of our work, were we wasting our time? I had to address this immediately. I asked Lily to take over the rehearsal, and I walked with Oscar to the backstage area to talk.

He opened with a brief personal narrative, detailing how he didn't like his role, he was missing his friends, and his school work was suffering. I listened carefully and asked if he was afraid of having to defend his sexuality to his schoolmates. He responded by painting a dismal picture of violence and retaliation from family, peers, and faculty. I froze, remembering my own youth, then reluctantly admitted my own uncertainties about the possible effects of our project. Then I drew us into the present moment, where twenty peers waited in rehearsal for his return, school faculty had helped us organize four assembly performances, and his parents had signed a waiver form supporting his decision to join the TSJ group. Finally, since he had already drawn a fairly complete picture of the worst-case scenario, together we worked on visualizing a best-case scenario of accomplishing our lofty goals to change school culture. I reminded him that, as a well-respected and well-liked student leader, he could be a powerful advocate for respect and could inspire others to join him. After our long talk and a short silence, Oscar rejoined the cast and announced his decision to stay.

Where's the Safety Net?

During all four of our performances of We Are Who We Are, *at the moment in the play when the football player comes out as gay, the audience jeered, practically tearing down the roof with excitement and shouting. I had a sinking feeling that the audience wanted to see blood.*

The riotous responses were evidence of the intolerance some students must endure just to go to school. The school was, in fact, not safe for LGBTQ students. Was it a majority of Wilson students who acted out against their LGBTQ peers? Was it mainly the "jocks"? Or was it *everyone*? I looked around the packed cafeteria to get a fuller understanding of the reactions. Many seemed pressured into jeering along with the loudest bullies. And yet there was one show during which a student hit a shouting bully in the shoulder with her purse. The hollering lasted five minutes.

In preparation for such a response, as the starting point for our post-show discussions, we asked the students in the audience to raise their hands if they had witnessed or experienced anti-LGBTQ behavior on their campus similar to what they had seen in the play. Many, many hands were raised. We then asked the students to clarify how their understanding of LGBTQ experiences related to the characters' experiences. We also invited them to share how the play affected their perspectives. Some empathized with the characters, others continued to vocalize their disdain toward LGBTQ people, and many remained silent or whispered among themselves. When one student cited the Bible as a reason for his refusal to accept the LGBTQ community, Vera responded quickly. She took the microphone, reminded everyone of the title of the play, and explained that "no matter what you believe, everyone deserves a safe school." Another TSJ participant quoted AB-537.[3] The ninety-minute discussion following each performance provided an opportunity for everyone to express their varying perspectives and created common ground.

I'm happy to report that—with the exception of the shouting bully who was hit in the shoulder with a purse—no one got hurt on the days of the assemblies. And when we returned months later for an end-of-year celebration, we found out that no one had been hurt or harassed in relation to the show at all.

Nevertheless, I still find myself questioning how best to define the nature and scope of my role and my responsibilities as the facilitator of a TSJ project. My primary responsibility as a lead facilitator of the Wilson project was to guide the development of a play and post-show discussion designed to foster constructive dialogue about school safety. The students, brave enough to tell true stories from their hearts, wanted to see genuine safety at school and risked their own safety and social acceptance by working on this project to achieve it. My colleagues and I did our best to supply the students with the appropriate tools to achieve their goals as effectively and as safely as possible. We sought to empower them with an expanded vocabulary to cut through the confusion of bullying, harassment, and discrimination and to create a powerful, transformative theatre and activism experience. But what happens if our work doesn't lead to constructive dialogue or to the creation of a safer campus? And what happens after we leave? Is it our responsibility to keep the kids safe beyond our program? If so, how do we go about ensuring their safety?

Although it's impossible to hold precious teenagers in safe bubbles as they travel to their adulthood, we did our best to work with them to assemble alliances among peers and adults and to develop a range of strategies for dealing with bias and discrimination, including policies and laws they could invoke when necessary.

In our play, we directly addressed the issue of faculty ignoring harassment of LGBTQ youth. This resulted in the principal taking responsibility and demonstrating her solidarity during the discussion, promising to hold faculty accountable for student safety. To rally additional support for the youth, Fringe Benefits invited LGBTQ allies from the community to attend the performances. ACLU lawyers, school board members, educators, friends, and neighbors strengthened our position by bearing witness to the recurring cycle of hate that can undermine a student's ability to achieve. Their presence helped legitimize the struggle for acceptance and validated theatre as a tool to move toward solutions. Perhaps their presence also confirmed the abundant support for LGBTQ youth not only on campus but in the greater community as well.

Continuing on the Path

The Wilson High School project was one of three TSJ Institutes that I co-led. In each of these Institutes, we set out to create and present theatre that changes discriminatory behavior, sometimes even policies and laws. I believe we can move toward these goals more effectively when we aim for authenticity in the process, doing our best to remain consistent with our values, purposeful in strategizing, and committed to our goals . . . never letting up.

As I charge through my current work, I attempt to continue on this path of authenticity. I try to approach difficult situations with empathy, equanimity, flexibility, and a sense of humor rather than confront them like a drill sergeant. When I do feel the need to "soldier up" or to speak up for others, I do my best to listen carefully and address concerns instead of immediately becoming defensive or punitive. I try to approach worst-case scenario planning by utilizing all possible facets of imagination and courage. I hope to continue to expand my understanding and to build on the whispers of the unheard until a community of honesty and dignity can model positive change authentically.

Maybe I should keep a paper ball in my pocket as a reminder, just in case.

Notes

1. It is important to note that both self-identified and *perceived* LGBTQ students were experiencing harassment (or worse) at school, even though they were

supposed to be protected by the California Student Safety and Violence Prevention Act of 2000. California State Legislature, CA Education Code Section 220, AB-537, Sacramento, CA, October 10, 1999, http://www.cde.ca.gov/re/lr/sv/.

2. To protect anonymity, I have fictionalized all names.

3. See note 1 for more information about AB-537.

Bricks and Stones: Bashing Back
with a Fistful of Words

CRYSTAL GRILLS WITH FLINT

I came to the Institute because I was pissed off, and I wanted to put my two-cents in with people who were working to find a way to put a stop to all the bullshit and hassles LGBT people deal with just for being gay. I used to be quite shy, and I didn't expect to tell my story—certainly not to a roomful of strangers where the only familiar face was my mum's. I'd already come out to her, and she'd come around to being really understanding and supportive, but there were some things I'd never told her.

I think something strange happens when people who don't know each other share similar experiences and come together for a common reason, and I found myself saying things I never thought I'd say. I think the Institute was a safe place for me to speak, as well as a safe place for Mum to hear, in a way that could never have happened between the two of us alone, with shame and blame always getting in the way. With the group there, neither of us could take things too personally, and Mum wasn't put in the position of having to respond right off the bat. She could take in the information and just sit with it, and nobody—including me—would read her silence the wrong way. We were all just following the Institute guidelines, speaking in turn, one at a time around the circle.

The stories just came out of me. Each time it was my turn to speak, I told a little bit more, and a little bit more. First, I told the group about the years of daily taunts and ridicule from classmates and kids down the street. Then I told them about the group of girls that liked to corner me and my friend and threaten us. And then I told the worst story of all, the one I'd never wanted Mum to hear, because how could I expect her to see my being gay as something positive when I'd already been bashed bloody once, and I was afraid it would happen again?

But in that space, my story was just one of many stories, all of them with the same undercurrent of violence, and all sounding so familiar. It was difficult to say it but good at the same time, and four years after the bashing my mum finally heard what happened to me. I told the group that I'd been walking a lesbian friend home from school so she wouldn't get the shit kicked out of her, then that same group of girls cornered us again and kicked the crap out of us and absolutely mauled us with trolley bars (metal handles from shopping carts) and bricks. My mum had to hear about the blood pouring out of us, all because we were gay, and about the way our attackers said that being gay is against everything and we should burn in hell, and the way they booted us one more time and told us to die in the gutter. Mum had to hear how I'd hidden the cuts and bruises under long sleeves and long pants until they healed, and how I had explained away my busted eyebrow as a freak sports injury from a really rough game.

When we got down to the business of actually writing the script that would become *Game On!*, a lot came up about violence and about how bashers really fight, what kind of insults they spit out at LGBT kids, what it really feels like to be hit—and it hurts like bloody hell to have somebody blacken your eye or break your nose or split your lip. If you really look at the way LGBT haters and bashers fight, right away you can see that they pull the same crap all the time. It's always the same slurs and insults: they're always yelling *faggot, dyke, pervert, lemon, fairy queen, lezzo, homo, poofter, queer, pansy, fudge packer, sinner,* and *freak* like a broken record. They make the same threats over and over again, telling you they are going to beat the shit out of you and fuck you up but good, telling you they are going to kill you for being a fairy-homo-poofter-freak. And they always have that pack mentality, with three or four or twelve of them against one, maybe two, LGBT kids.

Their safety-in-numbers strategy works really well, and so does their down-and-dirty tactic of fighting with anything they can get their hands on—belts, rocks, broken bottles, trolley bars, steel bats. They'll fight with their bare hands, if necessary. But they *are* going to fight. So we've got to decide how we are going to fight back. And we've got to find a better way to fight them than with fists and bricks and broken glass.

With *Game On!*, the only weapon we had was our words. But we figured, at the end of the day, a punch is a punch is a punch. It's a one-shot deal. You make a fist and haul your arm back and take a swing with all the weight of your hatred behind it. But people can throw only so many punches at a time before their arms get too tired, and they wear themselves out. Not like words, which never tire out. They keep hitting hard, where it hurts, and the way people need to hear them most. So all of us, LGBTs and straight allies alike—and my mum!—worked together and used the Institute to find the very best words to fight back against violence and discrimination.

In fact, my story became one of the cornerstones of the plot. And we used something Mum said as a line in *Game On!*: "She's still my daughter. It doesn't change who she is. I still love her the way she is." It really meant a lot for me to know that people in the audience were hearing my mum's words; maybe they could imagine it was their own mum saying them and get some feeling of hope or support from that.

After the Institute, we toured *Game On!* to public high schools across Queensland, and I worked on the production as set designer and builder, stage manager, and one of the post-show facilitators. I also shared my experiences with the public through a bunch of press interviews—including an interview and a big photo of me that made the front page of the Bundy municipal newspaper.

Suddenly, my face was everywhere in Bundaberg. I seriously considered quitting the project right then, not so much because I was afraid of being bashed again (and I *was* afraid to get bashed again, but the worst thing that happened to me after that news story was a bunch of guys yelling, "Dyke!" and throwing Coke bottles at me through the car window), but because my nephew was getting hassled, and kids at his school were picking on him and throwing bottles at him because of that newspaper article. I told him I was going to stop doing the show because I didn't want him to get hurt, but my nephew was great about it. He told me, "Don't stop. *This* is the reason why you are doing the play." And he stood up to those kids and said, "This is why my auntie is doing it. Because people like you don't have an open mind, and still think in the old-fashioned way where gays are dirty and disgusting and should be thrown in the gutter." I figured if he could be brave enough to deal with getting hassled, I had to be brave enough to keep going and not quit or give up in the middle of things.

It was a strange experience to be in the paper like that, because it all felt so personal again, and also like I was a cardboard cutout standing in for every gay person in Bundaberg. I wish I knew more about how the newspaper story really affected people, and if people recognized themselves in the story, or felt comforted or inspired, or found the courage to come out to their family and their friends. But if I am going to be on the front page of the newspaper, I'd rather it be in a story like that, as someone strong and proud and not beaten down, than be on the front page as a victim.

Going on tour with *Game On!* was great because we got immediate feedback from people in the audience. We had lots of kids come up to talk to us or drop off little notes thanking us for putting on the play, saying that we'd given them the confidence to tell their friends they are gay or bisexual or lesbian or transgender. They really got the message that their friends should accept them for *who* they are, not *what* they are.

I am glad I stuck it out and glad I told my story, because when it comes to violence and discrimination against LGBT people, I am not shy anymore, and I am not afraid to speak up when I hear someone call a kid a dyke, or see some ignorant bashers ganging up on someone and threatening to kick the crap out of them. I feel like a warrior, in a community of warriors, fighting the good fight with the mightiest weapon of all—our words.

A Few More Thoughts about Transformation

NORMA BOWLES

A great majority of participants found the Institute experience to be very positive and empowering. They felt that their voices were heard and included, and they believed that they had created exciting and powerful activist theatre.

> We did it! I have never felt more tired, yet more alive in my life, because inside of me there is something that is screaming "YEAH!" I am finally taking a stand against all the things that I have had to face in the past, but could never really say anything about because I felt that I would be the only one. Now I know that I am not the only one. So thank you!
>
> *Vanessa, university student, Texas*

> The last two weeks have been the most wonderful two weeks of my life. What we have done here has given me a really big wake-up call for what I need to stand up and do, to protect my family and friends, and my future, [to be] a political ally for everyone here.
>
> *Opal, middle school student, California*

> This project made me step back and take a look at my life and what I need to change. I have lived with people that are still disgusted by LGBT people and have had great in-depth conversations on this topic. I shared what I have done, spoke up, and did not just sit in the corner letting things be said that I knew to be wrong. I may have done that a few years ago, but no longer.
>
> *Jessica, university student, Ontario, Canada*

It did my heart so good to see not only my kids get involved and be so brave as to share their life, and to hear everybody else's life, and it has made a profound change in our family and in the way that we talk to each other and share our views.

Gary, parent, California

This class and this production made me want to continue to do theatre for social change, because I want to be part of more positive transformations.

Mallory, university student, California

This project was for me the most rewarding, as well as exhausting and scariest time in my life. I would not change it for the world. The feeling of knowing that you are probably saving someone's life is something which can't be expressed, but it is something which will stay with you for life. I have little doubt that this is what we accomplished.

Helen, community member, Queensland[1]

Still, while many participants felt excited about and empowered by the work, a number of participants felt frustrated, even disempowered or betrayed. Xanthia Angel Walker describes one of these situations quite compellingly in her essay in this volume. Another example involved a group of students who left one of the pro–marriage equality Institutes because they felt the project goals went against their moral code; in other instances, participants left Institutes early, feeling overwhelmed, disheartened, and/or offended by the discrimination stories presented by participants and/or frustrated or disenfranchised by the devising process. On the penultimate day of one collaboration, the participants voted to scrap the entire script and the devising process and to start again from scratch on their own. And after working tirelessly on a play to encourage employers to hire formerly incarcerated women, one participant wrote Fringe Benefits that she found herself "eighteen months later . . . no job, no resources and no collective support" (anonymous, personal communication).

Though I have devoted many, many hours to self-reflection and have continuously worked to fine-tune the devising process, I have found that there are no clear answers as to what can be done to guarantee that profound ruptures such as these never occur. Nevertheless, it does seem clear that each of these ruptures argues for the importance of *transparency* (everyone needs to be very clear, from the beginning and throughout the process, about project goals, procedures, and protocols) and *empowerment* (everyone needs to feel engaged as a uniquely important agent at every moment of the process).

Still, even when everyone is genuinely committed to transparency and empowerment, fully embodying these values throughout the course of a project often proves dishearteningly challenging. The director of one of the community organizations with which we worked saw the Institute as an opportunity for that organization's youth to benefit from what promised to be a very empowering experience. After the successful completion of the project—including an influx of life-saving support from the audience—she shared with us a sobering tale of an Institute that almost wasn't, as project leadership had been passed from one youth to another (and ultimately to an adult ally) like the proverbial hot potato.

One of the key lessons of which I am reminded as I think about this story is the importance of *infrastructure*. It can be very dangerous to place too much responsibility for the success of a collaboratively developed activist theatre project with any one individual, youth or adult. More important, perhaps, it is crucial for each participating organization to have a bulwark of relevant expertise, experience, and resources to support such projects. In this specific case, the partnering organization did not have theatre experience, expertise, or resources built into its infrastructure. It was not in a strong position to support an "empowering" experience for youth leadership of a theatrical endeavor. This, again, is why I have found it crucial to help build at least a three-pronged cosponsorship/infrastructure for the Institutes: between a theatre group (preferably part of a university theatre department), a community organization (with a track record for successful activism on the social justice issue to be addressed), and Fringe Benefits.

Since founding Fringe Benefits in 1991, I have wrestled with how best to think about and prioritize my own goals for this work. What should be the primary focus: activism, education, community building, empowerment, aesthetics, or . . . ? In our early years, during one of our first collaborations with homeless LGBTQ youth, one of the contributing writers, a transgender woman named Marcella, shared the following story: "I was a fresh-faced innocent once, too . . . back in the Stone Age, when I wasn't yet wearing makeup and miniskirts. . . . Before the time I became EMPLOYABLE. I'd go to interviews in a coat

& tie . . . and they'd be, like, trying to figure out if I was a faggot or a dyke. They were all so confused and uptight about whether or not I had a dick, they never even bothered to ask if I could type! So, after 6 or 7 months of pointless interviews like that, I chucked the coat and tie, beat my face, and found work on the boulevard" (in Bowles 56–57). As I considered Marcella's experience, I thought, Marcella doesn't need to be empowered; she's already formidably powerful! Like so many of the homeless youth we encountered, she was extremely bright, gifted, and capable of making significant contributions to society. She—they—did not need to be changed; the society that rejected them needed to be changed! As Jan Cohen-Cruz puts it so eloquently, "Empowerment lies not only in how subjects feel about themselves, but how they are seen within a social framework" (116).

Building on Jan's wise words, I decided it was important to frame Fringe Benefits' work from that point on as primarily activist in nature and to focus on conscientizing and dynamizing audiences, on transforming the way oppressed people are viewed and treated by society—on empowerment through activism. In the two decades since meeting and working with Marcella, I have enjoyed collaborating with countless other extraordinary, lovely human beings in diverse Fringe Benefits projects, including our Institutes in the United States, the United Kingdom, Australia, and Canada. I have been profoundly moved by their stories, their creativity, and their expressions of excitement and gratitude about their involvement in the projects. I have also witnessed the ripple effect of this work: Institute plays have changed hearts, minds, even votes. Innumerable activists-turned-artists and artists-turned-activists, new networks and alliances, and new Theatre for Social Justice groups, courses, and programs have sprung up in the wake of our Institutes.

Collaborating to create theatre for social change is profoundly transformative! It constantly inspires me to examine, reexamine, and rededicate myself and my work. Whether we see ourselves as artists, activists, scholars, concerned citizens, and/or as members of one or many communities, including the global community, we all have the power to transform and be transformed by this vital work!

Note

1. These comments were shared by participants in letters and Institute participant feedback forms gathered by Fringe Benefits (unpublished).

Bibliography

Bowles, Norma, ed. *Friendly Fire: An Anthology of 3 Plays by Queer Street Youth.* Los Angeles: A.S.K. Theatre Projects, 1997.

Cohen-Cruz, Jan. "Mainstream or Margin? US Activist Performance and Theatre of the Oppressed." In *Playing Boal: Theatre, Therapy, Activism,* edited by Mady Schutzman and Jan Cohen-Cruz. London: Routledge, 1994. 110–23.

APPENDIXES
CONTRIBUTORS
INDEX

Appendix A: Theatre for Social Justice Institute Overview

Pre-Institute Planning

For six to twelve months before an Institute, the partnering organizations work together to determine the discrimination issue on which they wish to focus, the target audience they want to reach, and the measurable outcomes they intend to achieve. For example, a disability rights organization might want to address able-ism in a specific university by creating a play for an audience of that university's administrators and board members with the goal of persuading them to improve accessibility to campus buildings and classrooms.

The partnering organizations then develop an expanded list of partnering organizations and departments; a work plan, timeline, and division of responsibilities; and a detailed budget, including available in-kind resources such as workspace and potential performance venues, equipment, copying, and potential cast and crew. Once all of these issues and logistics have been worked out, a Memorandum of Understanding is written and signed by representatives of all partnering organizations.

The partnering organizations then gather a diverse group of about thirty-five people interested in using activist theatre to address the selected issue. To continue with the above-mentioned example—addressing able-ism in a university setting—an ideal group for this project might include seven or more university students (students of diverse abilities, races/ethnicities, genders, academic and extracurricular interests, and so on); five or more diverse university educators and staff; as many members of the target audience as possible (in this instance, people with the ability to authorize improvements to campus infrastructure, such as administrators, board members, and trustees); seven or more theatre majors (actors, writers, improv troupe members, and the like); a counselor or social services professional; someone with legal expertise; and several people with knowledge about the disability rights movement and disability issues.

The Institute/Dramaturgical Quilting Bee Structure

Two theatre activists/Institute facilitators, trained by Fringe Benefits, travel to the work site (usually a school or community center) and conduct five days of intensive four-hour workshops with a group of approximately thirty-five participants. In between each workshop session, the FB teaching artists and as many project participants as possible transcribe audiotapes of stories, discussions, and improvisations from the workshops, flesh out the dramatic structure determined by the group, transform the transcribed improvisations into a first draft of the play, and use the group's dramaturgical input to refine and polish the script through several drafts.

Day One: Introductions and Story Sharing

The workshop begins with an opportunity for participants and facilitators to introduce themselves, an overview of the process and goals of the day and of the Institute, and an explanation of participation guidelines. The participants then share put-downs, jokes, stereotypes, and stories (leaving out names) of incidents wherein they've witnessed or been involved in teasing, name calling, bullying, intimidation, violence, and/or other forms of discrimination against members of the particular group of people whose concerns are the focus of the Institute—continuing with our example, university community members who have disabilities. The participants then share stereotype-busting stories about people with disabilities. At the end of the day, we devote about thirty minutes to facilitator-led improvisations based on some of the participants' stories. The session ends with a "Closing Circle" in which all are invited to share briefly how they're feeling or to state a hope they have for the play.

Day Two: Determining Which Stories and What Structure Will Work Best for the Target Audience

Everyone has about twenty minutes to review the transcripts from Day One. We then take time to think about our target audience, to develop a "demographic profile" of the "Movable Middle"[1] of that audience, and to consider our own stereotypes and fears about the

Movable Middle. We go on to consider possible common ground we share with target audience members and what kinds of entertainment they might prefer—what films, plays, television programs, and the like. At this point, each participant writes down on his or her own private "ballot" the three stories—from among the discrimination and stereotype-busting stories shared on Day One—that he or she thinks will be most likely to open the mind and heart of "John and/or Jane Q. Movable Middle" and change their discriminatory behavior (or encourage them to change discriminatory policies or laws).

The group then brainstorms various ways the stories might be dramatized using some of the dramatic structures, styles, devices, and characters of the shows we think the target audience would find most appealing. Together, we narrow the selection down to about five promising approaches and then divide ourselves into small groups to flesh out the ideas a little more fully. The day ends with each small group presenting a brief "pitch" of its concept to the full group. Following each pitch, the full group has a few minutes to respond with comments about what aspects of the proposed concept might work well for the target audience and what aspects might be problematic, as well as with some ideas about how to build on or improve the approach. Participants then add their first, second, and third choices for dramatic structure to their private ballots and turn these in to the facilitators. We end, as always, with a brief Closing Circle.

Day Three: Using Improvisation to Develop Draft One

The facilitators bring in a detailed script outline based on the structure and three stories democratically selected by the participants (the facilitators do not have a vote on this). The group has an opportunity to revise the outline vis-à-vis accomplishing our activist goals more effectively. Participants might change plot points, setting, tone, and/or character descriptions, including personality, interests, age, gender, ethnicity, and so on. To create the first draft of the play, the facilitators then guide the group through about three hours of improvisations based on this dramatic structure. Anyone can jump into an improvisation at any time, sometimes with multiple people simultaneously playing the same character. Anyone can call "Stop!" at any point to suggest a change in tone, plot, and/or approach. In the Closing Circle, everyone is invited to offer suggestions to the facilitators and other volunteers from the group who will be transcribing the audiotapes of the improvisations and developing the second draft. These suggestions tend to run the gamut from "Angela is starting to sound a little preachy—try rounding her out a bit, and *definitely* give her more of a sense of humor" to "I still think the exposition is too long" or "Try switching scenes 4 and 5."

Day Four: The Zen Cuisinart

The group reads through draft two (about twelve to fifteen pages) and discusses general dramaturgical issues. We then read the draft again, but this time all of the participants are invited to call out "Stop!" any time they think something—a line, an action, and/or a character—should be changed. Everyone is encouraged to jump in with proposals for solutions, such as "She should say 'That really bites!' instead of 'That's so gay!' Otherwise she sounds either ignorant or homophobic or both!" The suggestions are then quickly voted on and, if necessary, discussed and voted on again. If someone has a strong ethical, moral, or legal concern about a solution, even if that person is in the minority, we defer to his or her proposal, devote more time to brainstorming other possible solutions, and/or mark the section for further review and reworking between sessions. In this manner, in the course of four hours, we collaboratively whip draft three into shape. This day, at best, works like a Zen Cuisinart, the democratic process at its finest. At worst, it's like the proverbial places that no one wants to visit—the places where sausages and/or laws are made. The Closing Circle may include wishes for the final draft, favorite moments of the day, frustrations, and the like.

Day Five: Zen Cuisinart #2, Post-Show Discussion, and Next Steps

As with each session, the participants are encouraged to invite any friends, colleagues, and/or family members who they feel might be able to contribute to the playwriting process in some way—perhaps because of their experiences with the issues and situations addressed in the play, perhaps because of their theatrical, political, marketing, or other related expertise, and/or because of their understanding of the target audience. A handful of the participants (generally no more than the number of actors who will be in the actual cast) read draft four aloud. We then go through the play very quickly—two to three minutes per page maximum—and do our best to resolve any remaining problems. Participants are asked to mark spelling, punctuation, and relatively insignificant grammatical errors in their scripts for us to correct *after the group session*. Everyone is asked to focus *during the group discussion* on any/all remaining problems that pose more difficult aesthetic, strategic, and/or ethical issues, such as "I'm worried that if Ryan pulls a knife on Shabzi, all anyone will talk about in the post-show discussion is all of the recent knife-related violence in London," or "He shouldn't say 'I need your help'; that makes him sound too much like a victim." The goal is to be sure we have "all hands on deck"—the artists, the legal representative, the counselor, the community members who have had direct experience with the discrimination issue at hand, the members of the target audience—to solve these kinds of script issues collaboratively. Sometimes if important issues (or even apparently minor ones) are left for the actors and director to resolve in rehearsal, solutions that may seem effective from their perspective—funnier, more realistic, and/or time-saving—might end up creating additional problems that the Institute collaborative might have been able to prevent.

After the final Zen Cuisinart, the participants divide themselves into committees to share ideas and come up with "next steps" for marketing and outreach, production design, handouts, the post-show discussion, and post-show surveys. Each group chooses or is assigned a leader, a timekeeper, and a secretary who emails meeting notes to the entire Institute team. At the end of this session, each committee takes about five or ten minutes to share its ideas, next steps, and proposed next meeting times with the full group. Following each of these mini presentations, the full group has a couple of minutes to chime in with additional ideas and/or questions. Participants are invited to share any closing thoughts, thank yous, and/or wishes for the play in the final Closing Circle.

After the Institute

Following the Institute, Fringe Benefits offers email and telephone consultation as the participants collaborate to rehearse, market, and produce the play. The partnering organizations perform the play they have created for an audience of their choosing in their school or community. Each presentation of the play is followed by a post-show discussion or workshop.

All of the Memorandums of Understanding stipulate that project partners must present their play to a minimum of five hundred members of the predetermined target audience and have each of these audience members fill in a post-show survey through which we all can determine if the play has had the desired effect.

Note

1. There is an unwritten rule about persuasive speaking: 20 percent of your audience ("the choir") probably already agrees with you; 20 percent of your audience might be too hard to reach; and the remaining 60 percent make up the "Movable Middle." On Day Two of the Institute, after briefly explaining this concept, the Institute facilitators ask the participants to consider who might be in the Movable Middle of our audience. Then, in order to zero in on who might be part of a more-difficult-to-reach subset of this group, we ask them to try to picture the audience watching our play and to imagine "Which audience members might have their arms folded in defiance? Who might be rolling their eyes, whispering to their friends, texting, etc.?"

For example, while collaboratively devising a play addressing a target audience of high school students with the goal of reducing homophobic behavior, one Institute group defined their "John Q. Resistant-but-Movable Middle" as an eleventh grade guy, probably into sports, someone who regularly peppers his conversations with "Fag!" and "That is so gay!" The group also felt that Latino and/or African American young men might be more difficult to reach about these issues because they thought that there was normally less discussion about and/or acceptance of LGBT people in their communities and because of the still-pervasive stereotype that "all gay guys are white." Generally, the discussion through which the group develops an image of "John or Jane Q." raises a lot of important questions and concerns about our own prejudices and stereotypes and about how much care we need to take to engage our audiences respectfully, appropriately, and imaginatively.

To read more about the Movable Middle concept, please refer to http://www.equalitymaine.org/blogs/dorian-cole/the-moveable-middle and http://content.thirdway.org/publications/144/Third_Way_Memo_Moving_the_Middle_on_Gay_Equality.pdf.

Appendix B: Measurable Outcomes Worksheet

The problem: Briefly describe the specific issue you wish to address. Be sure to include what specific group of people is being discriminated against, by whom, and where, as well as what form(s) the discrimination takes and how this problem is affecting your school or community.

The goal: Briefly describe the primary change in behavior, policy, and/or law you aim to achieve by presenting your play. Include the specific issue about which you would like to raise your audience's awareness, understanding, and motivation to address, as well as any tools you aim to offer the audience to accomplish this goal. How do you hope your school or community environment will change as a result of accomplishing these goals?

Target audience: Briefly describe the primary audience you need to reach in order to accomplish your goal. Is it more important to reach those who are engaging in the discrimination, those being discriminated against, or bystanders who could potentially become allies? If addressing laws you think should be changed, do you need to reach legislators or voters, people who already agree with you, people who are on the fence, or people who disagree with you on this issue? If addressing policy issues, do you need to reach owners, trustees, and/or top administrators of the institution in question, or employees, members, and/or clients? If addressing behavior issues in schools, do you want to reach youth, parents, educators, or administrators? Be as specific as you can in your description of your primary target audience.

Organizational capacity: Once you have determined the specific audience you need to reach, consider whether or not it is one you have the capacity to reach. Do you have a way to make sure they will come to your show, or that they will allow you to present your show in their venue, perhaps during a meeting, assembly, or conference? Provide detailed answers to the following questions:

1. What is your timeline for rehearsing, marketing, and presenting the show?
2. What are the venues where the show *can be* presented, including, but not limited to, theatres, classrooms, community centers, religious centers, public squares, dining facilities, and so on?
3. What are the times and dates when the show *can be* presented, including, but not limited to, all-school assemblies; Freshman Orientation Week; Cesar Chavez Day; town hall or other organization meetings; local, national, or international conferences; and so on? Keep in mind that it would be ideal to allot at least ninety minutes for your presentation, including the show, post-show discussion, and time for the audience to fill out post-show surveys.
4. When devising the play, it's important to make sure it's not "too big" for your organization to produce. With that in mind, what is the maximum number of performers you feel comfortable counting on to act in the show? What kind of theatre experience and/or knowledge of the issues do they have? Please describe this potential cast as thoroughly as possible. For example: *Eight actors, all college students, mostly theatre majors, all generally knowledgeable about the issue, specifically: two straight-identified females, one white and one Latina; one lesbian-identified African American female; one genderqueer white individual; one bi-identified Asian American male; two straight-identified males, one Arab-American and one white; and two gay-identified males, one African American and one white who uses a wheelchair.*

Measurable outcomes: Set clear and reasonably achievable outcome goals that can be measured through post-show audience surveys or through some other evaluation instrument. For example:

Post-show surveys responses should reveal at least at 20 percent improvement among in the audience regarding the following issues:

1. Concern about anti-LGBTQ behavior on campus
2. Desire and willingness to intervene
3. Confidence that they have helpful tools/strategies for dealing with these incidents
4. Ideas about how to proactively make their campus safer and more inclusive for all

Schedule: The host organization should determine all of the above at least two months prior to the Institute to allow sufficient time for marketing, outreach, recruitment, and production planning.

Appendix C: Some Suggested
Guidelines for Project Facilitators

1. Familiarize yourself with all applicable and relevant national and state laws and with the policies of any/all organizations with which you are working.

2. Clarify expectations, goals, procedures, and protocols (including insurance and liability responsibilities) with the institution(s) where and/or with which you are working. Document your agreements in a contract.

3. Communicate with participants ahead of time about any specific accommodations they might require regarding mobility, communication, and/or allergies, and join with the proprietors of the spaces in which you will be working to adapt the space accordingly as well as possible. For example:

- If you plan to offer food during sessions, you may need to label the contents.
- You might need to ensure that certain foods, such as peanuts, are not even in the room.
- It would also be helpful to email participants before the first meeting advising them, "In order to accommodate individuals who have serious medical sensitivities to the chemicals in scented products, we ask that you refrain from the use of products such as perfume, cologne, aftershave, and scented moisturizer on workshop days."

4. If movement and/or improvisation will be involved, let participants know ahead of time that they will be asked to wear loose-fitting clothes, or as Fringe Benefits specifies in an email to Institute participants, "clothes in which you would feel comfortable doing somersaults; no skirts, no high heels, no open-toe shoes or sandals." If possible, ask everyone to work without shoes and socks in order

to lessen the chance of injury. Be sure to inspect, clear, and sweep the floor thoroughly.

5. Make sure the workspace offers visual and auditory privacy and that the temperature is comfortable.

6. Set up the room to enable all participants and facilitators to sit in a circle so that they can easily see each other and so that the impact of any/all intragroup hierarchies is reduced. During activities that involve movement, try to be sure you never have your back to anyone and that everyone can see you and all other members of the group.

7. Create, distribute, and collect "Participant Agreement Forms" through which each participant can specify how he or she would like to be credited for contributions to the project and if his or her photo and/or video likeness can be used in conjunction with the presentation, marketing, and/or documentation of the project. Clarify that each individual's stories, comments, and improvisations *might or might not* be incorporated in the final product(s), and specify the time frame during which and the process through which those decisions will be made.

8. At the beginning of each session, post the day's agenda, including time frames. Also post and explain workshop guidelines. Ours can be found in the Solanos' "It's Safe to Say" essay in this volume.

9. *All of the posted guidelines apply to facilitators as well as to participants.* It is especially important to remember not to judge anyone's contributions in any way, verbally or nonverbally (through laughter, groans, grimaces, eye rolling, and the like).

10. Create multiple, diverse opportunities for participants to make creative and critical contributions, including verbally and nonverbally, openly and anonymously, around the room sequentially or loosely ("popcorn" style), and so on.

11. Whether dramaturgical decisions are made democratically or through modified consensus (as with Fringe Benefits) or in some other manner, clarify that any participant's serious moral, ethical, and/or legal concern will be given top priority.

12. Clarify before any writing, Image Theatre, and/or small-group discussion exercise whether or not participants will be asked to disclose to the larger group what they've written or discussed and/or the story behind the physical image they've created.

13. Set clear per-person or per-group time limits for sharing stories, ideas, comments, and the like. State why you're asking participants to

share such information and if and/or how the information might be used (for example, "We may use these stories in our script").

14. Underscore to participants the importance of speaking up in the workshop about any discomfort they may experience with anything you or other participants might say or do. For more complex, lengthy, or private matters, encourage them to talk to you and/or to the project leader or counselor outside of the workshop sessions and/or to put their anonymous or signed comments in the "Feedback" box.

Appendix D: Legal Considerations Overview

It is important to work with someone who has legal expertise when doing community-based activist theatre, especially in order to:

I. **Avoid violating libel and/or slander laws in the script or production.**
This is especially important when plays are based on personal stories, including firsthand experiences and secondhand accounts. *For example:* After participants shared their stories on the first day of one Institute and before we selected which stories to include in the play, the university's legal representatives listed thirteen stories that they recommended we not include without significant fictionalizing as they pertained to incidents currently under litigation.

II. **Avoid violating copyright laws in the script or production.**
The playwriting and/or production team might wish to include in their show ideas, words, images, music, characters, and so on drawn from media (TV, film, advertising, literature, videos, and the like) that are not in the public domain. *For example:* We wanted to adapt the lyrics of "New York, New York" for *If Yes, Please Explain...*, our play promoting the employment of formerly incarcerated women ("Start spreading the news! We're hiring today!") and to have a chorus of "employers" sing and dance to a karaoke version of the song.

III. **Ensure that any/all laws and/or policies referenced in the script, marketing materials, handouts, and/or post-show discussion are accurately represented.**
Most of our plays address discriminatory behavior, policies, and/or laws. Whether critiquing or encouraging compliance with

these policies or laws, it is crucial to get the facts straight.

For example: In *9 Digits Away from My Dream*, our play encouraging California educators to support the immigration rights movement, specifically the "Dream Act" (aka AB-540), which would allow undocumented students to pay resident fees instead of out-of-state tuition fees, we wanted to provide the teachers in our target audience with correct and comprehensive information about how the proposed law would support their students and about how, without the protection of AB-540, their students were currently at risk.

IV. **Avoid violating lobbying and grassroots lobbying restrictions.**
   For example: We needed to be sure the scope, wording, and budgets of our various pro–marriage equality collaborations fell within legal parameters.

V. **Successfully navigate potential legal/policy/ institutional obstacles to reaching the target audience.**
   Some of the issues that might be encountered include the following:
   A. *When performing in public spaces:* First Amendment parameters, as well as laws regarding insurance, congregation in public space, public nuisance, and private property, regulations against loudspeakers and/or blocking traffic, and so on.
   B. *When performing in public or private schools (K–12):* proscriptions regarding show and post-show language and/or content.
      1. Including people with legal expertise as well as empowered school staff and faculty in the planning and writing phases helps ensure that:
         a. The script and production will fall within legal and school policy parameters.
         b. Host schools will feel confident and have evidence to share with their boards, supervisors, and/or PTOs that hosting the show:
            1) Can help make their schools safer.
            2) Complies with and/or helps reinforce state and federal laws and school district policies and regulations regarding such things as discrimination, bullying, harassment, Title I, Title IX, and so on.
            3) Probably will not require them to obtain "Opt-In" forms from parents in order for students to attend.
      2. Appropriate and constructive contracts can be drafted

between the following entities:

    a. Individuals and organizations collaborating to create the play (ensuring that everyone is properly credited and empowered).

    b. The organization(s) touring the play and the school(s) hosting the play (protecting the touring artists from sanctions, cancellations, censorship, harassment, and the like, and providing the hosts with information supporting the legality of the work).

    c. The organization(s) devising and/or touring the play, the school(s) hosting the play, and the parent(s) of any/all underage youth devising and/or attending the play (protecting the organizations and schools from lawsuits and the youth from exploitation).

In conclusion, we feel it is important for a legal representative to be present for all collaborative devising sessions and, ideally, to be available for questions during project planning, between devising sessions, and throughout the rehearsal process, shows, and post-show discussions, as well as in conjunction with outreach and marketing efforts (especially press interviews). Such a person's *timely* advice regarding dramaturgical, production, and community liaising issues can be invaluable.

Appendix E: Pyramid of Hate

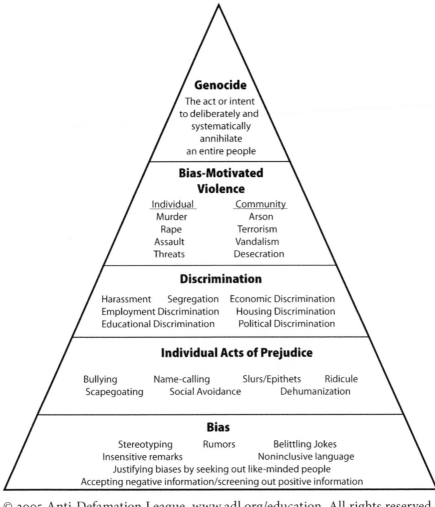

© 2005 Anti-Defamation League, www.adl.org/education. All rights reserved. Reprinted with permission.

Contributors

Amanda Dunne Acevedo is a theatre practitioner in Chicago, where she cofounded Genesis Ensemble. As a theatre teaching artist, she has worked in Chicago schools for Northlight Theatre, Writers' Theatre, Steppenwolf Theatre Company, and American Theater Company and works internationally and nationally with Fringe Benefits. She earned her BA in theatre from Miami University (Ohio).

Rod Ainsworth is a cofounder and a current director of Creative Regions, a production company working toward seeing regional communities thriving through creativity. He is a playwright, producer, and director based in Bundaberg, Queensland, Australia.

Jessy Ardern is a student at the University of Winnipeg and a co-artistic director of the Struts and Frets Players theatre troupe. In 2011, Jessy and writing partner Ariel Levine became the youngest playwrights ever to win the Harry S. Rintoul Award for Best New Manitoba Play at the Winnipeg Fringe Festival.

Ann Elizabeth Armstrong is an associate professor of theatre at Miami University of Ohio. She teaches directing, community-based theatre, and interdisciplinary studies and is a codirector of the "Finding Freedom Summer" project, a public humanities program on civil rights history. She has published on feminist pedagogy, community-based theatre, and intercultural theatre.

Norma Bowles, founder and artistic director of Fringe Benefits since 1991, has conducted Theatre for Social Justice, acting, and *commedia dell'arte* residencies throughout the United States and internationally. She edited Fringe Benefits' play anthologies *Cootie Shots* and *Friendly Fire*. Bowles is a recipient of the Association for Theatre in Higher Education's first Award for Leadership in Community-Based Theatre and Civic Engagement.

Natalya Brusilovsky has been a theatre practitioner, educator, senior center programs director, and café manager. She is currently an independent consultant, facilitating community and arts development programs, and a member of Theatre Action Group, promoting dialogue and celebrating lines of difference. She looks forward to opening a community arts café.

Selina Busby is a senior lecturer and the course leader of the MA Applied Theatre program at the Royal Central School of Speech and Drama (University of London). Her specialisms include prison theatre, youth theatre, Theatre in Education, and British theatre of the 1990s. At Central, she has developed and overseen projects with young people's theatre, both in the United Kingdom and internationally.

Tracey Calhoun teaches English at La Cañada High School in California and formerly taught at Woodrow Wilson High School in Los Angeles, where she served as coordinator of the Environmental and Urban Studies Small Learning Community and sponsor of the Gay-Straight Alliance. She has published articles on LGBT youth and education in *Alternative Network Journal* and UCLA's *Center X Forum*.

Michael Ellison is an associate professor at Bowling Green State University, where he created a program in musical theatre and the Humanities Troupe. He has taught master classes in the United States, Denmark, Germany, and the Philippines. His original musical *Key Changes* (book writer/lyricist, director/choreographer) had a showcase production in Brooklyn in 2010.

Diane Finnerty is a community educator and activist and directs faculty human resources and development in the University of Iowa's Office of the Provost. She holds a master's degree in women's studies and teaches as adjunct faculty in the UI School of Social Work. Diane currently serves on the Iowa City Human Rights Commission.

Flint teaches creative writing with an emphasis on the interplay between creative nonfiction, the limits of creative license, and critical theories of identity. Publications include *Chronometry*, *SPRAWL*, and *Two Hawks Quarterly*. Currently she is completing *Blood: A Memoir* and editing an anthology charting the spectrum of feminist ideologies of sexual desire.

Laura Reed Goodson has worked as an actor, director, voice coach, and playwright for more than twenty years. She currently works as a writer and therapist in Charlotte, North Carolina.

Crystal Grills lives in Hervey Bay, Queensland, Australia, where she works as a security guard.

Carly Halse trained at the Central School of Speech & Drama in London, where her research focused on the female body and autobiographical performance. Carly is now an actor, teacher, and facilitator working in London and the surrounding area.

Megan Hanley is an actor and activist who creates collaborative, physical, and political theatre. She has studied with the SITI Company, Grupo Cultural Yuyachkani in Peru, and the Hemispheric Institute for Performance and Politics. She received her master's degree in performance studies from New York University. Visit her website: meganhanley.weebly.com.

Susan V. Iverson is an associate professor of higher education administration and student personnel at Kent State University, where she is also an affiliate faculty member with the women's studies program. Her research explores multicultural competence, gender equity, civic consciousness, service learning, and the impact of change-oriented pedagogy on students' attitudes and thinking.

Kathleen Juhl is a professor of theatre at Southwestern University, where she teaches performance, acting, Alexander Technique, movement, and voice and mentors the Theatre for Social Justice student organization. She holds an MFA in acting and directing and a PhD in performance studies. She coedited *Radical Acts: Theatre and Feminist Pedagogies of Change.*

David Kaye is an associate professor of theatre at the University of New Hampshire, a cofounder of WildActs (UNH's Theatre for Social Justice troupe), and a 2011 Fulbright scholar. He has published several articles and devised numerous plays, in the United States and internationally, on a wide range of issues related to the struggle against oppression. He holds an MFA from Brandeis University.

Brooke Kiener is an actor, a director, and an educator in Spokane, Washington. She works extensively in the field of community-based theatre and has cowritten and directed productions about socioeconomic discrimination, injustice in the justice system, and food production and distribution. She is a member of the theatre faculty at Whitworth University.

Catherine McNamara is a cofounder of Gendered Intelligence and Pro Dean (Students) at the Royal Central School of Speech and Drama (University of London). Catherine teaches various undergraduate and postgraduate courses at Central and supervises at the doctorate level. She was a project coordinator of Sci:dentity, a twelve-month arts project involving young trans people (www.scidentity.com).

Bryan C. Moore is an associate professor at Concordia University, Nebraska, where he serves as director of the theatre program. His research and production interests include dramaturgy, storytelling in multicultural drama, and applied theatre techniques. He has participated in three Theatre for Social Justice Institutes, including twice as co-facilitator with Norma Bowles.

Daniel-Raymond Nadon is an associate professor at Kent State University, where he served for eight years as a co-coordinator of LGBT studies and coordinator of theatre at the Trumbull Campus. He teaches courses in theatre and social change, multicultural theatre, and LGBT theatre and has published essays and book chapters in the areas of LGBT theatre and LGBT studies.

Cristina Pippa is an award-winning playwright and teacher. Former Artist in Residence at Women's & Children's Hospital of Buffalo, Cristina wrote the book *Hippos at the Hospital* and is cofounding the nonprofit ArtCare. Her published play, *Cell Cycle*, explores a girl's fascination with cancer research amid national and personal crisis.

Jude Pippen is a cofounder of Creative Regions and currently a freelance theatre and arts worker. Jude has a doctorate in performance studies. She was named Cultural Development Worker of the Year by the Queensland Community Arts Network in 2006.

Bill Rauch is the artistic director of the Oregon Shakespeare Festival. Previously, he collaborated with communities nationwide for twenty years as cofounder and artistic director of Cornerstone Theater Company. His many awards include the Fichandler, TCG's Visionary Leadership Award, and the Margo Jones Medal. He lives in Ashland with his husband and two sons.

Rebecca M. Root is a freelance voice teacher with an MA in voice studies. Awarded VASTA's Clyde Vinson Memorial Scholarship, she has held workshops internationally; her writing has been published in *Voice and Speech Review, Magma,* and *Women and Environments International Magazine*. Her performance career spans more than twenty years and embraces theatre, television, and film.

Cynthia Ruffin (Lady Justice) is a theatre activist, playwright, director, teacher/student, and founder of Revolutionary Angel Productions. She studied with world-renowned theatre activist Augusto Boal and earned her liberal arts degree at Antioch University. Cynthia tours her one-person play called *Baggage,* which tells the stories of women survivors of domestic violence.

Lindsey Smith, inspired by the Theatre for Social Justice Institute, started the Theatre for Social Justice student organization at Southwestern University and served as director, stage manager, or facilitator for six different social change–based plays before graduating in 2009. She holds a masters in public policy and is currently working as a program evaluator.

Bernardo Solano is a recipient of national awards, grants, and fellowships from such institutions as the NEA, the Fulbright Program, the Rockefeller Foundation, and the Ford Foundation. His plays have been produced at theatres across the country, and his work in community-based theatre has been recognized both nationally and internationally. He serves as an associate professor of theatre at California State Polytechnic University, Pomona.

Paula Weston Solano is an actor, writer, solo performer, and educator. She is an associate artist with Cornerstone Theater Company, a teaching artist with Center Theater Group, and an adjunct faculty member at California State Polytechnic University, Pomona. She performs in plays, episodic television, and independent films, and leads workshops throughout the country.

Erasmo Tacconelli is a chartered clinical psychologist working in East London Mental Health Services and at the University of Hertfordshire. He also specializes in and publishes widely on sexual health, having worked within a range of sex, gender, and sexuality-related health services and voluntary services in London.

Lindsey Barlag Thornton is a cofounder of Genesis Ensemble. As a teaching artist, she has worked for American Theater Company, Auditorium Theatre, the Gift Theatre, Steppenwolf Theatre Company, and Writers' Theatre in Chicago and nationally and internationally with Fringe Benefits. Lindsey holds a BA in theatre from Miami University (Ohio) and an MFA in performance from the Art Institute of Chicago.

Xanthia Angel Walker is a director, a facilitator, and an educator passionate about the intersections of theatre, community, and social change. She is the cofounding artistic director of Rising Youth Theatre in Phoenix, Arizona, and holds an MFA in theatre for youth from Arizona State University.

Index

THEATER IN THE AMERICAS

The goal of the series is to publish a wide range of scholarship on theater and performance, defining theater in its broadest terms and including subjects that encompass all of the Americas.

The series focuses on the performance and production of theater and theater artists and practitioners but welcomes studies of dramatic literature as well. Meant to be inclusive, the series invites studies of traditional, experimental, and ethnic forms of theater; celebrations, festivals, and rituals that perform culture; and acts of civil disobedience that are performative in nature. We publish studies of theater and performance activities of all cultural groups within the Americas, including biographies of individuals, histories of theater companies, studies of cultural traditions, and collections of plays.

Other Books in the Theater in the Americas Series

Shadowed Cocktails: The Plays of Philip Barry from "Paris Bound" to "The Philadelphia Story"
Donald R. Anderson

A Gambler's Instinct: The Story of Broadway Producer Cheryl Crawford
Milly S. Barranger

Unfriendly Witnesses: Gender, Theater, and Film in the McCarthy Era
Milly S. Barranger

The Theatre of Sabina Berman: "The Agony of Ecstasy" and Other Plays
Translated by Adam Versényi
With an Essay by Jacqueline E. Bixler

Messiah of the New Technique: John Howard Lawson, Communism, and American Theatre, 1923–1937
Jonathan L. Chambers

Composing Ourselves: The Little Theatre Movement and the American Audience
Dorothy Chansky

Ghost Light: An Introductory Handbook for Dramaturgy
Michael Mark Chemers

The Hanlon Brothers: From Daredevil Acrobatics to Spectacle Pantomime, 1833–1931
Mark Cosdon

Richard Barr: The Playwright's Producer
David A. Crespy

Women in Turmoil: Six Plays by Mercedes de Acosta
Edited and with an Introduction by Robert A. Schanke